The
1600s

HEADLINES IN HISTORY

Books in the Headlines in History series:

The 1600s

HEADLINES IN HISTORY

Louise I. Gerdes, *Book Editor*

Bonnie Szumski, *Editorial Director*
Scott Barbour, *Managing Editor*

Greenhaven Press, Inc., San Diego, California

12968731

Library of Congress Cataloging-in-Publication Data

The 1600s / Louise I. Gerdes, book editor.
    p. cm. — (Headlines in history)
  Includes bibliographical references and index.
  ISBN 0-7377-0634-1 (pbk. : alk. paper)—
  ISBN 0-7377-0635-X (lib. bdg. : alk. paper)
    1. Seventeenth century. 2. Civilization, modern—17th century. I. Gerdes, Louise, I. II. Series.

CB401 .A16 2001
909'.6—dc21

                                                    00-064682

Cover photos: (top) Taj Mahal, Agra, India, Digital Stock; (bottom, left to right) Japanese Shogun Tokugawa Ieyasu, © Stock Montage; Isaac Newton analyzing the ray of light, © North Wind Picture Archives; Indian welcome on the Charles River, Massachusetts (1635), © North Wind Picture Archives
Library of Congress, 31, 52, 65, 71, 143, 161, 169, 269, 293
North Wind Picture Archives, 42, 80, 95, 113

CONTENTS

Chapter 1: A Century of Discovery

1. The Scientific Revolution

Although historians agree that the Scientific Revolution reshaped the way Europeans looked at themselves and the natural world, some historians challenge traditional explanations of its source and influence.

2. The Experimental Method: A New Framework for Science

For two thousand years natural philosophers relied on Aristotle's writings to explain the natural world. Seventeenth-century natural philosophers, however, used observation and experiment, explaining nature in quantifiable terms. The experimental method gave the people of the seventeenth century a new perspective; they began to see the natural world as mechanical, rather than mystical.

3. From Mathematics to Microscopes: Advances in Biology

Like most science in the seventeenth century, biology was inspired by developments in mathematics and mechanics, and when scientists began to examine living organisms as they would machines, they could describe the way organisms functioned, forming the study of physiology.

4. On the Mechanism of the Human Mind

Based on the science of his time and his observations of human behavior, the seventeenth-century philosopher Baruch Spinoza concludes that the conscious mind alone does not control human action. Spinoza claims that desires, emotions, and unconscious thought work concurrently with the mind to influence a person's actions.

Chapter 2: Coming to America

Chapter 3: The Emergence of New Dynasties

the next decade, Royalists and parliamentary armies battled for power. After Charles I was executed, Oliver Cromwell, a leader of the successful parliamentary armies, was named lord protector, but disputes within Parliament paved the way for the restoration of Charles II.

Chapter 5: The Changing Face of Europe

ing his reign in the latter half of the seventeenth century. Whereas some argue that Louis wanted to rule all of Europe, others claim that, as a Catholic king, he simply wanted to lead a crusade against heretics. Although the peasants suffered during his reign, Louis was revered by his people until he was no longer the conqueror.

to accompany choruses and fill great auditoriums with sound. The music of the age became so much a part of life that in the court of Louis XIV, music accompanied the king and his court while they dressed, ate, worshiped, and danced.

2. The Vitality of Baroque Painting

Many great painters emerged during the baroque period, including Peter Paul Rubens, Diego de Silva, Nicolas Poussin, Frans Hals, Sir Anthony Van Dyck, and Rembrandt. In both landscapes and portraits, baroque artists captured man's vigor and lust for life, explored the conflict between reserve and passion, and revealed man's inner life and soul.

3. The Golden Age of the Theater

The plays of William Shakespeare, Ben Jonson, Lope de Vega, Pedro Calderón de la Barca, Pierre Corneille, Jean Racine, and Molière mark the seventeenth century as the golden age of the theater. Whereas the early dramatists wrote to the people, the later playwrights wrote to the king's court. In France, although patronage controlled the drama of the period, Molière's comedies forced the French court to laugh at themselves.

4. Literature of the Seventeenth Century

Although the literary works of John Milton, Miguel de Cervantes, and William Vondel reflect the social, political, and economic climate of the seventeenth century, these factors also determined what literature would be produced. Whereas salons allowed creativity to flourish, the dependence on patronage and the standards set by academies often limited literary development.

5. Matsuo Bashō: Master of Haiku and *Renga*

Once Shogun Tokugawa Ieyasu established peace early in the seventeenth century, Matsuo Bashō, born into the samurai class, turned to writing haiku, the poetry of Japan. Bashō, a student of Zen, wrote of his travel experiences throughout Japan and is known for developing a new haiku style known as *renga*.

FOREWORD

Chronological time lines of history are mysteriously fascinating. To learn that within a single century Christopher Columbus sailed to the New World, the Aztec, Maya, and Inca cultures were flourishing, Joan of Arc was burned to death, and the invention of the printing press was radically changing access to written materials allows a reader a different type of view of history: a bird's-eye view of the entire globe and its events. Such a global picture allows for cross-cultural comparisons as well as a valuable overview of chronological history that studying one particular area simply cannot provide.

Taking an expansive look at world history in each century, therefore, can be surprisingly informative. In Headlines in History, Greenhaven Press attempts to imitate this time-line approach using primary and secondary sources that span each century. Each volume gives readers the opportunity to view history as though they were reading the headlines of a global newspaper: Editors of each volume have attempted to glean and include the most important and influential events of the century, as well as quirky trends and cultural oddities. Headlines in History, then, attempts to give readers a glimpse of both the mundane and the earth-shattering. Articles on the French Revolution, for example, are juxtaposed with the then-current fashion concerns of the French nobility. This creates a higher interest level by allowing students a glimpse of people's everyday lives throughout history.

By using both primary and secondary sources, students also have the opportunity to view the historical events both as eyewitnesses have experienced them and as historians have interpreted them. Thus, students can place such historical events in a larger context as well as receive background information on important world events.

Headlines in History allows readers the unique opportunity to learn more about events that may only be mentioned in their history textbooks, or may be ignored entirely. The series presents students with a variety of interesting topics that span cultural, historical, and political arenas. Such a broad span of material will allow students to wander wherever their curiosity will take them.

Shifting Power and Perspective

During the seventeenth century western Europe experienced a social and philosophical revolution that shaped the century. During this period, science, politics, and the social structure changed drastically. Discoveries in science began to prove that the universe was not finite but expanded outward, infinitely; the world was not stable but dynamic. Philosophers began to speculate that human action was no longer merely a product of divine manipulation. Instead, many people began to evaluate their world by new methods and according to new criteria and became open to the possibility that the individual pursuit of knowledge and expression, not traditional doctrine, could be used to examine and explain the world. This focus on the importance of the individual prompted an increased sense of self-reliance, and people came to depend less on traditional authority, not only pursuing their own self-interest but also seeking a voice in how and by whom they would be governed. This shift in perspective was, as historian Frederick L. Nussbaum writes, "the central fact of the movement of the European spirit, which expressed itself in science, in politics and in the economic structure, as well as in the arts."[1]

This shift in perspective from dependence on and obedience to traditional authority toward self-reliance and self-expression was possible because both the church and the monarchy were loosening their grip on the people of western Europe. Prior to the seventeenth century, states usually were based on religious or dynastic ties; citizens owed loyalty to their church or ruling family, and the lives of most people were completely dominated and controlled by these forces. The power of the church, however, was the primary influence. Even the decisions of monarchs were dictated or at least closely monitored by the church. However, this control began to wane as early as the fourteenth century.

The Waning Influence of the Church

Historians generally agree that the influence of the church began to diminish when the population of Europe had been significantly depleted as a result of a succession of horrifying outbreaks of bubonic plague. Many clergy died as well, leaving many villages without religious leadership. In this weakened state, the Catholic Church suffered other blows. In 1517 the German priest Martin Luther fathered a historic religious reformation when he argued that individuals did not need a pope or priest to absolve their sins; through prayer, they could directly ask God for salvation. Luther believed that the ritual, hierarchy, and priestly intervention that typified the Catholic Church was unnecessary. Luther's Protestant Reformation spread, and by the seventeenth century western Europe was divided between the Roman Catholic and Protestant faiths.

Then, in 1543, the Polish theologian Nicolaus Copernicus touched off a religious-scientific revolution by questioning the authority of Aristotle; at the center of the universe was the sun, he claimed, not the earth. Although Copernicus's ideas would not reach the light of day until almost seventy years later, when Galileo began to explore them, the idea that religion opposed science and that one or the other must prevail remained an undercurrent during the Renaissance.

The Renaissance began at the end of the fourteenth century, and at its height during the fifteenth and sixteenth centuries, libraries, academies, and universities flourished. Scholars returned to a study of the classics and the intellectual focus, called humanism, began to shift from the religious to the secular. The Renaissance brought new importance to individual expression and self-awareness as well as an expanding worldview. Historian Christopher S. Chivvis remarks, "The impact of Renaissance thought on the development of modern politics was profound and enduring. When Renaissance humanists reconsidered humanity's place in the universe, they concluded that man had the unique power to better his own life."[2]

Challenging the Divine Right of Kings

The English challenge to the divine right of kings illustrates the growing sense of self-reliance that emerged as a result of the diminishing influence of the monarchy. The English Parliament of the seventeenth century was the primary legislative body of England. Composed of nobles and clergy, parliamentary members provided a voice for the interests of the people who elected them. However, both James I (James VI of Scotland) and his successor, Charles I, tried to rule without consulting Parliament, claiming that their power was absolute according to the doctrine of divine right. Neither monarch successfully decreased Parliament's role, however. The

English had been under the combined rule of both the king and Parliament for so long that they were unwilling to give all of the power of government to a single person. The merchants and landowning nobles supported Parliament because members could be elected and changed if necessary. An absolute monarch, on the other hand, had no such restraints.

In 1641 Parliament impeached several supporters of Charles I and attacked his policies. When Charles tried to arrest the leaders of his opposition while they sat in the House of Commons, supporters throughout England came to the opposition members' defense, and Charles was forced to flee London. For nearly a decade parliamentary and royal armies fought for power. The parliamentary armies finally defeated the royal army and, in 1649, a parliamentary tribunal tried and beheaded Charles I for treason and crimes against the English people. The monarchy was, for a time, abolished. This conflict was the major turning point against rule by divine right in England. Later seventeenth-century English monarchs realized the power of Parliament and knew they must work with, not against, it. Because Parliament was now such a strong element of English government, absolute monarchy, based on the divine right of kings, never gained a foothold in England. Parliament continued to gain power over the king through the end of the 1600s and would eventually become the leading governmental body of England.

It is important to note that this rejection of traditional authority was to a great extent limited to western Europe. The people of the East would continue to be dominated by the religious and imperial authority of emperors, shoguns, czars, and grand viziers. Expanding world trade would expose the people of the East to the Western perspective, and some Eastern leaders were attracted by Western developments. Peter the Great of Russia, for example, traveled to Europe to learn about Western military technology; however, Peter rejected Western political and cultural developments. Other Eastern governments feared the incursion of Western ideas and would close their doors to the West during the seventeenth century, adhering to the traditional structure of authority, both religious and political.

The Scientific Revolution

As a result of weakening religious and monarchic control and guided by the humanist spirit of the Renaissance, the people of Europe and England began to express their own ideas and assert their independence with less fear of attack by church and government. This gradual shift from dependence on traditional authority toward the individual pursuit of knowledge is most clearly reflected in the Scientific Revolution. During the seventeenth century scientists would develop an entirely new way of thinking. They would not only challenge traditional notions about the nature of the universe itself but also the methods used to explain it. They would develop the experimental method to test their theories, and gradually they came to believe that human reason, not faith in traditional church doctrine, could be used to explain the universe.

The Copernican theory that the earth revolved around the sun, for example, was unproven until the 1600s, when Galileo Galilei and Johannes Kepler developed the physics that would prove Copernicus right. This shift from observation and theory to measurement and proof and, ultimately, prediction, represented a new way of thinking. The seeds for this new way of thinking were planted during the Renaissance. Although scholars had returned to a study of Aristotle and his description of the structure of the universe, they began to examine nature itself rather than relying on Aristotle's authority alone. Hoping to peel away the secrets of nature by viewing it for themselves, Renaissance scholars drew conclusions from their observations. These conclusions, however, were only theoretical. It was not until the seventeenth century that natural philosophy would shift from observation to experimentation and natural philosophers would develop their own explanations for the nature of the universe.

In 1620, for example, Francis Bacon argued in *Novum Organum* that natural philosophy must use experimentation to prove scientific theories that had been reached through observation. Rather than just observe the laws of nature, Bacon suggested, natural philosophers must demonstrate their understanding of these laws. This shift from observation to experimentation also gave scientific theory a temporal dimension. Scientists developed hypotheses and theories, designing experiments to support, negate, or modify the theory or hypothesis, making science an active dynamic process.

Although the work of many natural philosophers contributed to the brilliance of the Scientific Revolution, the mathematical universe produced by Isaac Newton is perhaps the greatest achievement of the seventeenth century. Newton applied mathematics to his observations and developed a scientific explanation for the motion of the heavens. As scientist and historian Michael Guillen notes, Newton's *The Mathematical Principles of Natural Philosophy*, "with its powerful marriage of mathematics and experimentation, transformed natural philosophy into natural science."[3] In this text, Newton explained that the planets were held in their orbits by gravity. Newton not only explained gravity, but he also invented the calculus used to explain it. The universe had order and meaning, but this meaning was based on reason, not faith. In this way Newton represents the philosophy and spirit of the Scientific Revolution and the Enlightenment of the next century.

The Power of Human Reason

Another result of the failing marriage of religion and science was the development of the philosophy that people, now less dependent on church doctrine, could use their powers of reason to master the natural world. This philosophy attained its definitive expression in René Descartes's text published in 1637, *Discourse on Method.* Unlike Bacon and Newton, Descartes was more interested in rational thought than experimental observation. Descartes, the inventor of analytic geometry, was fascinated by the certainty of mathematical proof and distrusted sensory experiences. He believed that reason alone could explain the workings of the universe. According to Descartes, the world could be divided into a world of experiences and a world beyond experience—the dualism of mind and matter. The world beyond experience was the world of God, but the world of experience could be mastered by human reason.

The emphasis on experimentation and the individual pursuit of knowledge led to another seventeenth-century development. To demonstrate and disseminate the information gathered from their experiments, natural philosophers needed an environment that encouraged these new methods. Scientific societies such as the Royal Society of London for the Promotion of Natural Knowledge, chartered in 1662, and the Parisian Académie des Sciences in France, chartered in 1666, emerged to support scientific inquiry. The societies further developed the dissemination of scientific knowledge through the publication of the first scientific journals in which scientists would publish their observations, studies, and experiments.

Exploring Economic Independence

As the grip of church and government loosened, people also began to explore their economic independence, which contributed to another phenomenon that shaped the century—the colonization of America. News that vast riches might be found in the New World led James I of England to establish a colony in America that the colonists named Jamestown. This American colony was primarily established to bring gold and silver back to England. However, inspired by their desire for autonomy and independence, some people of seventeenth-century England hoped to shape their own destiny by seeking their fortune in the New World. After establishing the Jamestown colony on Chesapeake Bay in 1607, like many early colonists, they struggled to adapt to the weather and faced often strained relationships with native populations. Eventually, however, these colonists would develop Jamestown, Virginia, into a thriving community.

As colonies such as Jamestown grew, they chafed under imperial control. The imperial intent of colonization was to create markets for exports alone, and colonies were forbidden to become involved in manufacturing or to engage in any commerce other than with the mother country. These prohibitions frustrated colonists, who were enjoying their new freedom. They began to chafe at the authority of the king. The colonists first sought only a voice in their governance, but when that was denied, they chose instead complete independence from imperial authority, which ultimately led to the American Revolution that erupted in the next century.

The Emergence of the Middle Class

Another seventeenth-century development that illustrates the exploration of economic independence is the emergence of the middle class. Expanding world trade created opportunities for merchants and businesspeople such as lawyers, bankers, and shopkeepers needed to support the burgeoning economy. The new middle class exploited these opportunities, gaining power and influence. Although members of the middle class were not titled landowners, these merchants and businesspeople had more money to spend than ever before. For example, the middle class began to participate in the patronage of the arts, and the middle-class taste for realism is reflected in the works of such towering seventeenth-century Dutch masters as Rembrandt and Frans Hals.

This money also gave members of the middle class more power and control over their lives. Because governments need significant funds to protect and maintain their interests at home and abroad, the middle classes in the seventeenth century could now assert the power of the purse and take an increasingly important part in politics. In Holland, they became powerful enough to gain an effective authority within the state. The new representatives of the provinces were wealthy middle-class merchants, a development that coincided with a peak in Dutch capitalism. In France, these merchants wanted to rise to the aristocracy, and the monarchy took advantage of their ambition by selling official posts. The rising middle class often lent money to the king to support his ambitions to rule Europe, and Louis XIV deliberately employed bourgeois administrators as ministers, hoping to limit the power of the nobles who opposed him.

As the influence of the middle class grew, so did its members' sense of power, and they began to seek a greater voice in how they were governed. They demanded individual liberty, government under a constitution, and the abolition or reduction of class distinctions. Inspired by philosophers such as John Locke, their frustration with the rigid social and political order would contribute to the revolutions that erupted in the next century. To achieve their goals, they also needed to develop the concept of a nation with a national government that represented them all, which would contribute to the continued development of the nation-state.

With their new sense of power and self-reliance—their increasing need for independence from authority—the people of seventeenth-century western Europe began to reevaluate their world. They questioned the traditional methods of science and challenged the role of established governments. With this new perspective they not only challenged ancient ideas but paved the way for the revolutionary spirit of the Enlightenment. Historian Leo Weinstein remarks, "Rarely before had an age so thoroughly reevaluated all the past in terms of new criteria; rarely before or after have so many great thinkers and artists lived in one century."[4]

However, the seventeenth century cannot be evaluated by the rise and fall of empires or developments in science and commerce alone. The fact that historians struggle to characterize the seventeenth century suggests that the events that shaped the period cannot be easily unified. To identify unifying characteristics, some historians label the newfound perspective and sense of power the baroque period; meanwhile, others focus on the influence of the Scientific Revolution, characterizing it as the Age of Reason.

Whether the 1600s represents a revolution or a philosophical temperament, the events and people of the century steered the course of humankind. No longer members of a finite universe, the people of the seventeenth century began to chart a new place for humankind in an expanding world.

Notes

1. Frederick L. Nussbaum, *The Triumph of Science and Reason, 1600–1685*. New York: Harper Torchbooks, 1962, p. 28.
2. Christopher S. Chivvis, "The Ascent of the *Nation-State,*" *World & I,* March 1999, p. 20.
3. Michael Guillen, *Five Equations That Changed the World: The Power and Poetry of Mathematics*. New York: Hyperion, 1995, p. 55.
4. Leo Weinstein, *The Age of Reason: The Culture of the Seventeenth Century*. New York: G. Braziller, 1965, p. 19.

A Century of Discovery

People began to look at the world in a new way in the seventeenth century. With the aid of new instruments such as the telescope and microscope, European scientists explored their environment with new vision, discovering a world different from that conceived by ancient philosophers. Building on the then-revolutionary theory of Nicolas Copernicus that the earth was not the center of the universe but traveled around the sun, Johannes Kepler discovered that planetary orbits were elliptical and that planets did not move at constant speeds. Isaac Newton's theory of gravity held that the universe consisted of an infinity of material particles pulling on one another simultaneously. Seventeenth-century natural philosophers were challenging traditional notions of man's place at the center of God's perfect universe.

At the beginning of the century, the reaction to this newfound knowledge was mixed. In some parts of Europe, the Catholic Inquisition considered these discoveries heresy, and those who supported these new ideas were forced to either recant or face execution: Italian philosopher Giordano Bruno was burned at the stake and, facing a similar fate, Galileo recanted. Although still skeptical of developments in natural philosophy, other parts of Europe were more tolerant, and as the century progressed, countries such as England and France supported communities of scientists, founding academic societies such as the Royal Society of London for the Promotion of Natural Knowledge in 1662 and the Parisian Académie des Sciences in 1666, which encouraged exploration in natural philosophy.

These revolutionary natural philosophers began to use experiments rather than rhetoric to explain phenomena. René Descartes's analytical geometry, John Napier's logarithms, and Isaac Newton's calculus allowed scientists to describe the material world through mathematics and mechanics, and scientists tested their theoretical conceptions, recording their observations and using mathematical and mechanical concepts to explain them. Rather than using observation alone to determine the orbit of the planets, Kepler could test his observations using mathematics. William Harvey's theory on the circulation of blood was made possible by measuring the capacity of the heart's ventricle and applying a mathematical equation that determined the blood must circulate out into the body to return to the heart.

Technological development and scientific experimentation fostered a mechanistic view of the world. Since physical phenomena could be explained, seventeenth-century philosophers debated whether human thought and behavior could be explained using the same methods. Descartes distinguished matter and thought, concluding that everything in the material world could be explained except the human soul. Baruch Spinoza also questioned a totally mechanistic view of man, arguing that human behavior is influenced not only by conscious thought, but also by unconscious motives and desires. Thomas Hobbes, on the other hand, believed that even human thought could be explained mechanically, and he conceived of government as one giant machine designed to protect society from its natural state, which is war. Because the sovereign represents the whole, to revolt against the sovereign is self-destructive, Hobbes claimed. However, John Locke argued that people voluntarily contract with the government for the protection of natural rights and, therefore, have the right to revolt against a government that breaches this contract.

These new ideas, tools, and methods altered the way seventeenth-century Europeans saw themselves and the world around them, and for this reason the century is considered a revolutionary period in both thought and science.

The Scientific Revolution

Richard G. Olson

Most historians agree that the Scientific Revolution reshaped the way Europeans viewed the natural world. However, in the following article historian Richard G. Olson reveals alternative explanations to traditional conceptions of the origins and influence of the Scientific Revolution. According to Olson, Christian thought was not in opposition to science, but supported man's superior capacity for insight and reason. Moreover, Olson explains, authors whose texts some historians view as revolutionary actually found support in ancient thought and merely used new methods to expand traditional ideas. Earlier historians argued that the secular intellectual societies encouraged the revolution, but Olson claims that older institutions also supported some of the research that came out of the period, including the Catholic Jesuit colleges. Although twentieth-century thought has revised some of the ideas that emerged during the Scientific Revolution, the experimentation that was central to the revolution continues to influence the modern world. Olson is a professor of history at Harvey Mudd College in Claremont, California, and author of several books on the history of science, including *The Emergence of the Social Sciences, 1642–1792*.

It outshines everything since the rise of Christianity and reduces the Renaissance and Reformation to the rank of mere episodes, mere internal displacements, within the system of medieval Christendom. Since it changed the character of men's habitual mental operations even in the conduct of the nonmaterial sciences, while transforming the whole diagram of the physical universe and the very texture of human life itself, it looms so large as

Excerpted from Richard G. Olson, "The Scientific Revolution Reshapes the World," *The World & I*, April 1999. This article is reprinted with permission from *The World & I*, a publication of The Washington Times Corporation, copyright © 1999.

the real origin both of the modern world and of the modern mentality that our customary periodization of European history has become an anachronism and an encumbrance.

So wrote British historian Herbert Butterfield in 1949, when he popularized the notion that a "scientific revolution" had occurred in Europe during the sixteenth and seventeenth centuries. In his view, this revolution was the single most important set of events to shape the modern world.

Reinterpreting the Scientific Revolution

In the half century since Butterfield's call to attend to the importance of the scientific revolution, specialized historians of science have dramatically reinterpreted its character in several respects:

• We have come to realize that it was much more closely linked to features of medieval Christendom and to both the Renaissance and the Reformation than Butterfield imagined.

• We now see it less as the result of a few intellectuals "picking up the other end of the stick," as Butterfield phrased it, than as the outcome of social processes and practices (such as printing) that crossed class boundaries and led to many competing ways of understanding the world.

• Finally, we find that it was as much shaped by dramatic changes in the material and nonmaterial environments of early modern Europeans—such as the rise of commercial capitalism and the humanistic emphases of the Renaissance—as it was a shaper of subsequent attitudes and events.

Yet one crucial insight of Butterfield's seems as true today as it did 50 years ago: The set of events referred to as the scientific revolution not only refashioned how early modern Europeans understood and related to the natural world but subsequently had an enormous effect on the creation of our modern material and mental worlds.

The Christian Humanist Legacy

One of the most pervasive features of modernity is a threefold set of assumptions: (1) the natural world is rationally structured; (2) human beings can gain knowledge of that structure by applying their reason to information gathered through their senses; and (3) humans can and should use that knowledge to improve the circumstances of their lives. These assumptions came to dominate Western culture in connection with the theoretical and practical achievements of the scientific revolution, but key elements were appropriated from the Christian tradition.

According to the belief systems of many religions, humans are understood to be incorporated within the natural order. But in Christian teachings, humanity stands outside that order and to some extent above it, by virtue of human likeness to the Divine and a special injunction from the Divine to subdue the earth and to "rule over . . . every living thing that moves upon the earth" (Genesis 1:26–30).

Within medieval Christendom, intellectuals attached great importance to human rationality and its capacity to provide insights into the workings of the physical world, so as to illuminate the nature of the Divine. It was not until the Renaissance, however, that humanists shifted focus from the static life of contemplation to the dynamic life of action associated with ruling the earth. First in Northern Italy and then throughout Europe, scholars began to mirror the shift in social and economic leadership away from the military and landed aristocracy, whose ways of life were extremely stable, to a class of urban notables exemplified by the Medicis and Albertis, whose growing fortunes derived from the dynamic domains of trade and commerce. The scholars reemphasized the biblical injunction to subdue and rule, and they focused on knowledge that promised an element of human control over the natural world. . . .

Revolutionary Texts

It is common to date the beginning of the scientific revolution to 1543, when two pivotal texts appeared. The first of these was Nicolaus Copernicus' *De revolutionibus orbium coelestium (On the Revolutions of the Heavenly Spheres),* which shook up astronomy by proposing a Sun-centered universe to replace the long-held, Earth-centered model advocated by Ptolemy (Claudius Ptolemaeus), the respected astronomer of second-century Alexandria. The second was Andreas Vesalius' *De humani corporis fabrica (On the Fabric of the Human Body),* which challenged several established views of human anatomy that derived from Galen, a second-century Greek physician. For instance, Vesalius' observations led him to suggest that, contrary to Galen's view, blood could not pass from one side of the heart to the other through the septum—the wall between the left and right sides.

These two texts radically changed the ways by which astronomy and anatomy were done. But Copernicus and Vesalius may have scarcely considered themselves revolutionaries. In fact, each was acting as a good humanist scholar, responding to severe problems in his discipline by seeking help in the pure and uncorrupted texts of antiquity.

As Copernicus reflected on the growing disparities between observed solar and planetary positions and those calculated using Ptolemaic theory, he searched the ancient literature and discovered that some writers, including Cicero [the Roman orator, statesman, and philosopher], had assumed that Earth moved around the Sun rather than vice versa. Even more important from a technical standpoint, he found that the early Greek astronomer Hipparchus had measured the constant year in terms of successive passages of the Sun past a given star—what we would call the *sidereal* year. On the other hand, Ptolemy had measured the constant year as the interval between one vernal equinox (the first day of spring, when day and night are equally long) and the next—a period we call the *solar* year. Copernicus' great work was, in effect, a reworking of Ptolemaic astronomy using Hipparchus' assumption regarding the constant year; one major consequence of that reworking was the necessity of viewing Earth as revolving around the Sun.

The case of Vesalius' revolution in anatomy was only slightly different. Galen's work, *De Anatomicus Administrationibus (On Anatomical Procedures)*, had emphasized the importance of direct observation of the structure of the human body rather than acceptance of any textual authority. But this text was unknown to the West until it was recovered and translated from the Greek by Vesalius' teacher, Gunther von Andernach, in 1539. Vesalius then began to study it and to uncover Galen's errors, many of which had occurred because Galen used apes for dissection when human cadavers were difficult to get. In his great work of 1543, Vesalius followed Galen's text chapter by chapter, correcting its errors while reemphasizing Galen's original admonition to learn anatomy by direct observation of the body.

The Institutional Milieu

Until relatively recently, students of the scientific revolution argued that one of its central features was the movement of science out of the religiously dominated universities, which were thought to have been intellectual backwaters, and into the new context of secular, government-sponsored organizations such as the Royal Society of London for the Promotion of Natural Knowledge (chartered in 1662) and the Parisian Académie des Sciences (established by [French politician Jean-Baptiste] Colbert in 1666). Around the same time, the dissemination of scientific knowledge was transformed through establishment of the first scientific journals: the *Philosophical Transactions* of the Royal Society of London (in 1665) and the *Journal des Savants* of the Parisian Académie (in 1666).

Although learned societies did emerge as centers of scientific activity and (especially on the Continent) received government support in return for their technical advice to the state, older institutions remained extremely important centers of intellectual vitality. Advances in anatomy and physiology, for example, continued to be made primarily at universities. It should be noted, though, that William Harvey's experimental demonstration (in the early seventeenth century) that the heart serves as a pump that circulates blood through the body was presented in lectures to the Royal College of Physicians, an honorary society in London.

In both applied mathematics and experimental natural philosophy (the term used for much of experimental science), the network of Jesuit colleges played a particularly important role through the seventeenth century, contrary to the general and largely false impression that the Catholic Church was implacably hostile to science. The Jesuit order was wealthy enough to purchase scientific instruments that were beyond the reach of most scientists and many universities. Moreover, beginning in the 1560s, it developed the first institutional support for positions in which distinguished scholars were relieved of their teaching duties and allowed to devote their efforts to research and publishing for periods of up to six years.

Another major locus of scientific activity throughout the sixteenth century and much of the seventeenth was the individual aristocratic court, which often supported intellectuals partly for their services and partly for fame and glory. Near the beginning of the seventeenth century, for example, the court of Emperor Rudolph at Prague employed Tycho Brahe, Johannes Kepler, and Joost Bürgi. Tycho's precise measurements of planetary positions forced a reconsideration of the Copernican assumption that planets move in circular orbits. Using Tycho's observations, Kepler formulated a new theory, according to which each planet moves in an elliptical orbit with the Sun at one focus. Bürgi, a mathematician and maker of spectacular astronomical clocks, invented logarithms to ease Kepler's calculations. And Bürgi's clocks stimulated Kepler to think of the universe in the likeness of a clock rather than a living being—a central concept for the creation of Kepler's revolutionary theory.

One important group of scientists was supported by the Cavendish family in England, where philosopher Thomas Hobbes was the center of a group that included Lady Margaret Cavendish, one of the first women to publish on scientific subjects. Another group was supported by the Medici family in Florence, where Evangelista Torricelli, Giovanni Borelli, Francesco Redi, and several others did experimental work on heat and atmospheric pressure, using their new inventions such as the thermometer and barometer.

The Mechanical Philosophy

In terms of the cultural impact of the scientific revolution, one major feature was the growing pervasiveness of the so-called corpuscular or mechanical philosophy. In fact, this philosophy was formulated in several different versions, all of which shared the assumption that physical phenomena must be explained in terms of the impact of one body or particle upon another. In [German philosopher and mathematician] Gottfried Leibniz's words, "A body is never moved naturally except by another body which touches it and pushes it; after that, it continues until it is prevented by another body which touches it. Any other kind of operation on bodies is either miraculous or imaginary."

The mechanical philosophy in its various versions derived from two major sources. One was the atomic philosophy that ancient philosophers Epicurus and Lucretius had developed extensively. The other was the familiarity of scholars with engineered objects that increasingly dominated Europe's urban landscape.

René Descartes and Robert Boyle stand out as the leading proponents of the mechanical philosophy's "rationalist" and "empiricist" versions, respectively. Descartes' interest grew out of a special concern with the rational structure of the world and with a mathematician's fascination with the certainty of mathematical proof. Indeed, he had absorbed the ancient skeptic's distrust of sensory experience and sought to develop scientific knowledge through the faculty of reason, as uncontaminated by empirical elements as possible. In a series of works—including the *Discourse on Method* (1637), *Principles of Philosophy* (1644), *The Passions of the Soul* (1649) and *On Man* (published posthumously in 1664)—Descartes sought to derive practically all phenomena from basic assumptions about the properties of matter. In so doing, he concluded that everything in nature is mechanical. While Descartes continued to believe in an immaterial human soul, other rationalist mechanical philosophers, including Thomas Hobbes, advocated a complete mechanical materialism in which even human thought was mechanically explained.

Unlike Descartes, who was confident that the world was rationally explicable and that his mind was capable of explaining it, Boyle was convinced that God's choices in creating the universe were ultimately unconstrained and therefore inexplicable. In Boyle's view, experiential and experimental interrogation of nature was an important means to understand how God chose to structure the universe; however, one could not anticipate in advance how He chose to make things work. Initially, Boyle's empiricist emphasis led him into alchemical studies, but his experiments with air convinced him to take a corpuscular (or mechanical) view of matter. In 1660, his *New Experiments Physico-Mechanicall, Touching the Spring of the Air, and Its Effects* appeared, describing the results of many experiments carried out with his newly invented air pump. Two years later, he announced his famous experimental result, known as Boyle's law: At a given temperature, the volume of a gas is inversely proportional to its pressure.

Competing Approaches to Knowledge

Coexistence of the rationalist and empiricist versions of mechanical philosophy illustrates that the scientific revolution involved competing approaches to scientific knowledge. In addition, a number of alternative philosophies vied for attention and influence. One of these eventually had a greater impact on modern scientific practice than the mechanical philosophy did.

First, there was a revived and revitalized Aristotelian tradition that emphasized observational and contemplative means of understanding nature. This tradition was especially important among Catholic scholars and particularly fruitful in medicine and natural history, but it was bitterly attacked by those who favored more aggressive experimental and applied approaches. . . .

Second, there was the Hermetic/Neoplatonic tradition that emphasized the "occult" or hidden connections among phenomena and posited a life force in all of nature. This tradition, through its manifestations in alchemy and "natural magic," was important in the early growth of empirical approaches in the search for natural knowledge. By the end of the seventeenth century, it was on the wane, but such major figures as Isaac Newton continued to take it seriously.

Finally, there was an approach to natural knowledge that sought descriptive mathematical laws of nature and abandoned the traditional search for causal accounts of phenomena. This position is most often associated with Galileo Galilei and Isaac Newton, for it played a major role in their most spectacular successes. . . .

This approach can be found in Galileo's *Discourses and Mathematical Demonstrations Concerning Two New Sciences* (1638), in which he showed that when a body at rest near Earth's surface is made to fall freely, the distance fallen is proportional to the square of the time of fall. Here he openly acknowledged his inability to explain the cause. Similarly, in a paper published in 1672, Newton demonstrated that white light is composed of light of all colors of the spectrum, each color being bent to a different extent when it strikes a prism's surface; but he admitted that he did not know why. And in his masterpiece, *Philosophiae Naturalis Principia Mathematica (Mathematical Principles of Natural Philosophy)* (1687), Newton articulated the law of universal gravitation—that every particle of matter in the universe attracted every other particle with a force that was proportional to the product of their masses and inversely proportional to the distance separating the particles. Here again, Newton admitted being unable to discover why this was so, and he refused to speculate about the cause.

Isaac Newton

Newton expended great efforts in trying to devise a mechanical explanation for gravity. In the "Queries" to various editions of his *Opticks* (first published in 1704), he sought to give causal accounts for numerous optical, chemical, and physical phenomena. But Newton was careful to distinguish between what he considered as having been demonstrated—such as the law of gravity and the composition of white light—and what he considered as merely conjectural until it could, perhaps, be demonstrated.

A Cultural Transformation

One major consequence of the scientific revolution was the transformation of almost all premodern, commonsense notions about the character of the natural world. For example:

• Before the scientific revolution, people believed that Earth was at the center or bottom of the universe, at the maximum distance from God, Who resided in the empyrean above the stars. Afterward, they understood they lived on one planet among others circling the Sun, which was one star among an uncountable number.

• Before the scientific revolution, all living things were thought to have souls that allowed them to be self-moving. Afterward, the bodies of living things were considered by many scientists as complicated mechanical devices that moved only in response to external stimuli.

• Before the scientific revolution, people naturally thought that the speed of an object was proportional to the force acting on it. Afterward, they understood that it was the acceleration of an object that was proportional to the force.

A second consequence of the scientific revolution was a dramatic transformation in the material conditions of the lives of nearly every person in the Western world. When Butterfield wrote about it in 1949, scholars generally held the opinion that scientific knowledge did not lead to significant changes in medical care, agriculture, and industrial productivity until well into the nineteenth century. But this view has been radically revised. . . . It now seems clear that scientific attitudes, practices, and knowledge greatly stimulated agricultural and commercial growth as early as the seventeenth century. They certainly fueled the Industrial Revolution of the late eighteenth century, and that revolution provided the foundation for the unprecedented wealth of modern western Europe and North America,

Finally, the scientific revolution was immensely important in transforming Western views of the character of society and the human individual. Methods of observation, analysis, and quantification developed in connection with natural knowledge were almost immediately and consciously transferred to the domains of society and individual human behavior. Thus in 1644, Hobbes produced a major transformation in political philosophy, claiming that he was doing for "civil philosophy" nothing but what Galileo had done for natural philosophy and Harvey had done for the science of man's body. Drawing heavily on rational mechanical philosophy, Hobbes initiated a tradition of liberal, individualistic, secular, and sociopolitical theory that has dominated

Anglo-American ideology ever since.

A few decades later, John Locke began to apply the conceptual apparatus developed in connection with experimental mechanical philosophy to issues in what we now call psychology and moral philosophy as well. William Petty and his British and French followers drew from mechanical and mathematical concepts in creating "political arithmetic"—the foundation of modern economics—and grounded it in the assumption that each of us acts in such a way as to maximize our rationally calculated self-interest. And [seventeenth-century English political theorist] James Harrington responded to Hobbes' political theory by initiating social analyses that began to identify political authority with economic power.

While these ideas, for better or worse, continue to underpin much of the Western view of self and society, our twentieth century . . . brought extraordinary revisions to established scientific concepts about nature, challenging the foundations of mechanical philosophies. From the work of such scientists as Max Planck, Albert Einstein, Louis de Broglie, and Erwin Schrödinger emerged radical views: that energy does not flow like a continuous wave but takes the form of discrete units (quanta), that waves can behave like particles, and that particles can have the properties of waves. From Einstein's famous equation, $E = mc^2$, came the realization that matter and energy are interconvertible, and his General Theory of Relativity explained the phenomenon of gravity as a manifestation of the curvature of space. These concepts run contrary to the notions consolidated at the time of the scientific revolution, but acceptance of the new theories is grounded in the argument that they provide the best known explanations for experimental observations. Thus, the formula of establishing theory based on careful experimentation, which was so central to the scientific revolution, continues to guide scientific research in the modern world.

The Experimental Method: A New Framework for Science

Philip K. Wilson

The experimental method evolved from a shift in the way scientists perceived the natural world, writes Philip K. Wilson, professor of the history of science. In the fifth century B.C., Aristotle provided natural versus supernatural explanations for phenomena based upon his observations, and his explanations of the universe formed the basis of natural philosophy for nearly two thousand years. During the Renaissance, however, philosophers turned away from Aristotle's writing and began to examine the natural world itself. In 1620 Francis Bacon argued that if people wanted to master nature, they must understand the laws of nature. Rather than use Aristotle's deductive reasoning, Bacon claimed, philosophers must use inductive reasoning—shifting from observation to experimentation. Scientific societies such as the Royal Society of London furthered the use of this new method because they provided a place where natural philosophers could gather not only to share ideas but to demonstrate their experiments. As a result of this new method of examining the world, people of the seventeenth century began to see natural phenomena in mechanical ways. Using mathematics, for example, Isaac Newton explained that celestial bodies moved according to the same gravitation forces as objects on earth. This mechanical philosophy conflicted with religion be-

Excerpted from Philip K. Wilson, "Origins of Science," *National Forum: The Phi Kappa Phi Journal,* vol. 76, no. 1, Winter 1996. Copyright © 1996 Philip K. Wilson. Reprinted with permission from the publishers.

cause it weakened the belief in miracles and divine inspiration. Nevertheless, this philosophy continued to inspire the testing of new theories and the reduction of natural phenomena to quantifiable terms. Wilson is professor of the history of science and biology at Truman State University in Kirksville, Missouri.

W hen perusing a science textbook, one can easily envision science as a body of knowledge. But more than knowledge, science is a process in that people "do" science. Scientists work according to a specific method of inquiry, a method that invites participants to interact with the world by asking questions, evaluating situations, and comparing experiences. Paraphrasing the British philosopher Bertrand Russell, it is not what scientists believe about natural phenomena that distinguishes them from others, but rather how and why they believe it. When did such a system of beliefs actually begin?

More than a focus upon any one epoch of time, the *origin* of science may be construed as the beginning of a new way of envisioning, perceiving, interpreting, and ultimately understanding the natural world. In this sense, science as a process has actually had several beginnings. Each of these beginnings may be seen as a shift in one or more of the concepts that characterize science: observing, collecting, rationalizing, organizing, hypothesizing, interpreting, and communicating. . . .

The Scholastic Approach

Western thinkers credit the Greek philosophers Plato and Aristotle with establishing the natural and physical sciences. These "originators" argued in the sixth and fifth centuries B.C. that phenomena such as planetary motion, changes in the physical composition of matter, and life itself should no longer be described as supernatural events, but were all explicable according to nature. Aristotle, for example, was an individual who, like the naturalists of more recent centuries, spent much time "in the field"—actually on the Aegean Isle of Lesbos—observing the habits and habitats of living organisms. He collected many marine specimens, scrutinized their similarities and differences, and placed the organisms on particular conceptual rungs of a continuous *scala natura* or "Great Chain of Being," according to their degrees of "perfection." In *De Generatione Animalium,* Aristotle described his concept of perfection as based on an individual organism's state of development at its birth. Humans achieved the supreme link of the chain, not only because of their fully perfected form at birth, but also by their superior ability to reason. The powerful legacy of this concept from the Hellenic through the Romantic periods constituted what Arthur Lovejoy described in his monumental *The Great Chain of Being: A Study of the*

History of an Idea (1936), as "one of the most grandiose experiences of the human intellect."

Aristotelian thought dominated natural philosophy for nearly two thousand years. *Questiones* drawn from Aristotelian texts formed the basis of the science that scholastics read, taught, and disputed in medieval universities. Students were expected to comprehend and respond to any proposed objections to Aristotle's description of the structure and operations of the universe. This scholastic approach exemplified a new origin of science. No longer were observing, collecting, and interpreting part of the individual scientist's endeavors. Rather, knowledge of the natural world was to be taken upon the authority of Aristotle, and upon university- (in other words, Church-) approved commentaries of the canonical writings. In this sense, science more clearly resembled *scientia,* its Latin etymological root meaning knowledge, understanding, or wisdom.

Roman and medieval natural philosophers made little if any distinction between what twentieth-century thinkers would view as science and pseudoscience. In reading Pliny the Elder's encyclopedic *Naturalis Historia,* compiled in the first century A.D., one finds, for example, his advice to soak seeds in wine to prevent certain fungal diseases juxtaposed with his recommendation to touch the tops of trees with "the gall" of a green lizard to protect them from the ravage of caterpillars. If this is not successful, he suggests that a crayfish or skull of a female horse or ass hung in the middle of the garden will chase away the pests. As an encyclopedist, Pliny sought, with apparently insatiable curiosity, to uncritically gather as much knowledge as possible, be it sound wisdom or specious folklore, into one place to serve as the source book of all natural philosophy.

The coexistence of *scientia* and pseudoscience in medieval natural philosophy is also exemplified by the interconnection of science, religion, and magic. Medieval scientists described the universe in terms of a divine plan. The world and its inhabitants typically operated according to, but were not confined to, the "laws" of nature. Christian doctrine secured Aristotle's teleological interpretation of nature in its own terms. When any disruption of the "natural" flow of things was encountered, Christianity empowered "scientists" to invoke God as the cause of a miraculous event. Thus, the concept of supernatural causes of phenomena, which the Greeks had displaced, was reintroduced into medieval science.

Magic used occult forces—forces explained to be either supernatural or natural, but hidden—to achieve some practical end. Extending the natural philosophers' desire to increase their understanding of nature, magicians desired ways of actually controlling nature. This utilitarian goal indicates that medieval magicians probably created an environment more conducive to the later development of experimental science than did contemporary natural philosophers in their quests to increase knowledge for knowledge's sake. Despite several attempts to curb Aristotle's influence, a solid knowledge of Aristotelian writings remained at the heart of science education through the Renaissance. Gradually, however, the Church acknowledged several problems in its authorized version of Aristotle. For instance, Aristotle's claim that the cosmos was eternal, that it had always been and could not cease to be, was inconsistent with the biblical creation account. Aristotle's teleological argument that the *primum mobile* set the cosmos in motion but was incapable of intervening left no room to account for miracles. Was reform imminent?

The Scientific Revolution

Renaissance thinkers, in magic and natural philosophy as well as in art, turned their gaze away from scholastic writings toward nature and the natural world. Nature's secrets, they exclaimed, were to be revealed by peeling away its structure layer by layer: "The present discoveries in science are such as lie immediately beneath the surface of common notions." To further advance knowledge, it was "necessary . . . to penetrate the more secret and remote parts of nature, in order to abstract both notions and axioms from things by a more certain . . . method," writes Francis Bacon, in *Novum Organum* (1620). This dissection or display of nature allowed individuals to view nature's "parts" for themselves, and to rationalize and interpret correlations between structure and function independently of theological constraints.

The change from science as merely received knowledge to an active questioning of the natural world required a shift in the framework—or a new origin—in the way of thinking about natural phenomena. The period between Nicolaus Copernicus's 1543 publication of *De Revolutionibus Orbium Coelestium* through Isaac Newton's *Philosophiae Naturalis Principia Mathematica* (1687), roughly demarcates what has, since the seventeenth century, been referred to as the scientific revolution.

Key examples of the type of conceptual changes that are labeled as revolutions are Copernicus's mathematical demonstration of a new sun-centered astronomical system in which the earth actually moved and Newton's mathematical explication that celestial motion operates according to the same gravitational forces and physical laws as terrestrial motion. They certainly meet the common qualifications that Roy Porter and Mikulas Teich described in *Revolution in History* (1986). Revolutions, these authors argue, result from a challenge and eventual overthrow of long-entrenched orthodoxy; demonstrate a triumphant, visible break from the past; and exemplify how, from the outset, reformers were consciously acting toward some grandiose intention.

For the past three decades, historians and philosophers of science have described the underlying conceptualization of the changes that took place during the scientific revolution as a paradigm shift. Indeed, discussion of "paradigms" and "paradigm shifts"—two phrases that originated in Thomas Kuhn's historical examination of *The Structure of Scientific Revolutions* (1962)—has permeated scholarship in myriad academic fields. Kuhn claimed that works by scientists including Aristotle, Copernicus, and Newton, and later Benjamin Franklin, Antoine-Laurent Lavoisier, and Charles Lyell demarcated particular periods of science. They served, he argued, to "define the legitimate problems and methods of a research field for succeeding generations of practitioners." In particular, their "achievement was sufficiently unprecedented to attract an enduring group of adherents away from competing modes of scientific activity," whereas their writings were "sufficiently open-ended to leave all sorts of problems for the redefined group of practitioners to resolve."

Francis Bacon's *Novum Organum* (1620) is typically given credit for the origin of the scientific revolution's new framework for science: the experimental method. Bacon, though not a scientist himself, was influential in generating a new paradigm for science. If the purpose of science was, as Bacon and many contemporaries believed, to give humans mastery over nature, thereby extending the powers of humans, then the laws of nature must be better understood. This level of understanding, so Bacon proposed, would be achieved through shifting natural philosophers from deductive to inductive reasoning and through the application of experimentation.

The Royal Society

Bacon's seventeenth-century model for organizing science around specific modes of inquiry may be viewed as the origin of other developments of the "new philosophy." It has been convincingly argued that the environment within the Royal Society of London—one of the first scientific societies—was designed after Bacon's description of a utopian "college of experience," a college that encouraged discussion and collaboration among investigators. This Society adopted the motto *Nullius in Verba* ("on the word or authority of no one") in an explicit attempt to distinguish the new science from the long Aristotelian-dominated tradition.

Early Fellows of the Royal Society designed experiments to demonstrate their knowledge of mechanics and became able to predict with certainty the actions of chemicals, magnets, and electricity. Others described their experiences with navigation and ballooning. Physicians, surgeons, and anatomists reported experiments upon patients whom they deemed to be remarkable cases. Because these results were published through the Society's regularly printed *Philosophical Transactions*, the Baconian dream of fostering the "Improvement of Natural

Knowledge" became a reality. Some, like Charles Darwin's staunch supporter Thomas Henry Huxley, later claimed this record of communication to be the actual origin of modern science. "If all the books in the world except the *Philosophical Transactions* were destroyed," Huxley asserted, "the foundations of physical science would remain unshaken."

The Mechanical Universe

The scientific revolution, what science historian Richard Westfall considered "the most important 'event' in Western history," originated, in part, from the triumph of another paradigm: the mechanical view of the universe. Mechanical philosophy and materialism grew out of the writings of natural philosophers including Galileo Galilei, Pierre Gassendi, René Descartes, Thomas Hobbes, William Harvey, Robert Boyle, John Locke, and Isaac Newton. Typically they used mechanically based deductive reasoning in their explanations of natural phenomena. Some revitalized the Pre-Socratic belief that all life was reducible to atoms, the actions of which were deducible from the laws of motion. Opponents argued that the mechanists' reductionist accounts removed or displaced God from the central position in their depiction of natural phenomena.

This shift in philosophical paradigms created a divisive rift between believers of supernatural cause and believers of natural cause. Keith Thomas in his classic *Religion and the Decline of Magic* (1971) argued that the "notion that the universe was subjected to immutable natural laws killed the concept of miracles, weakened the belief in the physical efficacy of prayer, and diminished faith in the possibility of direct divine inspiration."

Modern science has been dominated by two types of investigation: 1) the increasing importance of testing theories and hypotheses by experiment, and 2) the recognition of an underlying mathematical simplicity in nature. The dogmatic edicts so prevalent in earlier science writing were replaced with theories of science. Scientists sought to devise specific experiments to test a working hypothesis or tentative theory. Experimental results began to be interpreted as either supporting, negating, or modifying a particular hypothesis. In general, theories and hypotheses gained a temporal dimension. People can do no better, claimed experimental physiologist Claude Bernard in his *Introduction to the Study of Experimental Medicine* (1865), than "to follow the indications of natural phenomena, using theories as torches intended to illuminate the path and needing to be replaced as they were consumed."

The new science also demonstrated an increasing reliance upon expressing the substance of science in quantifiable terms. No longer was Aristotle's description of one starfish acceptable as a definitive explanation to the scientific community. Multiple experimental subjects needed to be tested to determine an average response. Standard, normative, and average became part of the vocabulary of the "new" science.

From Mathematics to Microscopes: Advances in Biology

Charles Singer

The attempts to measure physical phenomena that dominated the science of the seventeenth century are reflected in its study of biology, writes the late historian Charles Singer. In the following overview of the century's biological advances Singer provides a glimpse into some of the century's major biological discoveries as well as the changing attitudes that made these discoveries possible. For example, William Harvey's discovery that the blood circulates through the body depended not only on developments in mathematics but also on the philosophy that living organisms operated like machines. Using mathematics, Harvey determined the volume of blood, and believing the heart acted as a pump, he concluded that such a quantity of blood could only be possible if the blood went out into the body and came back again. Singer also explains the importance of developments like the microscope, which provided scientists with the ability to see the development of life-forms once believed to come into existence as a result of spontaneous generation. Singer has written many books on the history of science, medicine, and technology.

B iological science, it is often said, always lags behind physical science and is always in a more elementary stage. The statement is hardly borne out by history. It depends for any truth that it may possess upon a particular conception of the nature of science. In antiquity, in the hands of Aristotle, biological science was far ahead of physical. . . . The treatise of [Nicolaus] Copernicus is medieval by comparison, and contains very few original observations. To justify the doctrine of the relative backwardness of biological science it is necessary to postulate that the aim of biology is to represent biological phenomena in physical terms. Thus expressed, the statement becomes a self-evident proposition for, if the postulate be granted, biology can never advance beyond its physical interpretation. A large school of biological thinkers does not accept this postulate. Even more numerous are those who, taking no philosophical stand in the matter, hold that, until we know far more of the chemistry and physics of the so-called "life processes," living organisms can be profitably treated as things apart from the inorganic world. Nevertheless, it is true that the most significant biological advances of the insurgent century were attempts to express biological findings in physical terms.

The First Physiologists

The first to apply the new physical philosophy to biological matters was Santorio Santorio (1561–1636), a professor of medicine at Padua, in his little tract *De medicina statica* (1614). Inspired by the methods of Galileo who had been his colleague at Padua, he sought to compare the weights of the human body at different times and in different circumstances. He found that the body loses weight by mere exposure, a process which he assigned to "insensible perspiration." His experiments laid the foundation of the modem study of "metabolism." Santorio also adapted Galileo's thermometer to clinical purposes. It marks the medieval character of much of the thought of the day that his account of this (1626) is concealed in a commentary on a work of Avicenna.

The Englishman, William Harvey (1578–1657), is also to be regarded as a disciple of Galileo though he himself was, perhaps, little aware of it. Harvey studied at Padua (1600–2) while Galileo was active there. By 1615 he had attained to a conception of the circulation of the blood. He published his demonstration in 1628. The story of that discovery is very accessible. We would emphasize that the essential part of its demonstration is the result not of mere observation but of the application of Galileo's principle of measurement. Having shown that blood can leave the ventricle of the heart only in one direction, he turns to measure the capacity of the ventricle. He finds it to be two ounces. The heart beats 72 times a minute so that

William Harvey demonstrates the circulation of blood.

in the hour it throws into the system 2x72x60 ounces = 8,640 ounces = 540 pounds, that is to say about three times the body weight! Where can all this blood come from? Where can it all go to? The answer to that is that the blood is a stage army which goes off only to come on again. It is the same blood that is always returning.

The knowledge that the blood circulates has formed the foundation on which has since been built a mass of physical interpretation of the activities of living things. This aggregate forms the science of *physiology*. The blood is a carrier, ever going its rounds over the same route to return whence it came. What does it carry? And why? How and where does it take up its loads? How, where, and why does it part with them? And what does it bring back? The answering of such questions as these has formed the main task of physiology since Harvey's time. As each generation has obtained a more complete answer for one organ or another, so it has been possible to form a clearer picture of some part of the animal body as a working mechanical model.

Yet despite triumphs of physical methods in physiology, we cannot suppose, with [René] Descartes, that the clearest image—which is certainly at first sight the most satisfying—is of necessity also the truest, for the animal body can be shown on various grounds to be no mechanical model. A machine is made up of the sum of its parts. An animal body, as Aristotle perceived, is no more the sum of its parts than is a work of art. The Aristotelian world-system was falling. The Aristotelian biology held. Perhaps it still holds.

Descartes's Views on Man

Nevertheless, the physical discoveries of Galileo and the demonstrations of Santorio and of Harvey gave a great impetus to the attempt to explain vital workings on mechanical grounds. A number of seventeenth-century investigators devoted themselves to this task. The most impressive exponent of physiological theory along these lines was Descartes himself. His account of the subject [*L'Homme*] written by 1637 appeared posthumously in 1664. It is important as the first modern book devoted to the subject of physiology.

Descartes had not himself any extensive practical knowledge of physiology. On theoretical grounds he set forth a very complicated apparatus which he believed to be a model of animal structure. Subsequent investigation failed to confirm many of his findings. For a time, however, his ingenious scheme attracted many. A strong point in his physiological teaching was the stress laid on the nervous system, and on its power of co-ordinating the different bodily activities. Thus expressed, his view may sound modern, but it is grotesquely wrong in detail.

An important part of Descartes's theory is the position accorded to man. He regarded man as unique in his possession of a soul. Now in the view of Descartes the special prerogative of the soul is to originate action. Animals, he thought, are machines, automata. Therefore, given that we know enough of the works of the machine, we can tell how it will act under any given circumstances. But the human soul he regarded as obeying no such laws, nor any laws but its own. Its nature he believed to be a complete mystery forever sealed to us. Descartes conceived that the soul governs the body through the action of the nervous system, though how it does so he again left as a mystery. The two insoluble mysteries come, he believed, into relationship to each other in a structure or organ in the brain, known to modem physiology as the "pineal body." This organ he wrongly believed absent in animals other than man. All their actions, even those which seem to express pain or fear, are automatic. It is modern "behaviourism" with man excluded. Anatomically he was refuted by [Neils] Steno in a famous lecture at Paris in 1665.

The word "mystery" is not popular among modern men of science. It is, therefore, right to point out that the processes by which a sensory impression passes into sensation, by which sensation educes thought, and by which thoughts are followed by acts, have been in no way elucidated by physiological science. In these matters we are in no better case than Descartes. If we have abandoned his terminology we are no nearer a solution of his leading problems. The basic defects of Descartes's system were errors in matters of fact. It was on account of these that he ceased to have a physiological following in the generation after the publication of his essay *On Man*.

Descartes is often credited with the idea of reflex action which simply means the automatic response of the body to certain external stimuli without consciousness being (necessarily) involved. This conception, however, was implicit in the works of [Andreas] Vesalius, Galen, Herophilus, and perhaps of yet earlier writers. Nevertheless, Descartes certainly emphasized and illustrated reflex action. Moreover, like most of his contemporaries and predecessors he believed the nerves to be tubular and that they conveyed a "nervous fluid," distension by which inflated and thus shortened the muscles. He imagined that the movements of this fluid were controlled by an elaborate system of valves. The existence of such a fluid was disproved by his younger contemporary, [Jan] Swammerdam.

Exploring the Living Organism

One of the ablest critics of the physiological system of Descartes was the Dane, Niels Steno (1648–86), whose scientific work was done mostly in Italy and France. Steno, like Descartes, was a mechanist, but unlike Descartes applied himself to the exploration of bodily structure. He found a pineal gland like that of man in other animals, and he could not persuade himself that it had the connexions, material or spiritual, described by Descartes. His criticism of Descartes in detail was very damaging.

More constructive was the achievement of Giovanni Alfonso Borelli (1608–79), an eminent Italian mathematician, astronomer, and polymath, a friend of Galileo and [Italian anatomist Marcello] Malpighi. Borelli's work *On Motion of Animals* (1680) is the classic of what is variously called the "iatrophysical" or "iatromathematical" school. It stands as the greatest early triumph in the application of the science of mechanics to the working of the living organism. Stirred by the success of [Simon] Stevin and Galileo in giving mathematical expression to mechanical events, Borelli sought to do the like with the animal body. In this undertaking he was very successful. That department of physiology which treats of muscular movement on mechanical principles was effectively founded and largely developed by him. Here his mathematical and physical training was specially useful. He endeavoured, with some success, to extend mechanical principles to such activities as the flight of birds and the swimming of fish. His mechanical analyses of the movements of the heart, or of the intestines, were less successful, and he naturally failed altogether in his attempt to introduce mechanical ideas in explanation of what we now know to be chemical processes, such as digestion.

The Chemical Theories

Just as Descartes and Borelli sought to explain all animal activity on a mechanical basis, so others resorted to chemical interpretation. Forerunners of this point of view were Paracelsus and [Jan Baptista] van Helmont. A more coherent attempt was made by Francis de la Boe (Sylvius, 1614–72), professor of medicine at Leyden. That university had become by the second half of the seventeenth century the most progressive scientific centre. It was the seat of the first university laboratory, which was built at his instance.

Sylvius devoted much attention to the study of salts, which he recognized as the result of the union of acids and bases. Thus he attained to the idea of chemical affinity—an important advance. With a good knowledge of anatomy and accepting the main mechanistic advances, such as the doctrine of the circulation of the blood and the mechanics of muscular motion, Sylvius sought to give a chemical interpretation to other vital activities, expressing them in terms of "acid and alkali" and of "fermentation." In this attempt he made no clear distinction between changes induced by "unorganized" ferments, as gastric juice or rennet, and changes induced by microorganisms, as alcoholic fermentation or leavening by yeast. Nevertheless, he and his school added considerably to our knowledge of physiological processes, notably by their examination of the body fluids, especially the digestive fluids such as the saliva and the secretions of stomach and pancreas.

The views of yet another group of biological theorists were best expressed by another expert chemist, Georg Ernest Stahl (1660–1734). He is remembered in connexion with *phlogiston* [a substance believed to be given off during burning] and also stands as protagonist of his age of that view of the nature of the organism which goes under the term *vitalism* [the doctrine that phenomena are in some part self-determining]. Though expressed in obscure and mystical language, Stahl's vitalism is in effect a return to the Aristotelian position and a denial of the views of Descartes, Borelli, and Sylvius. To Descartes the animal body was a machine, to Sylvius a laboratory. But for Stahl the phenomena characteristic of the living body are governed neither by physical nor chemical laws, but by laws of a wholly different kind. These are the laws of the *sensitive soul*. This sensitive soul in its ultimate analysis is not very dissimilar from the *psyche* of Aristotle. Stahl held that the immediate instruments, the laboratory tools, of this sensitive soul were chemical processes, and his physiology thus develops along lines of which Aristotle could know nothing. This does not, however, alter the fact of his hypothesis being essentially of Aristotelian origin.

Studying Plant Physiology

Most of the physiological discussion of the seventeenth century turned on the vital process of animals and especially those of man. The plant physiology of the age was of a more elementary character. Van Helmont had shown that plants draw something of nutritive value from water. This was contrary to the Aristotelian teaching that plants draw their food . . . from the earth. The generation following van Helmont sought to erect a positive scheme of plant physiology without, however, very much success. Marcello Malpighi (1628–94), the great Bolognese microscopist, held wrongly that the sap is brought to the leaves by the fibrous parts of the wood. The leaves, he thought, form from the sap the material required for growth. This, he knew, is distributed from the leaves to the various parts of the plant. He conceived a wholly imaginary "circulation of sap" comparable to the circulation of the blood in animals. The respiration of plants, he falsely believed, is carried on by the "spiral vessels" which bear a superficial resemblance to the breathing tubes or *tracheae* of insects with which he was familiar.

The earliest experimental work on the physiology of plants was that of the French ecclesiastic, Edmé Mariotte (died 1684). This able physicist observed the high pressure with which sap rises. This he compared to blood pressure. To explain the existence of sap pressure he inferred that there must be something in plants which permits the entrance but prevents the exit of liquids. He held that it is sap pressure which expands the organs of plants and so contributes to their growth (1676).

Mariotte was definitely opposed to the Aristotelian conception of a vegetative soul. He considered that this conception fails to explain the fact that every species of plant, and even the parts of a plant, exactly reproduce their own properties in their offspring, as with "cuttings." He was, so far as plants are concerned, a complete "mechanist," and, therefore, anti-Aristotelian. All the "vital" processes of plants were for him the result of the interplay of physical forces. He believed, as a corollary to this view, that organisms can be spontaneously generated.

The Microscopic Investigations

The interpretation of vital activity in chemical and physical terms has had a continuous history to our own time. It is far other with the very striking microscopical researches with which the second half of the seventeenth century is crowded. Five investigators of the front rank, Marcello Malpighi (1628–94) at Bologna, Robert Hooke (1635–1703) and Nehemiah Grew (1641–1712) in London, Jan

Swammerdam (1637–80) at Amsterdam, and Antony van Leeuwenhoek (1632–1723) at Delft, all busied themselves with microscopic investigations on the structure and behaviour of living things. Their results impressed their contemporaries as deeply as they have some modern historians. But none of these microscopists inspired a school, and we have to turn to the nineteenth century for their true continuators. On this account the "classical microscopists" must be accorded a less prominent place in a general history of science than the great interest of their biological observations might suggest. We briefly consider the general ideas that they initiated.

The infinite complexity of living things in the microscopic world was nearly as philosophically disturbing as the unexpected complexity and ordered majesty of the astronomical world which Galileo and Kepler had unveiled to a previous generation. Notably the vast variety of minute life gave at once new point and added new difficulty to the conception of "Creation." This was specially the effect of Hooke's pioneer *Micrographia* (1665).

In a few notable respects the microscopic analysis of the tissues of animals aided the conception of the living body as a mechanism. Thus Harvey had shown that the blood in its circulation passed from arteries to veins. The channels of passage were unknown to him. They were revealed as "capillary vessels" by Malpighi and Leeuwenhoek. These observers discovered the corpuscles of the blood, the secretory functions of "glands," and the fibrillary character of muscles, thus helping to complete details of the "animal machine."

The nature of sexual generation had long been in dispute. The discovery (1679) in the male element of "animalcules"—"spermatozoa," as we now call them—aroused new speculations. The sperm then was organized. But how? The eye of faith, lit within by its own light, looking through an imperfect lens lit without by a flickering flame, saw many a "homunculus" in many a spermatozoon and even the piercing eye of a Malpighi or a Leeuwenhoek saw that which was not. The faith of others claimed that the homunculus should be carried by the female element, by the germ rather than by the sperm. That, too, was seen by the eye of faith. The more conservative Harvey insisted that the complex embryo in the simple substance of the egg was a "new appearance," excited by that imponderable ghost, the "generative force."

Microscopic analysis revealed some similarity between the structures of plants and animals. False analogies were drawn and carried at times to fantastic lengths. The "loves of the plants," on which poets had dwelt, were not wholly fables. It was slowly realized that flowers contain sexual elements, and a parallel was perceived between their reproductive processes and those of animals.

Theories of Spontaneous Generation

Lastly, there is an aspect of minute life that came to the fore in the later seventeenth century that requires some special discussion. It is the theme of *spontaneous generation* of living things, that is, the origin of living things from non-living matter.

Neither ancient nor medieval nor renaissance scientific writers doubted that spontaneous generation took place on occasion. Corpses were said to "breed" worms, dirt to "breed" vermin, sour wine to "breed" vinegar eels, and so forth. Spontaneous generation is often fathered on Aristotle and is in his writings, but it was not so much a doctrine as a universal assumption. When the reality of spontaneous generation was first questioned, the authority of Aristotle— or rather the contemporary misunderstanding of him—was a very real obstacle to scientific advance. It is also true that Aristotle gave spontaneous generation a place in his biological scheme. But his error was shared by every naturalist until the seventeenth century, and it is hard to see how any other view could then be taken.

With the advent of effective microscopes in the second half of the seventeenth century, new tendencies set in. On the one hand, exploration of minute life showed many cases of alleged spontaneous generation to have been falsely interpreted. Hooke watched the formation of spores in moulds (1665), [Christiaan] Huygens (c. 1680) and others (1702) saw the division and multiplication of certain microscopic organisms. On the other hand, the microscope revealed minute organisms which seemed to appear out of nothing. Thus Leeuwenhoek saw excessively small creatures in infusions of hay and other substance. Such infusions become in a few days or even hours turbid with actively moving microscopic forms. These seemed to be spontaneously generated.

Refutation by Experiment

In 1651 Harvey had pointed to the heart of this matter when he added to the frontispiece of his book *On the Generation of Animals* the words *Ex ovo omnia* ("All living things come from an egg"). Yet the first scientific treatment of the matter was made by Francesco Redi (1621–97), a physician of Florence. He tells us (1668) that he

> began to believe that all worms found in meat were derived from flies, and not from putrefaction. I was confirmed by observing that, before the meat became wormy, there hovered over it flies of that very kind that later bred in it. Belief unconfirmed by experiment is vain. Therefore, I put a (dead) snake, some fish, and a slice of veal in four large, wide-mouthed flasks. These I closed and sealed. Then I filled the same number of flasks in the same way leaving them open. Flies were seen constantly entering and leaving the open flasks. The meat and the fish in them became wormy. In the closed flasks were no worms, though the

contents were now putrid. Outside, on the cover of the closed flasks, a few maggots eagerly sought entry. Thus the flesh of dead animals cannot engender worms unless the eggs of the living be deposited therein.

Since air had been excluded from the closed flasks I made a new experiment to exclude all doubt. I put meat and fish in a vase covered with gauze. For further protection against flies, I placed it in a gauze-covered frame. I never saw any worms in the meat, though there were many on the frame, and flies, ever and anon, lit on the outer gauze and deposited their worms there. [Abbreviated.]

Redi continued to believe that gall insects were spontaneously generated. This subject was taken up by another eminent Italian physician, Antonio Vallisnieri (1661–1730). Correcting Malpighi, he showed that the larvae in galls originate in eggs deposited in the plants (1700). Vallisnieri compared the process of gall formation, as well as infection of plants by aphides, to the transmission of disease. Other investigators showed that fleas and lice are bred only by parents like themselves.

Thus the matter stood in the early eighteenth century with the general balance of opinion against spontaneous generation. The possibility had been disproved—so far as a universal negative can be disproved—for larger organisms. The question was still open for the minute creatures encountered in infusions.

In summary we may say that for biology the insurgent century closed with a strong mechanistic bias. The microscopic world, however, remained an enigma, a land of wonders where all laws seemed at times to be broken. *De minimis non curat lex,* "The law does not concern itself with the most minute things" was often quoted, but *lex* of the lawyer was quite different from *lex naturae.*

On the Mechanism of the Human Mind

Baruch Spinoza

Long before Sigmund Freud explored the conflict between the conscious and unconscious mind, the seventeenth-century philosopher Baruch Spinoza spoke of the struggle between man's emotional and intellectual life. The following is an excerpt from Spinoza's *The Road to Inner Freedom: The Ethics,* edited by Dagobert D. Runes, a lifelong student of Spinoza. Using seventeenth-century science and his observation of human behavior to support his philosophical ideas, Spinoza concludes that the conscious mind alone cannot dictate human behavior. For example, Spinoza explores the act of speech, claiming that people often wish that they could restrain their own tongues, but are unable to do so. From this and other examples, Spinoza deduces that the mind, or conscious awareness alone is insufficient to explain behavior. Spinoza argues that desires, emotions, and unconscious thought as well as conscious thought work together to influence human behavior. Having fled the Spanish Inquisition, Spinoza did not dare print the *Ethics* in his lifetime, and even when published posthumously in 1677 Spinoza's ideas met with disapproval by representatives of Christian churches.

O ur mind is in certain cases active, and in certain cases passive. Insofar as it has adequate ideas it is necessarily active, and insofar as it has inadequate ideas, it is necessarily passive.

Body cannot determine mind to think, neither can mind determine body to motion or rest or any state different from these, if such there be.

This is made more clear by the statement, namely, that mind and body are one and the same thing, conceived first under the attribute of thought, secondly, under the attribute of extension. Thus it follows that the order or concatenation of things is identical, whether nature be conceived under the one attribute or the other; consequently the order of states of activity and passivity in our body is simultaneous in nature with the order of states of activity and passivity in the mind.

Nevertheless, though such is the case, and though there be no further room for doubt, I can scarcely believe, until the fact is proved by experience, that men can be induced to consider the question calmly and fairly, so firmly are they convinced that it is merely at the bidding of the mind that the body is set in motion or at rest, or performs a variety of actions depending solely on the mind's will or the exercise of thought.

However, no one has hitherto laid down the limits to the powers of the body, that is, no one has yet been taught by experience what the body can accomplish solely by the laws of nature, insofar as she is regarded as extension.

No one hitherto has gained such an accurate knowledge of the bodily mechanism, that he can explain all its functions; nor need I call attention to the fact that many actions are observed in the lower animals, which far transcend human sagacity, and that somnambulists do many things in their sleep, which they would not venture to do when awake: these instances are enough to show that the body can by the sole laws of its nature do many things which the mind wonders at.

Again, *no one knows how or by what means the mind moves the body*, nor how many various degrees of motion it can impart to the body, nor how quickly it can move it. Thus, when men say that this or that physical action has its origin in the mind, which later has dominion over the body, they are using words without meaning, or are confessing in specious phraseology that they are ignorant of the cause of the said action, and do not wonder at it.

But, they will say, whether we know or do not know the means whereby the mind acts on the body, we have, at any rate, experience of the fact that unless the human mind is in a fit state to think, the body remains inert.

Moreover, we have experience that the mind alone can determine whether we speak or are silent, and a variety of similar states which, accordingly, we say depend on the mind's decree. But, as to the first point, I ask such objectors, whether experience does not also teach, that if the body be inactive the mind is simultaneously unfitted for thinking? For when the body is at rest in sleep, the mind simultaneously is in a state of torpor also, and has no power of thinking, such as it possesses when the body is awake.

Again, I think everyone's experience will confirm the statement that the mind is not at all times equally fit for thinking on a given subject, but according as the body is more or less fitted for being stimulated by the image of this or that object, so also is the mind more or less fitted for contemplating the said object.

But, it will be argued, it is impossible that solely from the laws of nature considered as extended substance, we should be able to deduce the causes of buildings, pictures, and things of that kind, which are produced only by human art; nor would the human body, unless it were determined and led by the mind, be capable of building a single temple. However, I have just pointed out that the objectors cannot fix the limits of the body's power, or say what can be concluded from a consideration of its sole nature, whereas they have experience of many things being accomplished solely by the laws of nature, which they would never have believed possible except under the direction of mind: such are the actions performed by somnambulists while asleep, and wondered at by their performers when awake.

Baruch Spinoza

I would further call attention to the mechanism of the human body, which far surpasses in complexity all that has been put together by human art, not to repeat what I have already shown, namely, that from nature, under whatever attribute she be considered, infinite results follow.

As for the second objection, I submit that *the world would be much happier, if men were as fully able to keep silence as they are to speak.* Experience abundantly shows that men can govern anything more easily than their tongues, and restrain anything more easily than their appetites; whence it comes about that many believe that we are only free in respect to objects which we moderately desire, because our desire for such can easily be controlled by the thought of something else frequently remembered, but that we are by no means free in respect to what we seek with violent emotion, for our desire cannot then be allayed with the remembrance of anything else.

However, unless such persons had proved by experience that we do many things which we afterwards repent of, and again that we often, when assailed by contrary emotions, see the better and follow the worse, there would be nothing to prevent their believing that we are free in all things. Thus an infant believes that of its own free will it desires milk, an angry child believes that it freely desires vengeance, a timid child believes that it freely desires to run away; further, a drunken man believes that he utters from the free decision of his mind words which, when he is sober, he would willingly have withheld: thus, too, a delirious man, a garrulous woman, a child, and others of like complexion, believe that they speak from the free decision of their mind, when they are in reality unable to restrain their impulse to talk.

Experience teaches us no less clearly than reason, that *men believe themselves to be free, simply because they are conscious of their actions*, and unconscious of the causes whereby those actions are determined; and further, it is plain that the dictates of the mind are but another name for the appetites, and therefore vary according to the varying state of the body.

Everyone shapes his actions according to his emotion. Those who are assailed by conflicting emotions know not what they wish; those who are not attacked by any emotion are readily swayed this way or that. All these considerations clearly show that a mental decision and a bodily appetite, or determined state, are *simultaneous,* or rather are one and the same thing, which we call decision, when it is regarded under and explained through the attribute of thought, and a conditioned state, when it is regarded under the attribute of extension, and deduced from the laws of motion and rest.

For the present I wish to call attention to another point, namely, that we cannot act by the decision of the mind, unless we have a remembrance of having done so. For instance we cannot say a word without remembering that we have done so.

Again, it is not within the free power of the mind to remember or forget a thing at will. Therefore the freedom of the mind must in any case be limited to the power of uttering or not uttering something which it remembers. But when we dream that we speak, we believe that we speak from a free decision of the mind, yet we do not speak, or, if we do, it is by a spontaneous motion of the body. Again, we dream that we are concealing something, and we seem to act from the same decision of the mind as that whereby we keep silence when awake concerning something we know. Lastly, we dream that from the free decision of our mind we do something, which we should not dare to do when awake.

Now I should like to know whether there be in the mind two sorts of decisions, one sort illusive, and the other sort free? If our folly does not carry us so far as this, we must necessarily admit that the decision of the mind, which is believed to be free, is not distinguishable from the imagination or memory, and is nothing more than the affirmation, which an idea, by virtue of being an idea, necessarily involves. Wheretofore these decisions of the mind arise in the mind by the same necessity, as the ideas of things actually existing. Therefore those who believe that they speak or keep silence or act in any way from the free decision of their mind, do but dream with their eyes open.

The activities of the mind arise solely from adequate ideas; the passive states of the mind depend solely on inadequate ideas.

Chapter 2

Coming to America

PREFACE

L ife in seventeenth-century Europe offered little hope for many who lived there. Religious persecution, political oppression, and poverty provided sound motives for those who chose to abandon their homeland and migrate to America. For some, America offered the promise of a new start in a utopian setting where colonists could practice their religion unmolested. For others, America held the temptation of untold riches: gold, silver, and unlimited natural resources. Those who sought either refuge or riches relied on the reports of those who had come before, and often these reports were either exaggerated or incomplete. Europeans who traveled across the Atlantic to establish colonies early in the century faced incredible hardships coming to America.

The life of these early colonists depended on many factors, including the character of the colonists, the location of the colony, and even the timing of their arrival. Although the colonists who established Jamestown, Virginia, arrived in the spring, they were distracted by the search for gold and, as Jamestown was located in a swamp, disease quickly reduced their number. On the other hand, the colonists who traveled on the *Mayflower* landed in Plymouth Harbor in December, and although more organized, they faced the fury of a New England winter, but the hearty Pilgrims survived. Later colonists, such as the Quakers who settled in Pennsylvania, had the benefit of those who came before and also more realistic reports of colonial life that began to arrive from the colonies.

Relationships between colonists and the native population also varied in the different colonies, depending on the character and motives of the various tribes that surrounded the colonial outposts. Fearful of the Englishmen, the Native Americans captured and killed several colonists in Jamestown before they reached an uneasy peace with the colonists. In New England, however, with the help of the English-speaking natives Samoset and Squanto, the Pilgrims reached a treaty with Chief Massasoit that lasted almost fifty years. The colonization of America during the seventeenth century made mythic figures of Chief Powhatan, Pocahontas, Captain John Smith, Squanto, and Miles Standish.

Colonization created an opportunity for those who traded in slaves, and the seventeenth century saw the development of America's slave trade. Seen by seventeenth-century traders as goods, Africans sold into slavery were packed together on slave ships in such numbers that many of them died while crossing the Atlantic. For slaves America was not a haven for hope and opportunity but rather death and despair.

Life in the colonies did not always live up to the expectations of those who settled in America. The promise of a utopian world failed to materialize for the Puritans of New England, and one response to colonial disappointment was an increase in accusations of witchcraft. Although these accusations were made throughout the colonies, the majority of witch-hunts and executions occurred in New England. Greed eroded the philosophy of tolerance and harmony that William Penn had hoped would flourish in his Pennsylvania Quaker society.

Although the path to colonization was not an easy one, many people remained to face the challenge of independence from colonial domination that was to come in the next century.

In Search of Riches: The Colonization of Jamestown

Alden T. Vaughan

In the following excerpt from his book, *American Genesis: Captain John Smith and the Founding of Virginia*, historian Alden T. Vaughan tells of the voyage and early experiences of the first settlers in Jamestown, Virginia, in 1606. Vaughan explains that having heard stories of the riches to be found in the New World, many of these early English colonists spent their energy looking for gold rather than evaluating the advantages and disadvantages of their location. Within months, disease, malnutrition, and Indian attacks killed nearly half the original company. According to Vaughan, the London Company that sponsored the colonists hoped to trade with the Indians, and Captain Christopher Newport resolved to treat them kindly, but some local tribes were not friendly. John Smith, a controversial leader of the colony, was captured by the Indians while exploring the interior and, Vaughan notes, Smith's conflicting accounts of his relationship with the Indian chief Powhatan and the Indian princess Pocahontas continue to be controversial. Vaughan is a retired professor of colonial American history at Columbia University.

O n Friday, 19 December 1606, John Smith boarded ship at Blackwall, London. By nightfall most of the other passengers and crewmen had crowded into the hundred-ton flagship *Susan Constant* and her smaller escorts, the forty-ton *Godspeed* and twenty-ton *Discovery:* early next morning they slipped down the Thames and made their way to the east coast of England. There contrary winds, the frequent bane of expeditions to America, held them in sight of land for six weeks. Before the small squadron finally sailed into blue water its provisions had been partly exhausted, its preacher lay perilously ill, and bitter quarreling had broken out among the passengers—an inauspicious start for England's new effort to colonize America.

The Voyage to America

Once at sea, Smith and his companions faced an arduous and circuitous trip to Virginia. The preferred trans-Atlantic route of the early seventeenth century led southward to the Canary Islands, then southwest to a point off the African coast where the north equatorial current flowed to the West Indies; from there ships could ride the Gulf Stream up the coast of North America. That route had the advantage of generally fair winds, relatively short hauls between ports, and confidence engendered by a familiar path. The disadvantage was duration: a journey of more than five thousand miles took from twelve to twenty weeks. At best colonists reached their destinations low on energy and ill-prepared to resist unfamiliar diseases; at worst the ships ran out of food and water, or epidemics struck on the high seas. Smith's shipmates knew many tales of disaster. They realized too that on arrival in America they faced the likelihood of illness or violent death. Yet they pushed on, encouraged by the hope that this expedition, unlike others, would survive and prosper.

It did survive, but not without a heavy share of the hardships that accompanied most seventeenth-century ocean crossings. The voyagers endured abysmally cramped quarters in low-ceilinged cabins with foul air and no privacy. They subsisted on barely edible rations: scant portions of salted meat and fish, stale biscuits, rancid cheese and butter, and beer of dubious quality—while it lasted. Long voyages never had enough fresh water for drinking and cooking. (One of the travellers later recalled that on his trip back to England the water "was so stencheous thatt . . . I cold nott endure the sentt thereof.") Seasickness racked many of the passengers. Others suffered more serious illnesses, while nutritional deficiencies drained human energy and spirit. So did the monotony of week after endless week of inaction, eased only by petty chores and an occasional exchange of rumors or tall tales. For more than four months the Virginia expedition pitched and rolled across the Atlantic; brief stops at the Canaries and at some of the Caribbean Islands offered temporary relief and fresh food. Almost everyone survived—only one man is known to have died among the more than one hundred fifty prospective colonists and crewmen—but the frightful mortality of the first years at Jamestown bore poignant testimony to the human cost of colonization.

The Character of the First Settlers

Command of the expedition rested in Captain Christopher Newport of *Susan Constant*, a veteran of sea dog raids on the Spanish West Indies, whose missing arm evoked bitter reminders of the New World's perils. Commanding the other ships were Bartholomew Gosnold, equally experienced in American waters, in *Godspeed;* and John Ratcliffe, about whom little is known except that he had a penchant for trouble, in *Discovery*. In Virginia the three captains would share leadership of the colony with Edward Maria Wingfield, a veteran soldier and the only settler named in the royal charter; Captain John Martin, a soldier and lawyer; Captain George Kendall, another troublemaker; George Percy, a veteran of the Low Countries and youngest brother of the Earl of Northumberland; and John Smith. Newport would stay only briefly. The company expected him to load a saleable cargo and return to England.

There is no complete roster of the men who composed the expedition of 1606–1607, but partial lists published later by John Smith reveal that it included more than fifty gentlemen, among them Reverend Robert Hunt, the only clergyman; also four carpenters, twelve laborers, two bricklayers, a blacksmith, a mason, a tailor, a surgeon, a sailmaker, a drummer, and four boys, with, one account concludes, "diverse others, to the number of 105." These were "the first planters"; not included in that category were the ships' crews and perhaps some disgruntled passengers who went back to England with the return voyage. The list throws little light, however, on the character of the first settlers. The enterprise called for men of skill, energy, and self-sacrifice; from what is known of the events of the first few years, both the leaders and the followers fell far short of that mark. Virginia survived not because of its first settlers but in spite of them. . . .

By late April the three small ships had reached the latitude of Chesapeake Bay, almost in sight of land, when "God, the guider of all good actions, forc[ed] them by an extream storme . . . to their desired port. . . ." They arrived none too soon. Captain Ratcliffe of *Discovery* already counselled return to England. Now, with the ocean crossing behind them, this latest contingent of Englishmen could begin the job they had been sent to do: to create in the American wilderness an outpost of British power and Christian civilization. That, at least, was their reputed mission. Most of the passengers had more mundane objectives: to get a fat share of Virginia's reputed riches and to enjoy for a while the American Garden of Eden.

The more realistic passengers, including John Smith, had doubts about easy wealth and easy living. Almost matching reports of the New World's grandeur were tales of its pitfalls: horrendous storms, deadly plants, ferocious animals, and man-eating natives. The Indians painted by artist-governor John White at Roanoke appeared peaceful, but they lived farther south and did not belong to the tribes of the Chesapeake region. Similarly, the Roanoke settlers had found fertile soil, but they had been in a different locality. No European had explored extensively the area Newport's men were about to settle; its benign reputation rested on sparse reports. Closer examination might reveal unexpected terrors. The Virginia colonists therefore felt anxiety as well as hope; some perhaps harbored silent fears, especially when pondering the mysterious fate of the Roanoke colony.

Belief that the Virginia venture would succeed where others had failed hinged partly on geography—Chesapeake Bay was expected to be a far better location; and partly on diplomacy—this colony would treat the Indians kindly, Captain Newport resolved. His intention received an early jolt: when he took a party ashore at Cape Henry (which he tactfully named for the Prince of Wales), a band of Indians assaulted the English, wounding two of them "very dangerously." Confident that other Indians would be friendlier and that the interior would fulfill earlier predictions, Newport led his squadron across the bay and up the nearest large river. After some preliminary exploration the leaders found an acceptable spot to unload and begin settlement. There, on 13 May 1607, the resident councillors, whose names had been brought in a sealed box to prevent jealousies en route and to avoid undercutting Captain Newport's authority at sea, took their oaths of office. The London Company had named seven men: Newport, Gosnold, Ratcliffe, Wingfield, Martin, Kendall, and Smith. In its first official act the resident council voted to have Wingfield its president and to exclude Smith, who was under suspicion.

The council's assignment was formidable. It had, first of all, to force a disparate collection of Englishmen to work in harmony lest they perish—no small task in light of the settlers' obstinate individualism and the forest's abundant perils. Moreover, the council had to meet the company's demand for profits. The London Company had hired men to build an outpost where the discovery of gold, trade with the Indians, or the raising of crops would bring a fair return on the stockholders' investment. After seven years the settlers would be given land, plus other benefits, and could do more or less as they pleased. In the meantime they worked for the company; in return they received passage, food, shelter (which they, of course, must build), and protection (which they must provide). They would labor as the company directed, be fed from its storehouse, live in its communal lodgings, and worship in accordance with its ecclesiastical preferences. Such conditions did not have wide appeal, and some of the men who accepted them in England changed their minds after a few weeks in Virginia. But they had made a bargain and must live up to it—if the council could make them.

The Natural Riches of Virginia

Despite the wrangling over Smith's place on the council and the discouraging first encounter with American Indians, prospects for success were bright in the early months. The country appeared bountiful, the climate salubrious. Observers compared the weather in Virginia to that of balmy Spain. Chesapeake Bay itself offered shelter from ocean tempests, yet with an entrance nearly twenty miles wide it promised ready access to the interior. Into the bay flowed "5. faire and delightful navigable rivers" of which they named the southernmost after the King. And no doubt the James River seemed majestic to Englishmen who were familiar only with smaller streams. It could be followed by a ship of three hundred tons for one hundred and fifty miles inland; its breadth of one half to two miles allowed easy navigation. Everywhere seafood flourished in startling size and abundance: sturgeon up to seven feet in length, great crabs that four men could feed on, as well as oysters, mussels, and an almost endless variety of saltwater fish, including one "like the picture of St. George and his Dragon."

The land was equally generous. Near the mouth of the river "fayre pyne trees" promised pitch and tar; further inland the larger trees could be cut into clapboard, timber, and masts, or when cleared would give way to fertile gardens. And throughout the dense forests roamed an amazing array of fowl and fur-bearing animals, some of which the Englishmen had never seen: raccoons "almost as big as a Fox, as good meat as a lamb," and opossums "of the bignesse and likenesse of a Pigge, of a moneth ould, a beast of as strange as incredible nature. . . ." "Suche a Baye, a Ryvar and a land," wrote William Brewster, one of the gentlemen settlers, "did nevar the eye of mane behould."

What the settlers beheld, however, did not quite satisfy them. The hated Spaniards had found gold and silver; Englishmen would settle for no less. And at first Virgnia appeared to hold riches of infinite value. "If we maye beleve ether in wordes or Letters," Sir Walter Cope reported to Secretary of State Salisbury shortly after Captain Newport's return to England, "we are falne upon a lande, that promises more then the Lande of promisse: In steed of mylke we finde pearle. / & golde Inn steede of honye. Thus they saye, thus they wryte." Cope, in England, had doubts about the mineral riches, as did Smith in Virginia. But they were exceptions. Englishmen on both sides of the Atlantic clung tenaciously to their greedy hopes, swallowing every Indian tale of precious metals. The mountains above the falls, most of the settlers and the adventurers back home believed, "Prommyseth Infynyt treasuer." Newport himself lent credence to the rumors by insisting to Lord Salisbury that Virginia was "verie Riche in gold and Copper."

The Distraction of Gold

Had the chimera of gold been merely an idle hope, no harm would have been done except to individual expectations. But the search for gold involved time and energy that other projects sorely needed. "There was no talke, no hope, no worke," Smith complained, "but dig gold, wash gold, refine gold, loade gold. . . ." Smith recognized the "guilded durt" for what it was. He realized too that the men could not live indefinitely in tents, nor could they exist for long on the scanty supplies they had brought along. And however plentiful the rivers and forests seemed at first view, the settlers had neither the tools nor the skill to feed themselves exclusively on fish and game. Worse still, the lust for valuable metals so dazzled the London Company that it included in the first supply expedition several appallingly irrelevant artisans: two goldsmiths, two refiners, a jeweler, and a perfumer. Virginia needed builders and tillers of the soil; it got gentlemen and practitioners of aristocratic crafts.

The Seat of the New Colony

The quest for quick riches unfortunately coincided with another fundamental error: the selection of Jamestown as the principal seat of the new colony. At first glance the choice seemed sound enough. Situated fifty-seven miles up river from the ocean, the narrow-necked peninsula, virtually an island, offered relative safety from incursions by Spanish or French warships. At the very least an enemy fleet would be spotted long before it could reach the settlement. Jamestown's peninsular location also protected the settlers against Indian attacks from the mainland, though at first the fifteen-hundred-acre tract was too large to defend; for many years English settlement covered only a small corner of the island. Defense, then, was a major consideration but not the only one. More important, tall pines close to the shore and the deep channel of the river at that point permitted ships to be tied up to the banks, thus dispensing with the laborious task of loading and unloading by small boats. And situated more than a third of the way to the fall line, the island would become a convenient point from which to send search parties for gold.

More than offsetting Jamestown's advantages was its threat to health. The colonists had fortunately arrived in mid-May, probably the most comfortable season in the area, and thus had not noticed the potential dangers of their location. Besides, an almost endless list of tasks needed immediate attention. As one settler reported, the colonists "falleth every man to worke, the Councell contrive the Fort, the rest cut downe trees to make place to pitch their Tents; some provide clapboard to relade the ships; some make gardens, some nets, etc." Within a few weeks the settlers had sown fields of wheat, constructed a few crude buildings and loaded *Susan Constant* and *Godspeed* with clapboard, sassafras roots ("our easiest and richest comodity" because of its reputation as a cure for syphilis and other maladies), and samples of ore. Intent on their labors and lulled by congenial weather, the colonists failed to notice that they inhabited an unhealthy swamp and that the brackish water they drank would eventually undermine their stamina. For the moment, however, they had energy enough. On 22 June 1607 the two ships, Captain Newport again in command, set sail for England. He left behind approximately one hundred men and several boys, and the pinnace *Discovery*. The colonists appeared in good health and spirits and eager to continue exploring the mainland.

Trouble in Paradise

Ten days later only a handful were well. Disease hit with frightening suddenness, brought on by a crippling combination of hot weather, hard work, foul water, and skimpy diet. Gone were the meat and ale to which husky Elizabethan appetites were accustomed; daily rations now consisted of half a pint of wheat and as little of barley, both wormy from months at sea. Even the kegs of hard tack were empty; sailors before their departure had pilfered them from the ships' storage and sold the precious biscuits to unwary settlers who had too little foresight to save for the lean months ahead. In August the death rate climbed alarmingly. Captain Smith later recalled that "God (being angrie with us) plagued us with such famin and sicknes that the living were scarce able to bury the dead. . . ."

By September half the company had died, including Bartholomew Gosnold. A few had fallen victim to Indian arrows, a few had succumbed to the immediate effects of inadequate diet, and one had been executed for treason. Most died from infections to which English bodies had little immunity, especially after a rugged year of travel, work, and malnutrition. John Smith took ill but recovered, probably because his earlier life had exposed him to a wide range of diseases.

Then came winter. In both Europe and America an unusually heavy frost lasted from late 1607 to early 1608. Frozen feet and chilblains [swelling from exposure to cold] joined the growing list of ailments. On the second day of the new year Captain Newport arrived with 120 new, but equally unacclimated, settlers and badly neéded supplies. Still misfortune plagued the colony. On January 7 fire raced through its huddled cottages, burning the storehouse and all but three of the dwellings, and indirectly causing further mortality among the ill and the newly arrived. When spring brought respite from the cold and the end of the first year at Jamestown, only 38 of the original 105 colonists still lived.

Spring also brought another load of settlers. In April Captain Nelson, who had left England the previous fall with Newport, but separated from him by foul weather had wintered in the West Indies, brought *Phoenix* into port with more mouths to feed. Better preparations and a less wearing voyage helped to reduce the mortality among the newest colonists, yet between the spring and fall of 1608 death claimed another thirty victims, most of them from Nelson's ship. In the first eighteen months Jamestown had lost almost half its inhabitants.

Negotiating with the Indians

The danger of Indian attack vied with malnutrition and disease as the greatest threat to the survival of the English colony. The Indians, in all probability, had exterminated the brief footholds on Roanoke Island; now they seemed likely to doom the Virginia experiment as well, unless they could be persuaded to help rather than hinder the effort.

Early contacts proved inconclusive. Despite some scattered clashes many peaceful meetings had taken place. After the initial skirmish on Cape Henry, the Indians greeted the Englishmen cordially, feasting the newcomers and giving them tobacco and other symbols of friendship. Even the few who seemed unhappy at the foreigners' intrusion succumbed to kindness. While scouting for a place to settle in early May the expedition encountered "many stout and able Savages . . . in a most warlike manner, with the swords at their backes beset with sharpe stones, and pieces of yron able to cleave a man in sunder." Yet when the Indians "demanded of us our being there, willing us to bee gone," the English gave signs of amity, and in the end the natives "let us land in quietnesse."

During the next few weeks relations vacillated. Part of the problem lay in the rivalries and conflicting interests of the various tribes. The hostility of some encouraged others to make peace with the white men; conversely, the friendship of some Indians assured the enmity of others. There were problems of communication too, stemming in many cases from the language barrier that throughout the seventeenth century proved insurmountable to all but a few of either race. And the cultural gap was even more formidable. There were striking contrasts in religion, in political structure, in economic systems, as well as lesser matters of clothing, hair styles, and eating habits. The significance of these and other differences would grow, rather than diminish, with time. For now, each race merely viewed with suspicion the other's customs. The English, for example, expressed astonishment and dismay at what they considered the indolence of Indian men and the drudgery of Indian women; the natives thought Englishmen performed "effemynate labour."

Building Trust

In spite of cultural and linguistic impediments, Newport persisted in allaying Indian distrust of the English, for a while even limiting fortification at Jamestown to a half moon of branches. The folly of that tactic became apparent in early June when two hundred warriors attacked the outpost, killing an English boy and wounding perhaps a score of the men. At the time, Newport, Smith, and twenty-two others were exploring the James River; on their return, work began on more substantial fortifications. By mid-June Jamestown boasted a triangular fort of upright logs, with "three Bulwarkes at every corner like a halfe moone, and foure or five pieces of Artillerie mounted in them." During the sweltering summer, when disease and famine hit hardest, the few healthy men kept constant watch lest a concerted attack or silent infiltration bring a sudden end to the colony. Englishmen who wandered outside the fort risked injury or death at the hands of lurking Indians. The toll mounted.

John Smith

On the whole, however, the trend of Indian-white relations appeared favorable. On June 14, a week before Newport's departure for England, several Indians came to Jamestown to explain that the recent attack on the fort had been perpetrated by minor tribes subservient to the great chief Powhatan; the friendly natives offered to help the English fight their enemies or make peace with them. They also warned the settlers to cut the weeds near the fort to reduce the danger of ambushes—advice that should have been unnecessary to a military man like Captain Smith. And in September, without supplication on the part of the colonists, several Indians arrived bearing corn. Though half ripe, it was a godsend to hungry men. This timely display of cordiality seemed to further vindicate Newport's conciliatory policy. For the moment all went well between Indians and whites. "But," noted John Smith, "our comaedies never endured long without a Tragedie." And in the colony's next tragedy, he played the central role.

The Capture of John Smith

After Newport's departure for England in the summer of 1607, John Smith became the principal negotiator with the Indians and leader of expeditions into the interior. In December he led a party up the Chickahominy River, a branch of the James that turned northwest about six miles above Jamestown. Taking a barge and a small contingent, Smith pushed up river as far as the vessel could go, then left seven men behind while he continued by canoe with two companions and two Indian guides. Disaster struck when the men on the barge disobeyed his instructions and went ashore; they were attacked and slaughtered. Other Indians ambushed Smith when he went fowling, and slew the guards he left with the canoe. Smith put up a stiff fight and killed two of his assailants before slipping into a quagmire. Waist-deep in muck and armed only with an empty pistol, he finally surrendered.

For the next several weeks Smith was once more a helpless prisoner. The events of his captivity are known only from his own writings or those of friends who reported what they heard from him, and it may be, as Smith's critics have contended, that he fabricated much of his story. But distorted or not, the episode would be crucial to Smith and to the Jamestown colony.

Smith . . . showed no fear of Indians, either individually or collectively. . . . Before his capture by the Indians, he had singlehandedly held off two hundred armed warriors (according to his account); thereafter he so impressed his captors with his courage and skill (again by his account) that in the end he gained not only his freedom but their high regard. Yet Smith had no strong affection for the American natives. Throughout his dealings with them the captain treated Indians like common adversaries, grudgingly giving them credit for strength or wisdom, but never trusting or cherishing them.

The Indians, in turn, considered Smith their principal enemy. They tried to kill him before his capture, and might have succeeded had he not used his guide for a shield. And they undoubtedly considered executing him in accordance with tribal customs—Smith later learned that one of his men had perished in a gruesome torture ceremony. But partly because Smith was a captain, and therefore a prize worth holding for ransom, and partly because he dazzled his captors with a pocket compass, they spared him for disposition by Powhatan. In the meantime he received kind treatment, and an abundance of venison and corn bread, while the Indians interrogated him about the English settlement. Smith put up a good bluff, exaggerating the strength of the English and predicting destruction of the Indians if they should harm him. The ruse worked. His captors not only spared his life but saved him from assassination by the father of an Indian he had shot before his capture. Smith now became a showpiece as the Indians took him from town to town and eventually to the great chief Powhatan.

Meeting with Powhatan

Powhatan impressed Smith, as he impressed all Englishmen, as a proud and majestic figure. That did not deter Smith from lying flagrantly about English intentions. "Hee asked mee the cause of our comming," recalled Smith. "I tolde him being in fight with the Spaniards our enemie, beeing over powred, neare put to retreat, and by extreame weather put to this shore . . . [and] our Pinn[a]sse being leake wee were inforced to stay to mend her, till Captaine Newport my father came to conduct us away." When Powhatan wanted to know why the English explored so far inland, Smith insisted that they intended to attack the Monocans, Powhatan's enemies to the west, for killing a child of Newport. That appealed to the chief; he regaled Smith with stories of his own domain and lands to the west, and invited the captain "to live with him upon his River," to engage in trade, "and none should disturbe us." "This request I promised to performe," Smith admitted, with no real intention of doing so—at least not in the sense the Indian meant. Powhatan released the Englishman and sent him back to Jamestown.

So reads Smith's initial version of his release, published as part of his "True Relation" of recent events in Virginia. He wrote it in early June of 1608 and sent it on *Phoenix* to England where it was printed later that year. It may originally have mentioned the intercession of Pocahontas and other events of his captivity that appeared only in his later writings, but the "True Relation" fell into the hands of an editor who deleted the parts he considered too personal or too detrimental to the reputation of the colony. In any event, the version published in 1608 mentioned no rescue by the Indian princess. Nor did Smith's *Map of Virginia* (1612), which told of his captivity in two sentences: "A month those Barbarians kept him prisoner. Many strange triumphes and conjurations they made of him: yet hee so demeaned himselfe amongst them, as he not only diverted them from surprising the Fort; but procure his owne liberty, and got himself and his company such estimation amongst them, that those Salvages admired him as a demi-God." This account showed Smith at his vainest; no room here for rescue by an adolescent girl.

The episode took on a far different appearance in 1624 when Captain Smith produced his *Generall Historie* of British America. Although Pocahontas had died several years earlier, she had become a legend: the savage princess who converted to Christianity, married an Englishman, visited England and met the royal family. There was no need then to suppress the story of her aid. Critics of Smith have seen the matter less generously: with Pocahontas and Powhatan dead,

no restraints prevented the captain from inventing an attractive anec-
dote. Who could deny Smith's claim that when the Indians had been
"ready with their clubs, to beate out his braines, Pocahontas the
Kings dearest daughter, when no intreaty could prevaile, got his head
in her armes, and laid her owne upon his to save him from death:
whereat the Emperour was contented he should live. . . ."? The truth
lies buried with the captain and his Indian captors.

A Bitter Homecoming

Whether through Pocahontas' intercession or his own negotiations
with Powhatan, early in 1608 Smith returned, accompanied by four
Indian guides, to the English outpost at Jamestown. His reception
there fell short of his expectations. On the Levitical grounds that he
had been responsible for the death of two of his men, and hence
should lose his own life, the council sentenced him to the gallows.
Only Smith's blunt refusal to submit to the hangman, and Newport's
timely return from England, rescued him once again from an igno-
minious death at the hands of his own countrymen.

With that event Smith's American career reached its perigee.
Thereafter his influence grew as that of Wingfield, Ratcliffe, and
Martin declined. Back in June Smith had gained his rightful seat on
the governing council through the intercession of Newport and Reverend Hunt, but since then his sole assignments had been to map the
area and barter with the Indians. Now, gradually and grudgingly, the
colony recognized Smith's considerable talents, especially in contrast to his fellow councillors'.

President Wingfield proved no leader. He rapidly lost the confidence of his followers by keeping for himself and his cronies the
colony's precious supply of sack and *aqua vitae*; at least the three surviving councillors—Ratcliffe, Smith, and Martin—were sufficiently
convinced of it to oust Wingfield from command less than six months
after his installation. John Ratcliffe, elected to succeed him, also
showed little skill at solving the colony's problems. Some new members joined the council in January 1608 when Captain Newport arrived with the "first supply," but as unseasoned colonists they played
a relatively passive role. As the need for firm leadership became more
apparent, both in dealings with the natives and in controlling the settlers, the colony increasingly turned to Smith. In September 1608 Ratcliffe's term as president, limited by charter to one year, expired. In
the ensuing election Smith won the office, "which till then," the captain later insisted, "by no means would he accept, though he was often importuned thereunto." Reluctant candidate or not, Smith now had
charge of England's only American outpost; its survival would depend
in large part on his judgment and strength of will.

The Puritans Migrate to Massachusetts

Bonnie L. Lukes

In the following excerpt from her book, *Colonial America*, Bonnie L. Lukes summarizes the events surrounding the early colonization of Massachusetts by two Puritan groups: the Pilgrims of Plymouth and the Massachusetts Bay Company. According to Lukes, both groups were fleeing religious oppression in England and established their own governments; however, the Pilgrims of Plymouth, who left England in 1620 aboard the *Mayflower,* were a small band of farmers who obtained permission, but not a charter, from King James I to settle in Virginia. Their ship, however, did not land in Virginia, but at Plymouth. Although the Pilgrims thrived after surviving the harsh winter and disease, the Puritans of the Massachusetts Bay Company, a much larger party who left England in 1630, were more successful, says Lukes. The Massachusetts Bay Puritans had a charter to establish their colony, and the colonists represented all levels of society, including wealthy gentlemen and middle-class merchants, the author explains. The original good will between the colonists and the Indians was broken with the Pequot War in 1637, Lukes writes, and the confederation of Puritan communities that arose following the war was the first glimmer of the colonial unity that would come in the next century. Lukes is a freelance writer who writes on a variety of topics, including colonial history.

Religion played only a small role in the settlement of Virginia, but in Massachusetts it was a crucial factor. The founding of Massachusetts grew out of a dissatisfaction with religious conditions in England.

At the beginning of the seventeenth century, England was officially Protestant. The majority of the people belonged to the state church—the Church of England. But certain members were troubled that the church retained traces of Catholicism. These people, who became known as Puritans, wanted to purify the church by doing away with rituals and church hierarchy—priests and bishops.

Looking for Land of Their Own

Within the larger Puritan group was a segment of believers called Separatists. They wanted to separate from the Church of England and establish their own church. This did not set well with James I, who, as king, was head of the Church of England. He had some of the Separatists jailed and vowed to "harry them out of the land, or else do worse." In 1608 they fled England for Holland.

In Holland the Pilgrims, as the Separatists came to be called, could worship as they pleased. But they were not happy to have their children growing up in a foreign country, speaking Dutch, and forgetting the English language and customs. Most of them were farmers who disliked living in the city. They wanted land of their own. And although they did not want to return to England itself, they wanted to live under the English flag. A further concern was that Catholic Spain might reconquer Holland and force the Catholic religion on them. So after twelve years in Holland, the Pilgrims decided to "dislodge . . . to some place of better advantage and less danger." Where better than the New World?

The Pilgrims had no money to buy and equip a ship, so they formed a joint-stock company with some London businessmen. The merchants agreed to finance the venture in exchange for half of all profits generated in the first seven years. Although the Virginia Company granted the Pilgrims a patent that allowed them to settle in Virginia, the Pilgrims were not employees of a company as the Jamestown settlers had been; the Pilgrims were partners with the merchants.

Although King James refused to give the Pilgrims a charter, he promised that if they returned to England to embark on their journey, he "would not molest them, provided they carried themselves peaceably." In September 1620 the Pilgrims boarded the *Mayflower* and set sail from Plymouth, England, with 101 passengers. Only 51 of the men, women, and children aboard were "Saints"—the name the Pilgrims called themselves; the others were of different faiths, and the Pilgrims called them "Strangers."

The Pilgrims of Plymouth

After sixty-five days at sea, the Pilgrims—either by accident or by intent—landed in New England instead of Virginia. They had no legal right to settle there because it was outside of their patent's jurisdiction. When the Strangers realized they had not reached their promised destination, they thought they had been tricked and threatened mutiny.

The Pilgrim leaders moved quickly to quell this rebellion and establish some form of government until their settlement could be authorized by the king. They assembled all the men who were aboard ship and drew up the Mayflower Compact. This document was an early indication of the self-governing spirit that would drive the English colonists who settled America. In it they agreed to obey majority rule in the colony. However, they were careful to include a pledge of loyalty to King James:

> We . . . the loyal subjects of our dread sovereign lord, King James . . . having undertaken, for the glory of God, and advancement of the Christian faith . . . a voyage to plant the first colony in the northern parts of Virginia, do . . . combine ourselves together into a civil body politic . . . to enact, constitute, and frame such just and equal laws . . . as shall be thought most meet [proper] and convenient for the general good of the colony, unto which we promise all due submission and obedience.

Of the sixty-five adult male passengers, forty-one—strangers as well as Saints—signed the agreement that would become Plymouth's constitution.

After sixty-five days at sea, the first Pilgrims landed at Plymouth Rock in December of 1620.

Landing on the New England coast in the middle of winter proved costly. Freezing weather and disease soon took its toll. By the end of winter, half of the Plymouth settlers had died.

Fortunately, the Pilgrims enjoyed a peaceful relationship with the Native Americans. This was partly because the local tribe had been too ravaged and weakened by smallpox to pose a threat. But it was also due to an Indian named Squanto. Years before the Pilgrims arrived, Squanto had been kidnapped by a passing English ship and sold into slavery in Spain. He had eventually made his way back to New England. Squanto spoke broken English and served as an interpreter for the Pilgrims. He also taught them how to plant corn, catch fish, and trap beaver. Squanto played an important part in the little colony's early survival.

The colony at Plymouth became self-supporting, and the Pilgrims lived peacefully alongside the Indians for forty years, but Plymouth remained a simple agricultural society small in number. The brave little band of Pilgrims who succeeded in carving out a tiny foothold on the wild and rugged New England coast never obtained a charter of their own.

Consequently, Plymouth eventually ceased being a separate colony. It was swallowed up by a more powerful and successful neighbor. For in 1630, the first of the enterprising Puritans arrived from England to establish the Massachusetts Bay Colony.

The Massachusetts Bay Colony

The Puritans had tried to reform the Church of England. When it became clear that the reforms were not going to happen, they resolved to establish a holy community in the midst of the New England wilderness, where the lives of individuals would be regulated in harmony with the will of God. But the Puritans were practical people. They wanted to make sure that they had a clear title to land in New England. That required obtaining a royal charter from Charles I, the reigning king. This seemed an impossible task because Charles— who was married to a French Catholic—despised the Puritans. Nevertheless, influential Puritans in Parliament persuaded him to grant a charter that formed twenty-six investors into the Massachusetts Bay Company. The company and the colony were synonymous until 1684.

The migrating Puritans elected John Winthrop governor of the Massachusetts colony. Winthrop, a devout Puritan and an influential man in England, shared his fellow Puritans' vision of what could be accomplished in a "new" England. "We shall be like a City upon a Hill; the eyes of all people are on us," he wrote.

Late in April 1630 eleven ships—carrying more than 700 men, women, and children; 240 cows; and 60 horses—embarked for

America. The "Great Migration" had begun. Some 20,000 men and women would follow before the decade passed.

Unlike the Pilgrims, who came primarily from England's lower working classes, the Puritans represented all levels of English society. They included gentlemen of substantial means like Winthrop as well as merchants and lawyers, tradesmen and craftsmen, and a substantial number of yeoman farmers. But the "lesser sort," tenant farmers, unskilled workers, and servants, also joined the Puritan movement.

In June the Puritans got their first glimpse of New England, but before they saw it, they inhaled its aroma. "There came a smell off the shore like the smell of a garden," one wrote. They settled along Massachusetts Bay. A small number of Puritan and non-Puritan settlers were already scattered up and down the New England coast, and Winthrop began the process of governing approximately one thousand people. The Puritans would establish seven towns that first year, including Boston.

The terms of the Massachusetts charter put control of the colony into the hands of the governor, a deputy governor, and the seven freemen (members of the corporation) who migrated. They were authorized "to make . . . all manner of wholesome and reasonable . . . statutes" for the colony.

However, government of the Massachusetts Bay Colony could not be left in the hands of so few. Membership in the corporation was soon expanded to include other adult males. Being a member meant having the right to vote in the General Court, Massachusetts's representative legislature. A member of the General Court was called a "freeman," and the word soon became synonymous with "voting citizen."

The number of freemen was limited, however, by the General Court's ruling that "noe man shal be admitted to the freedom of this body politicke, but such as are members of some of the [Puritan] churches." This violated the charter, but for over fifty years no Massachusetts resident could vote in provincial elections unless he belonged to an accepted Puritan church. (Women were not allowed to vote under any circumstances.) But in an important step toward future separation of church and state, the Puritans barred ministers from holding political office.

A Representative Government Grows

By 1634 Massachusetts contained three to four thousand inhabitants distributed over sixteen towns. No one would have called its government a democracy, but that year the freemen in each town gained the right to elect two representatives annually.

Soon, however, the colony's leaders grew fearful that the number of elected representatives would become large enough to control the vote. As a result, the General Court split into two houses. The upper house consisted of the governor and his assistants and the lower house of the elected representatives. Any proposed law had to pass both houses. The General Court still allowed only male church members to vote, but the town meeting was becoming more and more popular. And at town meetings, all men could vote.

By 1640 New England included settlements in Rhode Island, Connecticut, New Hampshire, and Maine. The settlers had lived more or less peacefully with the Native Americans until the Pequot War in 1637—the first major struggle between the two cultures. That war, in which Massachusetts and Connecticut colonists all but eradicated the Pequot tribe, led to the formation of the New England Confederation. The confederation comprised Massachusetts, Plymouth, Connecticut, and New Haven. (Rhode Island was excluded because of the nonconformists there, and New Hampshire and Maine because they had no unified government.)

The purpose of the confederation was to defend the colonies against the Indians and from possible outside invasion by the French and the Dutch. (The colonists could not depend on the mother country to help them because England was embroiled in a civil war.) The confederation read in part,

> We live encompassed with people of several nations and strange languages which . . . have of late combined themselves against us; and seeing . . . we are hindered from . . . seeking advice, or protection [from England] . . . do conceive it our bounded duty . . . to enter into a . . . consociation [alliance] among ourselves, for mutual help and strength.

This confederation was the earliest sign of the colonial unity that would develop in the next century.

The Structure and Economic Development of Quaker Pennsylvania

Gary B. Nash

The Quakers hoped to establish a colony in America where they could live by their own laws. Unlike other colonists, however, the Quakers who arrived in Pennsylvania in 1681 had the benefit of the preparations of William Penn, who had planned the civil and criminal code, the distribution of land, and conditions of settlement. In the following excerpt from his book *Quakers and Politics*, author and historian Gary B. Nash explains how the structure of immigrant society and the economic development in Pennsylvania frustrated Penn's hope for a harmonious Quaker society. The large middle-class society of yeoman and artisans, whose ambition was not blocked by a strong upper class, competed with not only Penn's original investors, the Free Society of Traders, but merchants and traders outside Penn's society, creating discord among the colonists. Although the society had no problem finding buyers for their goods, they were forced to provide goods on credit, and investors in England failed to fulfill their financial commitments, putting the society in debt. These factors lessened the influence of the society, dis-

Excerpted from Gary B. Nash, *Quakers and Politics: Pennsylvania, 1681–1726.* Copyright © 1968 Princeton University Press. Reprinted with permission from the author.

crediting Penn and his colony. Nash is professor of history at UCLA and author of many books on early America.

In three-quarters of a century of English colonization no settler had come to a colony where more had been done to pre-establish the machinery of government than in Pennsylvania. Colonists in Virginia, Plymouth, and Massachusetts Bay had little more than a patent from the Crown or a preliminary social "compact" to guide them as they stepped ashore in the New World. New Yorkers and Marylanders had only their proprietors' instructions regarding the distribution of land and the general conditions of settlement. Some attempt at devising organic law had preceded settlement in the Jerseys and Carolinas, but the "Concessions and Agreements" of these colonies were not to be compared for comprehensiveness with William Penn's "Concessions and Conditions," the Frame of 1682, and the accompanying civil and criminal code—all fashioned in England.

From Harmony to Discord

Yet for all the preliminary work done in England, the first years in Pennsylvania were distinguished not by the orderly establishment of political institutions and purposeful development of the economy, but rather by wholesale confusion and chronic friction between sections, groups, and individuals. In the first rush of enthusiasm settlers wrote fervently of "the Joy of the wildernes, & . . . that gladnes that did break forth of the solitary & desolate Land"; or they saw in Pennsylvania "an honorable place within Zions walls" where the divine hand was "setting up a remnant in these parts as an ensign to the Nations." Similarly, Penn wrote letters, meant for consumption in England, that described a "precious Harmony" in the meeting of the legislature and a "heavenly Authority" which bound together in common purpose all members of the "holy experiment." But in reality, few things were more elusive in early Pennsylvania than "authority" and "harmony." The plans of the Free Society of Traders for a pivotal position in economic affairs were resented and resisted from the outset. In the political sphere elements of the legislature matched strength, the Lower Counties jockeyed for power with the three Quaker counties established around Philadelphia, pro- and antiproprietary factions emerged, and within factions individuals vied for position. "For the love of God, men and the poor country, be not so governmentish, so noisy and open in your dissatisfactions," Penn wrote only three years after the colony had been launched. A year later he was writing in disgust that he was tempted to give Pennsylvania back to the King and let "a mercenary government" tame the Quakers if it could.

The human ground swell that broke upon Pennsylvania's shores in the first four years of settlement was evidence of the hopes and aspirations which Penn had aroused with his strenuous promotional efforts. Twenty-three ships from England sailed up the Delaware between December 1681 and December 1682, disgorging some two thousand settlers. In 1683 twenty ships followed with an additional two thousand immigrants. James Claypoole estimated that toward the end of that year almost one thousand settlers arrived in one six-week period alone. By the close of 1685, when the first great wave of immigration ended, almost ninety ships had delivered about eight thousand immigrants to Pennsylvania, a population buildup unmatched in the annals of English colonization. Even the great Puritan migration to Massachusetts Bay Colony in the early 1630's did not quite equal the initial movement to Pennsylvania. It had taken Virginia three decades to reach the population Penn's colony attained by 1685.

The Structure of Immigrating Society

At the bottom of immigrating society, if one excludes the small number of Africans who were brought into the colony in the first two years, were the indentured servants. It is likely that at least one-third of all the early settlers were indentured, and probably one-half of the adult males arriving in the early years came as servants. This was no permanently depressed class of individuals, however. Frequently the indentured servant was an ambitious person whose only chance of reaching America lay in contracting his labor for a limited period. Though no statistical analysis of his progress is possible, one sees frequent evidence of a rapid ascent in society. John Clows of Cheshire, England, a purchaser of 1,000 acres of land, brought three indentured servants with him to Pennsylvania. One became a substantial landowner and constable of Newtown and Wrightstown in Bucks County; another was a constable in Bucks County by 1689 and later an innkeeper and operator of a Delaware River ferry; and the third became a yeoman farmer. Of Joseph Fisher's eleven servants, four became landowners, one a deputy sheriff of Bucks County, two were women who married landowners, and four died or dropped from sight.

Above the indentured servants stood the colonists of yeoman and artisan origin. These were typically men of skill and drive. For in seventeenth-century England the riffraff and ambitionless generally refused to trade their parish alms for the rigors of fashioning life anew in the American wilderness. When Penn proposed to transport poor Scots to Pennsylvania and "set them downe at easy raits," his chief agent and promoter in Scotland advised that "such is the humeur of that gang of people here" that none would "stir from home [for] such a journey." Those who sought land and wider opportunity in the New World were the craftsmen and farmers in whom the fires of ambition had not yet been snuffed out by years of destitution. This was especially true among Quakers. Friends in England were rarely recruited from the truly impoverished class. The Society's strongest appeal was to the urban worker or shopkeeper and in the country to the yeoman or husbandman.

One estimates that 80 to 90 percent of the nonindentured immigrants were of the artisan-yeoman class. A study of landholding in the first decade of settlement tends to support this view of a society in which the "middling sorts" predominated. It is tempting, upon analyzing land purchases made in England, to conclude that Pennsylvania began as a rather sharply stratified society. . . . Three-quarters of the purchasers, having invested no more than £20 in Pennsylvania land, were concentrated in the lower brackets where they accounted for about one-third of the total land purchased. At the other end of the scale were a relatively small number of men (10 percent of the total purchasers) who could lay claim to nearly half of the purchased land in Pennsylvania. What changed this picture markedly was the fact that whereas more than two-thirds of the smaller purchasers immigrated, less than one-third of the wealthy buyers did so. The first rent roll for Pennsylvania, completed in 1689, gives evidence of a far less stratified society than the list of First Purchasers would tend to suggest. . . . Landowners predominated in the countryside and the general absence of men with large estates. Kent and Sussex counties showed a somewhat more differentiated society, perhaps because the area had been settled a decade or more before Pennsylvania was founded.

The Society in Philadelphia

In the city of Philadelphia the preponderance of humble settlers was much the same. Penn had made a strong appeal in the urban centers of English society, for he knew that the Society of Friends had thrived in London, Bristol, Dublin, and smaller towns, and he recognized that men of the "laborious Handicrafts" would form the backbone of his "great city." In 1685 he boasted of the wide range of crafts represented in Philadelphia. Later statements confirm the impression that Philadelphia was typically a town of ambitious artisans and shopkeepers.

If society in Pennsylvania seemed to huddle on the lower and middle rungs of the ladder, though the bottom-most rung was scarcely occupied, it did not lack at least the nucleus of an upper class. Though unpretentious landowners and struggling urban artisans predominated, there was a small number of more substantial men among the initial immigrants. . . . Usually they had purchased at least 5,000 acres of land, had invested £50 or more in the Free Society of Traders, and had arrived with at least a half-dozen indentured servants. From an early date they were able to establish small commercial farms which produced grain and foodstuffs for the West Indian market. But in spite of their relative affluence, these men lived remarkably like their poorer neighbors. Because everyone started from scratch in the Delaware wilderness, the colonial gentry, if it can be called that at all, was distinguished chiefly for its rough-hewn appearance. It would take at least a generation in Pennsylvania for the wealthier immigrants to carve out estates which in size and appearance would clearly differentiate them from their neighbors.

More important in the formation of a colonial upper class was the rapid gathering of a community of merchants. About thirty-five traders, Quaker with few exceptions, converged on Pennsylvania during the first four years. . . .

Others outside of England also saw fortune awaiting them in Pennsylvania. . . . Merchants of Amsterdam and leaders of the Dutch migration, transferred their estates to the colony. . . . Men [were] quick to perceive the economic control which Philadelphia would soon exert over the entire length of the river. Most of these adventurers gravitated toward Philadelphia. Only a few . . . sought success down-river at Chester, the oldest settlement in the province, or in the lower Delaware ports of New Castle and Lewes.

The significance of the structure of immigrating society lay in the heavy concentration of yeomen and artisans and in the relatively narrow distance that separated the upper and lower classes. The effect of this telescoping of the social structure was ambivalent. In terms of economic development, the presence of so many sturdy yeomen and artisans, together with the general absence of a fixed upper class, which might block the ascent of ambitious persons of humble origin, was probably a major factor in Pennsylvania's phenomenally rapid growth. In political and social affairs, however, severe strains were placed on traditional concepts of political organization.

The Pattern of Economic Development

There are few parallels in colonial history to the economic success of Pennsylvania in the first two decades. Only three years after settlement, its capital city was firmly established in the Barbados provisioning trade and had cut deep inroads into New York's control of the middle-Atlantic fur and tobacco markets. By 1700 Philadelphia was second in size only to Boston in the English colonies. Prosperity stemmed not only from the fertile soil of the Delaware River Valley and Penn's effectiveness in promoting immigration to his colony. At least as important was the fact that from the outset Pennsylvania possessed a large number of highly skilled craftsmen, men who formed the nucleus of a thriving urban community and gave impetus to the infant economy. Equally important in the rapid economic development of the colony was the immediate arrival of an experienced body of merchants, men long established in other seaports of the English world, men with sound credit and reputation, men whose close mercantile contacts throughout the world of English commerce gave the economy a kind of headstart. Many were closely connected with a far-flung circle of Quaker merchants, some of whom had invested liberally both in Pennsylvania land and the Free Society of Traders. Almost automatically, Pennsylvania merchants took their place in this intercolonial and intercontinental league of Quaker commerce.

Pennsylvania's rapid growth and the general success of the economy in the first two decades should not conceal the fact that almost from the start there were tensions and at times even open conflict within the mercantile community. On the surface the emergent merchant class appeared homogeneous enough. Almost all of the merchants were Quakers. Most of them were English, proceeding to Pennsylvania from various way stations in the English mercantile world, but acquainted even before arrival through previous commercial and religious contacts. Those who took up trade on the lower Delaware mixed easily with the early settlers who had drifted into the region in the 1660's and 1670's. However, despite the outward appearance of unity, the merchants were deeply divided. The sources of tension related not so much to their ethnic or religious background as to other considerations. Only nine of the merchants had participated in the launching of Pennsylvania. As members of Penn's circle, they had received important provincial and proprietary offices and appeared to hold special claims to the proprietor's favors. Probably few of them doubted that once in Pennsylvania they would be uniquely situated to control the colony's trade. At least as important, only five of the early merchants belonged to the Free Society of Traders, which Penn had projected as a vital part of his plans. Finally, about one-quarter of the total had cast their lot in the down-river ports south of Philadelphia from which they gazed apprehensively at the burgeoning Quaker capital.

The seal of the colony of Pennsylvania

Division in the Free Society

The immediate difficulties of the Free Society of Traders can be taken as an indication of the divisions within the mercantile ranks. The hope entertained by the Society that it might assume a controlling role in the economic development of Pennsylvania was quickly lost. Only a handful in number, Penn's merchant associates found themselves swamped by a larger group of entrepreneurs who had no intention of allowing such a closed body to monopolize the colony's trade. Instead the early commerce fell largely into the hands of individual merchants, acting for themselves or as agents for merchants in England. This overshadowing of the Free Society had repercussions far beyond the economic realm.

In a sense the Free Society of Traders was defeated before it entered the race. The first phase of commercial activity involved provisioning the successive waves of immigrants that disembarked on Pennsylvania shores; by the time the Society was on the scene in late 1682 this function was already in the hands of other men. During the earliest stages of immigration merchants who had established themselves on the Delaware in the 1670's, when the region was still a part of the Duke of York's grant, assumed the leading role, selling supplies to the newcomers and capitalizing on the needs of those who arrived too late in the year to get crops in the ground. The "ancient lowly inhabitants come to sell their produce to their profit and our accomodation," reported Penn after his first winter.

Merchants in other colonies were also quick to exploit the new market on the Delaware. At first coin was plentiful, for most immigrants converted their assets into specie before leaving England. According to Penn, about forty ships came to trade in Pennsylvania during the first year, eager to exchange provisions for the always coveted money. "New York, New England and Road Island did with their provisions fetch our Goods and Money," he disclosed.

The Promise of Trade

Among those who came to trade, some found the promise of Pennsylvania irresistible. William Frampton was one. An established New York merchant with an eye to the main chance, he made his move early. During the first winter of settlement he was in Philadelphia selling cargoes on consignment from his friend, Walter Newberry, a Quaker merchant of Newport, Rhode Island. With two sloops, owned jointly with Francis Richardson of New York, another Quaker merchant and ship captain, Frampton also traded extensively in the Lower Counties where nearly every tobacco planter in Kent, Sussex, and New Castle counties was soon in his debt. Early in 1683 Frampton purchased the land rights for 5,000 acres and two city lots from one of Penn's earliest supporters and moved his family to Philadelphia. Two years later he was operating one of the largest wharves on the Philadelphia waterfront and had acquired a brewery, a bakery, and an inn. In addition, he became the Pennsylvania agent for Charles Jones & Company, Quaker merchants of Bristol, England, and for London merchants Walter Benthall and Thomas Hart.

Although neither a First Purchaser nor a member of the Free Society, few in Pennsylvania could match his success in the early years.

Another merchant who exemplified the pattern of early economic development was Samuel Carpenter. For ten years a Quaker merchant in Barbados, Carpenter arrived in Philadelphia in early 1683 and immediately set about spinning a network of enterprises that made him the wealthiest merchant in the province within a decade. His fine wharf, capable of accommodating ships of 500 tons, was the first in Philadelphia; by 1685 he had an interest in several grain mills, timber lands on both sides of the Delaware, and a lime burning business. His trade with the West Indies was extensive. Like other merchants he was deeply involved in land speculation, both in Pennsylvania and West New Jersey.

Even those who had launched the Free Society and invested substantial sums in it, merchants such as James Claypoole and Robert Turner, were quick to pursue their own mercantile interests apart from company affairs. Claypoole, who was treasurer of the Society, was one of Philadelphia's most eager entrepreneurs. More than a year before his departure from England, he had plied his brother, already in Pennsylvania, with questions about trade possibilities in the new colony and had sent a trusted servant ahead to launch his mercantile affairs. Once in Philadelphia he quickly established a vigorous trade, importing pork, beef, butter, cheese, and a variety of dry goods and tools from England and sending pipe staves, timber, silver, pelts, furs, and whale oil and bone in return. Trade lines were quickly opened to Barbados where another brother, a prospering planter-merchant, acted as correspondent.

By 1684, individual merchants had firmly established the Delaware River as a center of no small promise in the English mercantile world. Boston, Newport, New York, Bristol, London, and Barbados were all within the orbit of trade for Philadelphia and New Castle. Penn reported in July 1683 that since the previous summer almost sixty ships had put into Philadelphia to trade. "This we esteem a good beginning," he remarked. James Claypoole, no less optimistic, expressed the general belief that within a few years Pennsylvania would rival any of her neighboring colonies in matters of commerce.

Problems Within the Society

Amidst the buoyant beginnings of such individual enterprisers, the Free Society of Traders encountered little but adversity. From the beginning the company was crippled by the disinterest of some of its officers and the erratic behavior of others. Nicholas More, the president, was no man to lead the venture. Aristocratic, unstable, and condescending by nature, he was poorly equipped to guide the Society's affairs. Most of his time was spent establishing his manor outside of Philadelphia. Simcock, the vice-president, settled in Chester County, far away from the Society's offices, and became a farmer. Claypoole, the treasurer, did not arrive in Philadelphia until late 1683 and then, seeing the already fallen state of company affairs, followed his own trading interests while grumbling of the incursions which Society business made on his time. One of the committee men complained about the Society's governing board: "particular men do[e]th for themselves." Of the twelve members elected as resident commissioners, three decided to remain in England and three others took up land outside of Philadelphia, the Society's center of business.

Despite personnel problems, efforts were made to establish the Society at the heart of the province's economic life. The first cargo of English goods and about sixty indentured servants of the company arrived in September 1682 with President More. Eager buyers snapped up the wares. But already the necessity of buying provisions from other colonies was draining Pennsylvania of money and the Free Society was forced to take credit when the supply of coin was exhausted. A second cargo reached Pennsylvania the following summer. Again the shipment was quickly disposed of, but as before the goods had to be retailed on credit. "We are forced to trust most what we sell, and People will not pay in 6 or 9 months," the treasurer reported. Within a year he was obliged to admit that "we have neither credit nor money, and now must sue people at law, or be forced to loose all."

Compounding the financial difficulties of the Society was the unwillingness of English stockholders, apprehensive at reports of mismanagement in Pennsylvania, to pay in their full subscriptions. "Wee understand but halfe of the subscription money is paid in," wrote an alarmed member of the governing board in January 1684. Added to the growing shortage of specie in the province, the default of English stockholders was nearly a crushing blow. It was apparent that the Society lacked sufficient capital to sell goods on credit for the one or two years required until Pennsylvania could develop exportable commodities to balance her trade.

Although crippled by inadequate capitalization, the Society attempted to carry out some of the expansive schemes projected in London in 1682. Fishing and whaling expeditions were initiated at the mouth of Delaware Bay; a grist mill was purchased from early Swedish settlers and operated for a few years; a glass factory, a brick kiln, and a tannery were begun; and Lasse Cock, an early Swedish settler and experienced Indian trader, was engaged to launch the fur trade of which so much was expected. Two small vessels were purchased to establish a trade with the West Indies. But in spite of these attempts commerce in Pennsylvania after 1684 progressively fell into the hands of men who had played no part in the original promotion of the colony or who were steadily shying away from the proprietary group. Supplies from England were controlled not by the Free Society but by Charles Jones & Company of Bristol whose factors in Philadelphia, William Frampton and Andrew Robeson, remained aloof from the proprietary circle. The growing grain trade with the West Indies, which would become the foundation of Pennsylvania's economy for the next two decades, was likewise dominated by independent merchants who shunned any involvement with the Free Society. Their efforts only signified a continuation and reemphasis of the earlier attempts to outflank the proprietary-supported joint-stock company and its handful of London Quaker merchants.

A succession of suits brought against the Society between 1684 and 1686 caused its final collapse as a significant factor in Pennsylvania's trade. Thereafter, the Society functioned solely as a land company, gradually selling its extensive property to settle debts.

The Indians of New England: An Account from 1634

William Wood

Although reports came to seventeenth-century England providing news of America, not until 1634 did the English public have a thorough account of the New World and its inhabitants. In order to respond to English curiosity and to prepare future colonists, William Wood published *New England's Prospect*, an early description of the Massachusetts Bay Colony. In the following excerpt, Wood describes some of his observations of the various Indian populations who inhabited New England in the seventeenth century. For example, Wood describes the well-armed Mohawk, who lived west of Massachusetts, as treacherous, savage cannibals who would destroy the neighboring tribes without protection from the English. On the other hand, Wood describes the Pequot as courteous, fair, and industrious, pointing out that after trading with the English, the Pequot would profit from selling English goods to remote populations who were unaware of the goods' value.

Of the Connecticuts, Mohawks, or Such Indians as Are Westward

The country as it is in relation to the Indians is divided, as it were, into shires, every several division being swayed by a several

Excerpted from William Wood, *New England's Prospect* (Amherst: University of Massachusetts, 1977), edited by Alden T. Vaughan.

king. The Indians to the east and northeast, bearing the name of Churchers and Tarrenteens; these in the southern parts be called Pequots and Narragansetts; those who are seated westward be called Connecticuts and Mohawks. Our Indians that live to the northward of them be called Aberginians, who before the sweeping plague were an inhabitant not fearing, but rather scorning, the confrontments of such as now count them but the scum of the country and would soon root them out of their native possessions were it not for the English.

These [Mohawks] are a cruel bloody people which were wont to come down upon their poor neighbors with more than brutish savageness, spoiling their corn, burning their houses, slaying men, ravishing women; yea very cannibals they were, sometimes eating on a man, one part after another, before his face and while yet living, in so much that the very name of a Mohawk would strike the heart of a poor Aberginian dead, were there not hopes at hand of relief from the English to succor them. For these inhuman homicides confess that they dare not meddle with a white-faced man, accompanied with his hot-mouthed weapon. These Indians be a people of a tall stature, of long grim visages, slender waisted, and exceeding great arms and thighs, wherein they say their strength lieth; and this I rather believe because an honest gentleman told me, upon his knowledge, that he saw one of them with a fillip with his finger kill a dog, who afterward flead [flayed] him and sod [boiled] him, and eat him to his dinner. They are so hardy that they can eat such things as would make other Indians sick to look upon.

Being destitute of fish and flesh, they suffice hunger and maintain nature with the use of vegetatives. But that which they most hunt after is the flesh of man; their custom is if they get a stranger near their habitations not to butcher him immediately, but keeping him in as good plight as they can, feeding him with the best victuals they have. As a near-neighboring Indian assured me, who found what he had spoke true by a lamentable experience (still wearing the cognizance of their cruelty on his naked arm) who being taken by them, eat of their food [and] lodged in their beds, nay he was brought forth every day to be new painted, piped unto, and hemmed in with a ring of bare-skinned morris dancers, who presented their antics before him. In a word, when they had sported enough about this walking Maypole, a rough-hewn satyr cutteth a gobbit of flesh from his brawny arm, eating it in his view, searing it with a firebrand lest the blood should be wasted before the morning, at the dawning whereof they told him they would make an end as they had begun. He answered that he cared as little for their threats as they did for his life, not fearing death; whereupon they led him bound into a Wigwam where he sat as a condemned prisoner, grating his teeth for anger, being for the present so hampered and the next day to be entombed in so many living sepulchers. He extends his strength to the utmost, breaketh the bands from his hands and loosing the cords from his feet, thought at once to be revenged for the flesh of his arm, and finding a hatchet lays on with an arm of revenge to the unliving of ten men at first onset. Afterward taking the opportunity of the dead of the night, [he] fled through the woods and came to his native home where he still lives to rehearse his happy escapal. Of the rest of their inhuman cruelties let the Dutchmen (who live among them) testify, as likewise the cruel manner of leading their prisoners captive, whom they do not only pinion with sharp thongs but likewise bore holes through their hamstrings, through which they thread a cord coupling ten or a dozen men together.

These Indians be more desperate in wars than the other Indians, which proceeds not only from the fierceness of their natures but also in that they know themselves to be better armed and weaponed, all of them wearing sea horse skins and barks of trees (made by their art as impenetrable, it is thought, as steel), wearing head pieces of the same, under which they march securely and undauntedly, running and fiercely crying out *"Hadree Hadree succomee succomee"* (we come, we come to suck your blood), not fearing the feathered shafts of the strong-armed bowmen, but like unruly headstrong stallions beat them down with their right hand tomahawks and left hand javelins, being all the weapons which they use, counting bows a cowardly fight. Tomahawks be staves of two foot and a half long, and a knob at one end as round and big as a football. A javelin is a short spear, headed with sharp sea horse teeth; one blow or thrust with these strange weapons will not need a second to hasten death from a Mohawk's arm.

I will conclude this discourse concerning the Mohawks in a tragical rehearsal of one of their combats. A sagamore [chief] inhabiting near these cannibals was so daily annoyed with their injurious inhumanity that he must either become a tributary subject to their tyranny or release himself from thraldom by the stroke of war, which he was unable to wage of himself. Wherefore with fair entreaties, plausible persuasions, forcive arguments, and rich presents he sent to other sagamores, he procured so many soldiers as, summed with his own, made his forces six thousand strong; with the which he resolutely marched towards his enemies, intending either to win the horse or lose the saddle. His enemies, having heard of his designs, plotted how to confront him in his enterprise and overthrow him by treachery, which they thus attempted: knowing their enemies were to swim over a muddy river, they divided their bands, lying in ambush on both sides of the river waiting his approach, who suspected no danger, looking for nothing but victory. But immediately they were environed with their unexpected foes in their greatest disadvantage, for being in the water, shoot they could not, for swimming was their action. And when they came to the side, they could not run away, for their feet stuck fast in the mud, and their adversaries impaled them about, clubbing and darting all that attained the shore, so that all were killed and captived saving three, who—swimming farther under the waters (like the duck that escapeth the spaniel by diving) until they were out of sight of their bloodthirsty foes—recovered the shore, creeping into the thickets from whence after a little breathing and resting of their weary limbs they marched through the woods and arrived at their own homes, relating to their inquisitive survivors the sad event of their war, who a long time after deplored the death of their friends, still placing the remembrance of that day in the calendar of their mishaps.

Of the Tarrenteens or the Indians Inhabiting Eastward

The Tarrenteens [Abnaki], saving that they eat not man's flesh, are little less savage and cruel than these cannibals. Our Indians do fear them as their deadly enemies, for so many of them as they meet they kill. About two years ago, our Indians being busy about their accustomed huntings, not suspecting them so near their own liberties, were on the sudden surprised by them, some being slain, the rest escaping to their English asylum, whither they durst not pursue them. Their sagamore was wounded but presently cured by English surgery.

These Indians are the more insolent by reason they have guns which they daily trade for with the French, who will sell his eyes, as they say, for beaver. But these do them more credit than service; for having guns they want powder, or if they have that they want shot, something or other being always wanting; so that they use them for little but to salute coasting boats that come to trade, who no sooner can anchor in any harbor but they present them with a volley of shot, asking for sack and strong liquors which they so much love, since the English used to trade it with them, that they will scarce trade for anything else, lashing out into excessive abuse, first taught by the example of some of our English who to unclothe them of their beaver coat clad them with the infection of swearing and drinking, which was never in fashion with them before, it being contrary to their nature to guzzle down strong drink or use so much as to sip of strong-waters until our bestial example and dishonest incitation hath too much brought them to it.

From which I am sure hath sprung many evil consequents, as disorder, quarrels, wrongs, unconscionable and forcive wresting of beaver and wampompeag [strands of shells used as money], and from overflowing cups there hath been a proceeding to revenge, murther, and overflowing of blood. As witness Master Way's boat, which they sunk with stones after they had killed his son, with three more, buzzing the English in the ears that they see it bulged against the rocks and the men drowned in the beating surges. But afterwards, being betrayed, as many as were caught were hanged. Another who was situated on Richmond's Island, living as he list amongst them, making his covetous corrupt will his law, after many abuses was with his family one evening treacherously murthered under a fair pretence of trade; so that these that lived beside the law of God and their king, and the light of nature, died by their hands that cared neither for God, king, nor nature.

Take these Indians in their own trim and natural disposition and they be reported to be wise, lofty-spirited, constant in friendship to one another, true in their promise, and more industrious than many others.

Of the Pequots and Narragansetts, Indians Inhabiting Southward

The Pequots be a stately, warlike people, of whom I never heard any misdemeanor, but that they were just and equal in their dealings, not treacherous either to their countrymen or English, requiters of courtesies, affable towards the English.

Their next neighbors, the Narragansetts, be at this present the most numerous people in those parts, the most rich also, and the most industrious, being the storehouse of all such kind of wild merchandise as is amongst them. These men are the most curious minters of their wampompeag and mowhacheis [Indian Gold], which they form out of the inmost wreaths of periwinkle shells. The northern, eastern, and western Indians fetch all their coin from these southern mintmasters. From hence they have most of their curious pendants and bracelets. From hence they have their great stone pipes, which will hold a quarter of an ounce of tobacco, which they make with steel drills and other instruments. Such is their ingenuity and dexterity that they can imitate the English mold so accurately that were it not for matter and color it were hard to distinguish them. They make them of green and sometimes of black stone; they be much desired of our English tobacconists for their rarity, strength, handsomeness, and coolness. Hence likewise our Indians had their pots, wherein they used to seethe their victuals before they knew the use of brass. Since the English came, they have employed most of their time in catching of beavers, otters, and musquashes, which they bring down into the bay, returning back loaded with English commodities, of which they make a double profit by selling them to more remote Indians who are ignorant at what cheap rates they obtain them in comparison of what they make them pay, so making their neighbors' ignorance their enrichment. Although these be populous, yet I never heard they were desirous to take in hand any martial enterprise or expose themselves to the uncertain events of war, wherefore the Pequots call them women-like men. But being uncapable of a jeer, they rest secure under the conceit of their popularity and seek rather to grow rich by industry than famous by deeds of chivalry. But to leave strangers and come to declare what is experimentally known of the Indians amongst whom we live. . . .

Of the Aberginians or Indians Northward

First of their stature, most of them being between five or six foot high, straight bodied, strongly composed, smooth-skinned, merry countenanced, of complexion something more swarthy than Spaniards, black haired, high foreheaded, black eyed, out-nosed, broad shouldered, brawny armed, long and slender handed, out breasted, small waisted, lank bellied, well thighed, flat kneed, handsome grown legs, and small feet. In a word, take them when the blood brisks in their veins, when the flesh is on their backs and marrow in their bones, when they frolic in their antic deportments and Indian postures, and they are more amiable to behold (though only in Adam's livery) than many a compounded fantastic in the newest fashion.

It may puzzle belief to conceive how such lusty bodies should have their rise and daily supportment from so slender a fostering, their houses being mean, their lodging as homely, commons scant, their drink water, and nature their best clothing. In them the old proverb may well be verified: *Natura paucis contenta* [Nature is satisfied with a few things], for though this be their daily portion, they still are healthful and lusty. I have been in many places, yet did I never see one that was born either in redundance or defect a monster, or any that sickness had deformed, or casualty made decrepit, saving one that had a bleared eye and another that had a wen on his cheek. The reason is rendered why they grow so proportionable and continue so long in their vigor (most of them being fifty before a wrinkled brow or gray hair betray their age) is because they are not brought down with suppressing labor, vexed with annoying cares, or drowned in the excessive abuse of overflowing plenty, which oftentimes kills them more than want, as may appear in them. For when they change their bare Indian commons for the plenty of England's fuller diet, it is so contrary to their stomachs that death or a desperate sickness immediately accrues, which makes so few of them desirous to see England.

Their swarthiness is the sun's livery, for they are born fair. Their smooth skins proceed from the often annointing of their bodies with the oil of fishes and the fat of eagles, with the grease of raccoons, which they hold in summer the best antidote to keep their skin from blistering with the scorching sun, and it is their best armor against the mosquitoes, the surest expeller of the hairy excrement, and stops the pores of their bodies against the nipping winter's cold.

Their black hair is natural, yet it is brought to a more jetty color by oiling, dyeing, and daily dressing. Sometimes they wear it very long, hanging down in a loose, disheveled, womanish manner; otherwhile tied up hard and short like a horse tail, bound close with a fillet, which they say makes it grow the faster. They are not a little fantastical or custom-sick in this particular, their boys being not permitted to wear their hair long till sixteen years of age, and then they must come to it by degrees, some being cut with a long foretop, a long lock on the crown, one of each side of his head, the rest of his hair being cut even with the scalp. The young men and soldiers wear their hair long on the one side, the other side being cut short like a screw. Other cuts they have as their fancy befools them, which would torture the wits of a curious barber to imitate. But though they be thus wedded to the hair of their head, you cannot woo them to wear it on their chins, where it no sooner grows but it is stubbed up by the roots, for they count it as an unuseful, cumbersome, and opprobrious excrement, insomuch as they call him an Englishman's bastard that hath but the appearance of a beard, which some have growing in a staring fashion like the beard of a cat, which makes them the more out of love with them, choosing rather to have no beards than such as should make them ridiculous.

Accusations of Witchcraft in Seventeenth-Century New England

Bryan F. Le Beau

Although accusations of witchcraft were made in all the European colonies, in the following excerpt from his book *The Story of the Salem Witch Trials*, Bryan F. Le Beau examines some of the reasons he believes the majority of witch-hunts occurred in New England. Although some authorities blame Puritanism alone, Le Beau argues that belief in witchcraft was part of seventeenth-century life, and when Puritan society appeared to be decaying, many blamed witchcraft. According to Le Beau, women who challenged traditional male authority or men and women with criminal records were often accused of witchcraft. Moreover, the community's sense of charity also deteriorated and members who were dependent on the community were also subject to accusations, particularly older women and widows. Le Beau is a professor of history at Creighton University.

B elief in witchcraft in the European colonies of America was widespread, the specific nature of that belief and the response of the authorities in each group of colonies paralleling that of the mother country. In Dutch territory, there was only one case of an individual being charged with being a witch, and that occurred in the town of Easthampton, which was populated by Englishmen who had migrated south out of New England. Perhaps as many as forty-three individuals were charged in New France, but they were seldom convicted, and then only mildly punished. The single notable exception involved Daniel Vuil. Vuil, a Huguenot, was accused of casting a spell on a fourteen-year-old girl with whom he had fallen in love, after he had been rejected by her parents. He was executed.

In New Spain, the Holy Office of the Inquisition set out to destroy witchcraft, but, much as in Spain where the Holy Office dealt mostly with conversos [Jews], in the colonies it tended to focus on Native Americans and blacks. It was incorporated into the larger drive to evangelize Native Americans and to eradicate pagan religion in the process. Witch-hunts appeared irregularly, but they were pursued with fervor. Sentences were sometimes harsh, but as a whole the courts were lenient and the executions few, as they were in Spain. For example, in Mexico between 1536 and 1543, the Holy Office charged twenty people with witchcraft, including fifteen women, of whom at least five were lower-class blacks or "mixed bloods." All were punished, some by public whipping, but none were executed. In 1675, authorities hanged four Indians in what is now New Mexico for practicing sorcery, but they were accused as well of killing seven missionaries. The uncommonly harsh penalty helped trigger the Pueblo Revolt of 1680.

Witch-Hunts in British Colonies

Following England's example, the number of witch trials in the English colonies was low. There were several cases in the Bermudas during the second half of the seventeenth century, beginning, according to the principal historian of the event, with the arrival of Scottish servants with their "superstitions" into a dominantly Puritan environment, ruled by a governor sympathetic to attempts to ferret out witches. Fifteen individuals, twelve women and three men, were initially charged with witchcraft, the records of nearly all of their cases making mention of various forms of maleficia [the casting of spells out of revenge, spite, or malice] rather than heresy. Five were executed, including four women. By the end of the century, when the Bermuda trials all but ended (there was one incompletely recorded case during the early years of the eighteenth century), the number of accused reached twenty-one, including sixteen women. One more woman was executed, but most of the rest of the cases ended in dismissal. There is little in the records by which to draw a profile of the accused. All we have is the previously noted historian's comment that the trials involved "harmless old women and half-crazy men."

There were occasional trials in various British colonies of mainland North America, including Virginia, New York, New Jersey, Pennsylvania, and Maryland. In Virginia, between 1627 and 1705, nine cases of accused witches made it to court; ten defamation cases involving witchcraft accusations were heard as well, most of them after 1668. Only one of the accused, however, William Harding of Northumberland County, in 1665, was convicted, and he was whipped and banished. Unique to Virginia were three shipboard executions of women accused of witchcraft, but little is known of their cases.

Aside from Virginia's shipboard executions, Maryland has the distinction of being the only British colony of mainland North America outside of New England wherein an execution for witchcraft took place. Rebecca Fowler was hanged in 1685, but the details of her case have not survived. Otherwise, historian Francis Neal Parke has found only five cases in colonial Maryland, four occurring between 1665 and 1686, the last in 1712. Four of the five involved women, and although the records are incomplete, no more than two (including the man) were convicted. All other cases in British America, numbering well over 200, occurred in New England, over half during the Salem witch trials.

As was the case in the Spanish, French, and Dutch colonies of the Americas, the British colonists assigned Native Americans to Satan almost from the start. They too believed that prior to their arrival, New England had belonged to the Devil, and that the Devil had a grip on its native inhabitants—that the Devil "visibly and palpably reigne[d] there," as the Reverend William Crashaw of Virginia put it. As David Lovejoy has suggested, given their religious intensity, New England Puritans may have exaggerated the Devil's role, thereby providing themselves with an explanation for their minimal success in evangelizing the "heathen," as well as a rationale for the bloody Pequot (1637) and King Philip's (1675) Wars. But in British America, Native Americans were seldom actually charged with witchcraft; that crime was reserved almost exclusively for Christians.

Looking for Explanations

It is not entirely clear why the overwhelming number of witch-hunts in British America occurred in New England. . . . The reader might be tempted to blame it on the Puritans. As Karen Armstrong has recently concluded:

> [A]s Salem shows, they [the Puritans] brought their phobias and frustrations with them. They also brought from Europe an inadequate conception of religion. Instead of seeing compassion as the primary religious virtue, the Puritans of New England—latter-day crusaders—cultivated a harsh, unyielding righteousness that was quick to judge and condemn. Instead of seeing God as all-powerful and all-forgiving, the Puritans saw Satan everywhere.

Further, although their authority was beginning to wane by the 1690s, Puritans dominated seventeenth-century New England and, as some have argued, the ministry may have been anxious to use any pretext to reestablish their influence. There is no evidence, however, that levels of activity in New England followed lines of heightened religiosity.

In their sermons, especially at executions for witchcraft, ministers linked maleficia and diabolism [dealings or possession by the devil]. They occasionally interrogated the accused and provided advice for public officials and the courts. But over the course of the century, Puritan ministers were not disproportionately numbered among the proponents of the trials. The records show that many were opposed and even instrumental in controlling them. Perhaps, then, without exonerating the Puritan ministry from any culpability, George Lyman Kittredge was right in warning that to tie witch trials in New England to religious opinions alone would be a serious error; the people of seventeenth-century New England believed in witchcraft not because they were Puritan, but because they were men of their time. To quote John Demos, witchcraft "belonged to the regular business of life in premodern times; or at least it belonged to the belief system, the value structure, the predominant psychology of those times," but then that still leaves us with the problem of explaining the large number of cases in New England. . . .

European witch-hunts were most common in areas of great turmoil, whether it be political, social, economic, or religious, and of such tur-

A woman stands trial for witchcraft. In seventeenth-century New England, women who challenged traditional male authority were often accused of being witches.

moil the people of New England at the end of the seventeenth century had more than their fair share. That, combined with their unique sense of having been chosen by God to establish a New Jerusalem and their fear that they had failed in their mission, led Puritan New Englanders to establish blame for that failure. Upon their arrival in the wilderness, John Winthrop had warned them that if they failed, God's wrath would be turned against them, and there was evidence by 1692 that indeed that was happening. What they needed to do was find out who was responsible, punish them, and thereby return to God's path and merit His favor once again.

The Practice of Magic

New Englanders, as typical Englishmen, were steeped in the lore of witchcraft. As Richard Godbeer has found, "alongside Protestant Christianity, there co-existed a tangled skein of magical beliefs and practices that the colonists brought with them from England." To use the anthropological term, they were *magico-religious*, and it is that with which Puritan ministers were particularly concerned—not with those who had rejected Puritanism, for they were few. Puritan ministers emphasized God's absolute sovereignty, insisting that everything in the world was determined by God, and they urged people to submit to His sovereignty without exception. They made great strides in persuading their flocks to that point of view, but their victory over pagan practices was not absolute, largely because so many of the laity did not see any conflict between the two.

While Puritan ministers condemned any form of magic as blasphemous and diabolical, most of their flock continued to believe in astrology, fortune-telling, divining, and the use of charms and potions to ward off evil or attract good fortune, love, and wealth. Because such practices were informal and not part of any coherent doctrinal system or organized institutional structure, they were so elusive as to defy any counterattack. As long as they did not elicit any significant opposition, which was most of the time, the practices were a nearly indistinguishable part of everyday life.

New Englanders, then, added little to the concept of witchcraft they inherited from England. For ministers, witchcraft may have been about repudiating Christ and worshipping the Devil, but for the common people it was primarily about doing harm. Thus, although the laws of seventeenth-century New England embodied the theological views of witchcraft and demanded proof of direct contact between the accused and the Devil, lay folk tended to focus on the suspect's malevolence. They were more concerned with a witch's use of occult skills to do harm. And as Richard Godbeer has speculated, this "disjuncture between legal conceptions of witchcraft and popular testimony about witchcraft made conviction extremely difficult."

The Tension Among Neighbors

As was the case in England, most cases in New England were initiated by people charging their neighbors with using witchcraft to harm members of their family or to destroy their livestock and personal possessions. Charges were essentially face-to-face interactions within communities where relationships—familial, spatial, gendered, and economic—became charged with suspicion, anger, and revenge.

Moreover, the history of witch trials in seventeenth-century New England reveals a similar tendency on the part of accusers to project guilt upon, and expel, certain members of the community. Much as Keith Thomas and Alan D. Macfarlane have found in England, charges in New England followed lines of intrinsic tension and hostility. In England, such tension was especially common in the Early Modern Period, when the sense of community of the traditional English village was disintegrating. Change was hardest on dependent members of the community—the poor and widowed, for example—whose subsistence depended on the generosity of their neighbors. They were often the first to be charged with witchcraft, and their accusers were likely to be those who had denied the accused's request for assistance, thereby failing to conform to the traditional code of community behavior. In the process, they not only felt guilty about their moral lapse but also, when some misfortune befell them, they projected that guilt onto the accused by holding them morally culpable for the incident. Not surprisingly, the marginally better-off were particularly well-represented among the accusers.

There may have been fewer truly needy in seventeenth-century New England, but the same thesis applies. When the traditional mutuality or communal pattern of which we have spoken began to unravel, as it did in the late-seventeenth century, the same feelings emerged. In fact, it may have been even more pronounced in New England because of its emphasis on the covenanted community. John Winthrop had told the Puritans upon their arrival in Massachusetts that God required their harmony if His mission for them was to succeed, but as the century wore on in the face of the new social and cultural values and attitudes that accompanied New England's transformation from a traditional rural, agricultural society to a more cosmopolitan, urban, and commercial world, that harmony was lost. Whatever sense of responsibility and charity had characterized New England at its founding was declining.

The Characteristics of the Accused

Given all of this, John Demos has gathered the following statistics concerning those accused of witchcraft in seventeenth-century New England. Of all suspects for whom he could determine social class, 73 percent were below the midpoint on his social scale. Those with

declining fortunes, though not necessarily poor, were also disproportionately represented among the accused, and both were much more
likely to be aggressively prosecuted and convicted.

As was true in England, 80 percent of those charged with witchcraft in New England were women, and at least half of those men who
were charged were the husbands, sons, or close associates of women
cried out against first. Men among those charged were less likely to
be tried and convicted, and if convicted, their sentences were usually
less severe. The only partial exceptions to this rule, and it was a matter of degree in both instances, were the two large-scale witch-hunts
of Hartford and Salem. In the former case, the portion of females was
64 percent, in the latter, 73 percent, suggesting that, as in Europe,
when fear of witchcraft was particularly strong, stereotypes tended to
crumble but not to collapse.

As was the case in England, the accused of New England were
largely older women, but still middle-aged. At a time when sixty was
considered the beginning of old age, 67 percent of those prosecuted
for witchcraft were between the ages of forty and sixty. At the time
they were first suspected, 82 percent fell into that age bracket. As John
Demos has explained, women in their forties and fifties had reached
their peak in terms of authority or power in the Puritan community;
they had fully realized their role in society and had presided over a
household of several children, servants, and apprentices. The accused,
however, generally were not so accomplished. Never-marrieds were
not disproportionately represented among the accused in New England, but being a widow was clearly a liability, and even more vulnerable were those with fewer children than average. Twice the proportion of the accused as that of the general population were childless, and the percentage of those who bore fewer children was higher
as well.

Carol Karlsen has argued that women over age forty were singled
out because they lived in a society in which men exercised substantial legal, political, ideological, and economic authority over women.
Witch-hunting, therefore, was a means of reaffirming this authority at
a time when some women were testing those constraints. Especially
vulnerable, Karlsen notes, were women without brothers and widows
who remained single or remarried but who had no sons by their previous marriage. Both stood to inherit property, and they stood in the
way of the orderly transmission of property from one generation of
males to another and were resented for it.

The Criminalization of Witchcraft

Of particular importance in New England was the accused's relationship to the community and to his or her family. To use Demos's words,
"a peaceful household was seen as the foundation of all social order."

Thus, any suspicion that a man, or especially a woman, caused domestic disharmony invited unfavorable notice from neighbors, and if it persisted, suspicion of witchcraft. Not surprisingly, men and women who had criminal records were disproportionately represented among the accused witches of seventeenth-century New England. Demos set the rate at a minimum of 36 percent, but allowed that the figure could be as high as 63 percent. Either level is significant when it is compared to a crime rate for the general population of from 10 to 20 percent, and, among women, of only 5 percent.

Just as interesting, however, is the type of crime with which witches were charged. When Demos organized the specific charges brought against those included in his study, he found that the single largest group by far (41 percent) had been charged with assaultive speech, and the rest with theft, lying, sex offenses, physical assault, resisting authority, arson, and fraud. Assaultive speech included slander and defamation, mostly, but it also referred to "filthy" and "scandalous" speech, and as historian Jane Kamensky has found, "disorderly speech," when employed by women, was seen as especially disruptive of the social order and particularly damaging for seventeenth-century New England women on a number of different counts, including their being more likely to be charged with being a witch.

In sum, historians have drawn a composite image of witches in seventeenth-century New England as being comparatively poor, female, middle-aged, and married or widowed; having fewer than the average number of children; often being in trouble with the law or in conflict with friends and family; having practiced some form of medical healing; and appearing abrasive in style and contentious in character. Few suspects conformed to all of these specifications, but the better someone fit this description, the more likely she or he would be accused of witchcraft.

Seventeenth-Century Accounts of the Slave Trade in the New World

Charlotte and Denis Plimmer

In the following selection, Charlotte and Denis Plimmer introduce first-hand accounts of the slave trade that was developing in the New World during the seventeenth century. For example, letters to the Massachusetts Bay Colony describe the economic advantages of slavery and provide instructions on how to develop a slave trade. The editors include an early law providing for emancipation of slaves and a memorandum from a slave agent, known as a factor, describing the horrifying mortality on slave ships—the factor more concerned with the loss of salable goods than human life. The editors also provide excerpts from the journal of a slaver who describes the "factory" where slaves were procured, evaluated, and marked, as well as the problem of slave suicide.

By 1645, British settlers were well established in New World colonies of their own, and increasingly aware of the importance of slaves to their growing economies, both in the West Indies and in North America. George Downing, later Oliver Cromwell's spymaster and the developer of Downing Street, where British prime ministers now live, sent a letter from Barbados to his cousin, John Winthrop Jr, in Massachusetts.

If you go to Barbados, you shal see a flourishing Iland, many able men. I believe they have bought this year no lesse than a thousand Negroes, and the more they buie, the better able they are to buye, for in a yeare and halfe they will earne (with God's blessing) as much as they cost. . . .

The Origins of the Trade

In the same year, Downing's father, Emanuel, wrote a letter to Winthrop's father, governor of the Massachusetts Bay colony. The two older men were brothers-in-law.

To his evere-honored brother John Winthrop, Esqr. at Boston.

Sir, . . . If upon a just warre [with the Indians] the Lord should deliver them into our hands, wee might easily have men woemen and children enough to exchange for Moores [blacks in North Africa], which wilbe more gaynefull pilladge for us than wee conceive, for I doe not see how wee can thrive untill wee get into a stock of slaves sufficient to doe all our buisiness, for our children's children will hardly see this great Continent filled with people, soe that our servants will still desire freedome to plant for them-selves, and not stay but for verie great wages. And I suppose you know verie well how wee shall mayneteyne 20 Moores cheaper than one Englishe servant.

The ships that shall bring Moores may come home laden with salt which may beare most of the chardge, if not all of it. . . .

Although the British did not organise slaving on a substantial scale until after the restoration of Charles II, there were earlier sporadic attempts to structure a system of trade with West Africa. The operations of the Guinea Company, typified in the following Letter of Instructions *to a ship's captain (1651), anticipated those of two bodies later to operate under royal charter, the Company of Royal Adventurers of England Trading into Africa, and the Royal African Company.*

London, the 9 of December, 1651.

Mr. Bartholomewe Haward, First we pray you perform your dayly dutie unto Almightie God, that so we may expect a blessing upon your endeavours.

You are to hasten with your ship to Gravesend, and being cleered there into the Downes, and from thence with the first faire winde and weather, in Compa. with such ships as you shall finde, to saile directlie for the River Gambra in Guinny, where you shall finde the ship *Freindship* Capt. Jno. Blake Comaunder, upon w'ch ship Mr. James Pope is our cheif factor, to whome you are to deliver our Letter, and such Cargo as we have laden in you (excepting the cases of sugar chest boards belonging unto Mr. John Wood) unto whome we have written to buy and put aboard you so many negers as yo'r ship can cary, and for what shalbe wanting to supply with Cattel, as also to furnish you with victualls and provisions for the said negers and Cattel, as also with such Caske as Capt. Blake can spare, to be filled with water, all w'ch we have desired Mr. Pope to effect in as short a time as may be, and when he shall have laden your Cargo of negers or Cattel aboard, you are to signe bills of ladeing for what you shall receive desireing his letter to Mr. Francis Soane Mercht at Barbados unto whome we have written effectually for the sale of your negers, and ladeing your ship for London, whose order and directions you are to followe untill he shall give you your dispatch for London. Wee desire you to be veary carefull in the well stoweing of your ship and that none of the goods you shall take aboard be abused, and being dispatched from thence we pray you hasten for London, and when you come into our Chanell be veary vigilant and carefull for feare of surprysalls, not trusting any. And our ord'r is that all the while you lye in the River Gambra untill your Cargo be provided that you followe the directions of Mr. James Pope and from all places where you shall touch send us advice of your proceedings. There is put aboard your Pinck *Supply* 30 paire of shackles and boults for such of your negers as are rebellious and we pray you be veary carefull to keep them under and let them have their food in due season that they ryse not against you, as they have done in other ships.

When you shall come into the Downes you are to send unto Mr. Thomas Waad at Dover for a case of Cristall beads w'ch he will put aboard you there w'ch you are to cary with you for Gambra and deliver with the rest of the Cargo unto Mr. James Pope. So Comitting you to God's protection we rest Your loving freinds.

Row: Wilson
Thomas Walter
Tho: Chambrelan
John Woods
Maurice Thomson

The Early Efforts to Emancipate

There were occasional instances of consideration for the negro even in the early days. One of the first acts that tried to ensure emancipation for slaves in North America was passed by the General Court of Election at Warwick, Rhode Island, on 19 May 1652. There is no record, however, of this Act's ever having been enforced.

Whereas, there is a common course practised amongst English men to buy negers, to that end they may have them for service or slaves forever; for the preventinge of such practises among us, let it be ordered, that no blacke mankind or white being forced by covenant bond, or otherwise, to serve any man or his assighnes longer than ten yeares, or untill they come to bee twentie four yeares of age, if they bee taken in under fourteen, from the time of their cominge within the liberties of this Collonie. And at the end or terme of ten yeares to sett them free, as the manner is with the English servants. And that man that will not let them goe free, or shall sell them away elsewhere, to that end that they may bee enslaved to others for a long time, hee or they shall forfeit to the Collonie forty pounds.

Earlier that same year, the directors of the Dutch West India Company, whose nation then led the world's slave trade, had written to the thriving Netherlands colony 'at the Manhattans'.

And in order that you may be the more fully assured of our good intention, we do hereby consent that the commonalty yonder shall have liberty to repair to the coast of Angola and Africa, and transport thence as many negroes as they will make use of for the cultivation of their lands, on the conditions and regulations which are sent herewith to the Director.

Amsterdam, 4th April, 1652. . . .

The Factors in Africa

The mortality of slaves runs like a threnody through the trade's history. They died of melancholy, of disease, of torture, of the sheer impossibility of living on the stifling slave decks of the Middle Passage. A Memorandum From the Factors [*agents*] *at Cape Coast Castle to the company (1681):*

In answer to what your Honours are pleased to suggest concerning Capt. Woodfin's Negroes whereof 160 died and no complaint made of their Goodness wee are apt to beleive that had he taken in only 400 there had few miscarried and wee find that the Covetousness of Command'rs Crowding in their Slaves above their proportion for the advantage of Freight is the only reason of the great Loss to the Compa. If your Honours would be pleased to beate them down in their number though you gave them five shillings per head exterordinary Your Honours would be considerable gainers at the yeares end.

The same factors objected to unsaleable trade merchandise:

Wee are Sorry wee must complaine of our late deed trading att Cabo Corse occasioned by the want of goods we wrot your Honours for and it grived us the more to see our Neighbours att the Mine [the Dutch at Elmina Castle] . . . take great Pride to shew the English how well they are furnished with all sorts of goods and how their ware houses are cramed with Prodigious quantitys. . . .

Wee have added a Cattalogue of goods most vendible at this Place which by all opertunityes wee fail not to acquaint your Honours there being some small additions to what was in our last *vizt.* 500 P's Saies [type of serge], 1500 P's Perpetuanoes [English woollen cloth] (800 of which must be green, 600 blew and 100 red) but not any Printed for they will not sell Lett the collours be what they will . . . 600 Brawles [striped Indian cloth], 5 Callicoe Clouts, 500 one pound Pewt'r Basons, 150 2 lb. Ditto, 150 3 lb. Ditto, 150 4 lb. Ditto . . . 100 Ginghams, the Red Stript best, 5000 Sheetes, 600 broad Tapseiles [Indian cotton], 300 Narrow ditto, 500 Long Clothes white, 100 half firk's Tallow, 100 Dozen Knives ordinary. . . . Without your Honours are pleased to supply us with . . . good store . . . you will unavoidably Lose considerably by those Ships you send to take their Slaves in here upon the Gold Coast what for the greate scarcity of them and the extravagant pizes [prices] that are given by the commanders of ships. . . .

Log of a Slaver

One of the most vivid pictures of seventeenth-century slaving comes down to us from the Journal of Thomas Phillips *(1694), commander of the company's ship* Hannibal, *450 tons, 36 guns.*

. . . *May the 19th.* Steering along shore within three leagues, with fine easy gale, we spy'd a canoe making off towards us, whereupon we lay by and staid for her; when she came aboard the master of her brought in three women and four children to sell, but they ask'd very dear for them, and they were almost dead for want of victuals, looking like meer skeletons, and so weak that they could not stand, so that they were not worth buying . . . we were upon the Alampo coast, which negroes are esteem'd the worst and most washy of any that are brought to the West-Indies, and yield the least price; why I know not, for they seem as well limb'd and lusty as any other negroes, and the only difference I perceiv'd in them, was, that they are not so black as the others, and are all circumcis'd which no negroes else upon the

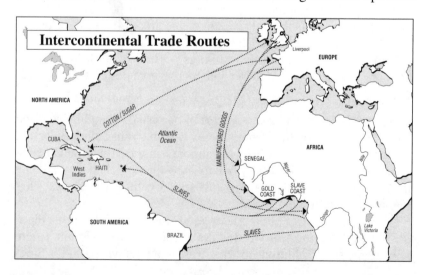

Intercontinental Trade Routes

whole coast (as I observ'd) are: The negroes most in demand at Barbadoes, are the gold coast, or, as they call them, Cormantines, which will yield 3 or 4 *l.* a head more than the Whidaws, or, as they call them, Papa negroes; but these are preferr'd before the Angola, as they are before the Alampo, which are accounted the worst of all. . . .

May the 21st . . . Our factory [at Whydah] lies about three miles from the sea-side. . . . [It] stands low near the marshes, which renders it a very unhealthy place to live in; the white men the African company send there, seldom return to tell their tale: 'tis compass'd round with a mud-wall, about six foot high, and on the south-side is the gate; within is a large yard, a mud thatch'd house, where the factor lives, with the white men; also a store-house, a trunk [main area] for slaves, and a place where they bury their dead white men, call'd, very improperly, the hog-yard. . . .

The factor, Mr. Peirson, was a brisk man, and had good interest with the king, and credit with the subjects, who knowing their tempers, which is very dastard, had good skill in treating them both civil and rough, as occasion requir'd. . . .

As soon as the king understood of our landing, he sent two of his cappasheirs, or noblemen to compliment us at our factory, where we design'd to continue, that night, and pay our devoirs [respects] to his majesty next day, which we signify'd to them, and they, by a foot-express, to their monarch; whereupon he sent two more of his grandees to invite us there that night, saying he waited for us, and that all former captains used to attend him the first night: whereupon being unwilling to infringe the custom, or give his majesty any offence, we . . . were carry'd to the king's town. . . .

We returned him thanks by his interpreter, and assur'd him how great affection our masters, the royal African company of England, bore to him, for his civility and fair and just dealings with their captains; and that notwithstanding there were many other places, more plenty of negro slaves that begg'd their custom, yet they had rejected all the advantageous offers made them out of their good will to him, and therefore had sent us to trade with him, to supply his country with necessaries, and that we hop'd he would endeavour to continue their favour by his kind usage and fair dealing with us in our trade, that we may have our slaves with all expedition, which was the making of our voyage; that he would oblige his cappasheirs to do us justice, and not impose upon us in their prices; all which we should faithfully relate to our masters, the royal African company, when we came to England. He answer'd that the African company was a very good brave man; that he lov'd him; that we should be fairly dealt with, and not impos'd upon . . . so after having examin'd us about our cargoe, what sort of goods we had, and what quantity of slaves we wanted, etc., we took our leaves and return'd to the factory, having promised to come in the morning to make our palavera, or agreement, with him about prices, how much of each of our goods for a slave.

. . . He and his cappasheirs exacted very high, but at length we concluded . . . then the bell was order'd to go about to give notice to all people to bring their slaves to the trunk to sell us. . . .

The Examination of Slaves

When we were at the trunk, the king's slaves, if he had any, were the first offer'd to sale, which the cappasheirs would be very urgent with us to buy, and would in a manner force us to it ere they would shew us any other, saying they were the Reys Cosa [king's property], and we must not refuse them, tho' as I observ'd they were generally the worst slaves in the trunk, and we paid more for them than any others, which we could not remedy, it being one of his majesty's prerogatives: then the cappasheirs each brought out his slaves according to his degree and quality, the greatest first, etc. and our surgeon examin'd them well in all kinds, to see that they were sound in wind and limb, making them jump, stretch out their arms swiftly, looking in their mouths to judge of their age; for the cappasheirs are so cunning, that they shave them all close before we see them, so that let them be never so old we can see no grey hairs in their heads or beards; and then having liquor'd them well and sleek with palm oil, 'tis no easy matter to know an old one from a middle-age one, but by the teeths decay; but our greatest care of all is to buy none that are pox'd, lest they should infect the rest aboard. . . .

. . . We mark'd the slaves we had bought in the breast, or shoulder, with a hot iron, having the letter of the ship's name on it, the place being before anointed with a little palm oil, which caus'd but little pain, the mark being usually well in four or five days, appearing very plain and white after. . . .

The negroes are so wilful and loth to leave their own country, that they have often leap'd out of the canoes, boat and ship, into the sea, and kept under water till they were drowned, to avoid being taken up and saved by our boats, which pursued them; they having a more dreadful apprehension of Barbadoes than we can of hell, tho' in reality they live much better there than in their own country; but home is home, etc: we have likewise seen divers of them eaten by the sharks, of which a prodigious number kept about the ships in this place, and I have been told will follow her hence to Barbadoes, for the dead negroes that are thrown over-board in the passage. . . .

We had about 12 negroes did wilfully drown themselves, and others starv'd themselves to death; for 'tis their belief that when they die they return home to their own country and friends again.

The Emergence of New Dynasties

PREFACE

Political history is often the story of the rise and fall of dynasties—a succession of rulers of the same line of descent. These powerful families maintain their position for a considerable time, influencing religious practices, national culture, economic development, and foreign policy. Dynasties end for many reasons. Some end because the family fails to produce an heir, others as a result of corruption and mismanagement, and still others because of political turmoil and drastic social changes. At the beginning of the seventeenth century, several dynasties had ended or were soon to end, making way for new dynasties that emerged to shape the century.

In Russia, the Rurik dynasty came to a close when Czar Fyodor I died without an heir in 1598. For a fifteen-year period known as the Time of Troubles, influences from within and outside of Russia vied for power until Michael Romanov was designated the new czar in 1613. The early Romanovs were faced with rebuilding Russian economics and defending Russia from encroachment by Poland and Sweden. The dominant personality of the Romanov family during the seventeenth century was Peter the Great, the grandson of Michael. Before Peter's reign, Russia remained isolated from Europe. However, Peter hoped to westernize Russia and develop his naval empire with European technology, and his travels in Europe in 1697 connected Russia with the West. The Romanov family continued to rule Russia for 304 years, the dynasty finally ending in 1917 with the Russian Revolution.

Toyotomi Hideyoshi, a brilliant commander whose family conquered and dominated Japan during the sixteenth century, died in 1598. In 1600 Tokugawa Ieyasu defeated the Toyotomi family in the Battle of Sekigahara, and the emperor of Japan designated him shogun, establishing the Tokugawa shogunate, which lasted until 1867. While shogun, Ieyasu elevated the samurai to the top of the social hierarchy and urged a return to traditional Japanese values and teachings. Ieyasu is known for maintaining control of his dynasty by forcing the feudal lords to maintain a residence in Edo (Tokyo), leaving a hostage in their absence. The Tokugawa rulers insisted on obedience and submissiveness under a strict hierarchy that molded values that persist in modern Japan. Ieyasu encouraged the study of Confucianism and discouraged foreign interference, particularly European influences. Between 1614 and 1640, many Christians were executed, and a later shogun, Tokugawa Iemitsu, completely closed Japan to the West in 1639.

A number of rebellions and financial problems weakened China's collapsing Ming dynasty early in the seventeenth century. At the same time, Nurhachi, a Manchu tribal leader, gathered together into "banners" the tribes that lived on the northern border of China, providing a unified force that invaded China, ultimately taking Peking (modern-day Beijing), in 1644. Once the Manchu captured Peking, they adopted many aspects of the Chinese culture, and many provinces were governed by both a Manchu and a Chinese governor cooperatively. The Manchu substantially expanded the Chinese empire and began trade with Europe under the leadership of Kang Xi, who was also a scholar and spiritual leader. The dynasty was overthrown in 1911, under the leadership of Sun Yat-sen and, after two thousand years, a republican form of government replaced monarchic rule.

All three new dynasties maintained their influence for several centuries, each making its own mark on the seventeenth century.

The Rise of
the Romanovs

Anatole G. Mazour

In 1598 Czar Theodore I of Russia died with no descendants, and for fifteen years a series of Russian and foreign leaders vied for the crown. During this period, referred to as the Time of Troubles, the Romanov family was in and out of favor with those in power, writes Anatole G. Mazour in the following excerpt from his book *Rise and Fall of the Romanovs*. While friendly with the false pretenders, who claimed to be the missing son of Czar Ivan IV, the Romanovs were unpopular with Boris Godunov, who ruled from 1598 to 1605, and opposed Prince Shuisky, who ruled from 1606 to 1610. After a revolt against Polish rule, a national assembly gathered to choose a new czar, and in 1613, selected the young Michael Romanov. The Romanovs had been popular during the tyrannical reign of Ivan IV and had a matrimonial tie with the royal family. Although some were hesitant, the assembly believed it unwise to introduce a totally new dynasty, and Michael Romanov became czar. His father Philaret (Fyodor Nikitch Romanov) became the patriarch of Russia, and both father and son governed Russia, beginning a dynasty that continued for 304 years.

W hen Tsar Theodore I died in 1598, the last descendant of the Riurik dynasty passed into history. This resulted in a fifteen-year social and political upheaval commonly referred to as The Time of Troubles. The successor to the throne (in February, 1613) was a young lad by the name of Michael Romanov, who was destined to initiate the new dynastic line that lasted precisely 304 years. Who were the Romanovs and how did the family come to be chosen as the new dynasty?

The Early Romanovs

The origin of the Romanov family is none too clear and is particularly complicated by the fact that during the early Muscovite period changing names was, for various reasons, a common practice. The earliest reference to what was destined to become the Romanov dynasty is to be found in the Chronicle under the date 6855, that is, 1346. The Chronicle reads:

> In the summer of 6855 [1346]. . . . Grand Prince Semyon Ivanovich, grandson of Daniel, was married for the third time; he married Mary, the daughter of Grand Prince Alexander Mikhailovich of Tver: and those who went to Tver after her were Andrei Kobyla and Aleksei Besovolkov.

Later the Chronicle has reference to another member of the family line under the name of Theodore Koshka, a prominent boyar [aristocrat] and associate of the Grand Duke Dimitri Donskoi (1359–89). His sons changed the name to Koshkin and two sons of Zakhari Koshkin adopted the name of Zakharin-Koshkin and later Zakharin. The star of the Zakharins quickly ascended when Anastasia, the daughter of Roman, married Ivan IV, thereby raising the family to the highest ranks (an honor some families came to frown upon). Of the latter's descendants, one Nikita Romanovich Zakharin played a most prominent part at the time of Ivan IV. The patronymic name eventually became the name of the new Russian dynasty—Romanov.

The Time of Troubles

The road of the Romanovs to the throne was strewn not only with roses but sharp thorns as well. During the brief reign of Theodore I, the grandfather of Michael Romanov, Nikita, acting as regent, came to share the responsibilities with Boris Godunov. The death of Theodore and the ensuing dynastic crisis terminated their friendly coöperation and soon the two became bitter rivals for political power. There was good reason for Boris to suspect the conduct of the Romanovs, cautious though it might have been. The Romanovs were friendly with the False Pretenders, [who claimed to be the son of Tsar Ivan IV, Dimitri Ivanovich, who died mysteriously], and they enjoyed far more popularity in the country than Boris ever did. It was the First Pretender, better known as False Dimitri, who appointed the father of Michael Romanov to the bishopric of Rostov. Small wonder that shortly after Boris attained the throne the Romanovs became the target of severe attacks. One of the first things

Boris did was compel Theodore Romanov (under the name of Philaret), and his wife Mary (as Martha), to take monastic vows.
Michael thus became separated from his father in infancy. From
about the middle of the reign of Ivan IV the masses regarded the Romanovs as a model boyar family who championed the cause of the
people only to become victims of political persecution.

If at the time of Ivan IV the Romanovs managed to hold aloof
from politics, from the time of Boris they became seriously embroiled. With the ascendancy of Prince Shuisky (1606–10) things
did not improve because the Romanovs had openly opposed him as
a candidate to the throne. After four years Shuisky was overthrown:
the candidacy of Ladislas, the son of the King of Poland, was advocated. In the midst of this struggle the Second False Pretender made
his appearance. The internal conflicts resulting in foreign intervention and invasion led to the inevitable outcome—the rise of a national movement that rebelled against all foreign orientations and
the establishment of order and peace by its own national forces. The
movement was headed by a humble burgher from Nizhni-Novgorod,
Kuzma Minin, and a nobleman, Prince Pozharsky. After their in-
spiring appeals to the people, the two leaders managed to form a national army that expelled the Polish invaders from Moscow. By October, 1612, Minin and Pozharsky had issued a call to elect deputies
to a national assembly for the purpose of electing a new tsar and
restoring peace and public order. The following February the
deputies—perhaps one of the most representative assemblies ever
gathered in Moscow—met to determine the future of Russia.

One of the first decisions they made was not to consider foreign
candidates to the vacant throne. They thought it particularly unde-
sirable to have a successor urged by the Polish king and backed by
the Polish army, a choice which might occasion political and religious problems later. For this reason the church as well as others
hailed the decision as a national triumph.

Election to the Throne

Having decided upon the selection of a native candidate the next
problem was the naming of such a candidate. This proved a far more
difficult task, since the preceding events had gravely thinned the
ranks of the old titled aristocracy: those who survived the last half
of the century of tyranny, error, and turmoil often compromised
themselves either by collaboration with the Polish invaders, or by
supporting other lost or suspect causes. Others who proved loyal
during the trying years were not socially qualified to be considered
for the establishment of the new dynasty. The Romanov family itself was not able to take an active part in the assembly: the father,
Philaret, was a prisoner of war in Poland; a brother, Ivan, remained

in Moscow during the occupation and was considered disqualified; Michael resided with his mother in a convent not far from Moscow. Other members of the Romanov family were scattered throughout the land. It was a family missing its head, lacking physical as well as political unity.

But in 1613 the national assembly thought of Michael Romanov for various reasons: the family's eminence, its unblemished record during the second half of the reign of Ivan IV, the popularity of certain of its members among the people represented at the assembly, and above all the fact of the matrimonial tie with the royal family. By considering Michael Romanov, a first cousin once removed of the last tsar, Theodore I, the assembly believed that genealogical continuity was confirmed. (Theodore I was the son of Anastasia, a sister of Nikita Romanov, the grandfather of Michael.) The Romanovs were wise enough to remain aloof from the tyrannical administration of Ivan IV, and so succeeded in cultivating popularity and later gaining respect. The masses considered Michael's grandfather, Nikita Romanov, as their champion. The candidate's father, Theodore (known better by his church name of Philaret), was a noted scholar of his day.

Maintaining Dynastic Continuity

Because of his high church office it was considered improper to offer Theodore the crown; his son Michael, therefore, was the logical candidate. Furthermore, in the absence of the father the young boy

Michael Romanov, the first of the Romanov czars, was only sixteen years old at the time of his coronation in 1613.

might be willing to follow the counsel of the assembly. Such was the feeling of the majority of deputies, who represented the burghers, the free peasantry, the Cossacks, the higher and lower clergy, and the greater and lesser nobility. After much debate only the greater nobility and the peasantry manifested some hesitance, while the lesser nobility, the Cossacks, and the burghers unconditionally supported the Romanov candidate. The assembly, being generally conservative, felt that it would have been politically unwise to introduce a totally new dynasty; on the contrary, it sought to give the impression that the disruption of the dynastic line was accidental and its restoration a natural act. Michael Romanov thus served as a symbol not only of legitimacy, but also of dynastic continuity. In essence the assembly sanctioned what Ivan IV had been aiming at with such fury: an absolute monarchy in which the new tenant landlords or lesser nobility, the burgher class, and the Cossacks constituted the backbone of the state.

Michael Romanov ascended the throne as hereditary sovereign of the Russian state, bearing the crown by divine right. The former concept of the state as a hereditary patrimony henceforth became invalidated by the new status of the crown. The Boyar Council shared the same fate: doomed by the nature of the resurrected state to political oblivion. Furthermore, upon the return from Poland of Michael's father, an illustrious figure was added to the high ranks of government. In June, 1619, in the presence of the Patriarch of Jerusalem, Philaret was consecrated as Patriarch of Russia. From that date on until his death in 1633, Patriarch Philaret played a prominent part not only as head of the church, but as a distinguished leader of the state as well. The country was virtually governed by both the father and the son. Secular and spiritual powers seemed to have merged into a single source of authority. Years of harsh experience had hardened Patriarch Philaret and turned him into a determined despot with a touch of bitterness as well as an aura of parochialism. Yet whatever one might say of Patriarch Philaret, the Romanovs' early success was largely due to him.

Peter the Great's Trip to the West

M.S. Anderson

In 1697 Europeans had their first encounter with Russian royalty when Czar Peter the Great traveled with his embassy to the West. In the following excerpt from his book *Peter the Great,* M.S. Anderson explains that Peter's primary motives for making his historic journey were to acquire knowledge of shipbuilding and develop alliances that would both preserve and expand his empire. For example, Peter hoped to develop an alliance of Christian powers to oppose the Turks so that he could expand his empire to the Black Sea. Peter hoped to travel in disguise, but he failed to deceive anyone, and although most Europeans found Peter intelligent and witty, many believed that he was ill-mannered—more like a sailor than a prince. Peter believed that a man should be measured by his knowledge and work rather than his title, so he worked on the docks while in Holland and England and studied gunnery in Prussia. According to Anderson, Peter was more impressed by the military power of Europe than its government or culture. Anderson is professor emeritus of international history at the London School of Economics.

In March 1697, Tsar Peter the Great left Russia and did not return until September 1698. In those eighteen months he travelled through Courland [Latvia] and Brandenburg, Germany, to the Dutch Republic, thence to England and, on his return journey, to Vienna. He did not see France and had to abandon an intended visit to Italy. But with these important exceptions he made the acquaintance of the most advanced regions of Europe. Ostensibly he travelled merely as 'Peter Mikhailov', a member of the 'great embassy' of which Admiral Lefort was the formal leader. This easily penetrated incognito deceived no one; but it was carefully maintained throughout the journey. It reflects Peter's deeply held belief that what really mattered was a man's innate worth, a compound of knowledge, energy and public spirit, not titles, ceremonies or outward appearances. The feeling which had led him to serve as a sergeant-bombardier and work as a shipwright now forbade him to travel abroad in the role of a tsar. The journey was the supreme illustration of his contempt for tradition and of his wide-ranging though somewhat superficial curiosity about the contemporary world. No Russian ruler had ever visited a foreign land; and apart from a few diplomats and merchants very few Russians of any kind travelled abroad. Now Peter was seen to be throwing down the barriers which had hitherto separated his country from the rest of Europe.

The Reasons for the Tsar's Journey

The dominant motives behind the embassy, as far as he himself was concerned, were almost certainly the acquisition of a deeper knowledge of shipbuilding and everything maritime, and the recruitment of foreign experts in these fields on a much larger scale than hitherto. He was unwilling to contemplate the possibility that the young Russians now being sent abroad for training might return with a knowledge of naval matters superior to his own, even though the 250-strong embassy included thirty-five 'volunteers' destined for the study of maritime affairs. It recruited, mainly in the Netherlands and England, about a thousand technicians and instructors—shipwrights, officers, navigators, even a few teachers of mathematics—some of whom were to play important roles in the carrying-out of Peter's plans.

At the same time, however, there were important political and diplomatic considerations underlying the great journey to the west. Peter hoped to press further the victories he had won over the Turks. In particular he was anxious to obtain, if possible, the fortress of Kerch, [a port in the Crimea], and with it free passage for his ships through the Straits of Kerch into the Black Sea. If this could be achieved the entire relationship between Russia and the Ottoman empire would be tilted, perhaps decisively, in favour of the former. It seemed possible, from the perspective of Moscow, that an enlarged and more effective coalition of the Christian powers against the infidel might be created; for the war of the Grand Alliance, which had absorbed the energies of France, England and the Dutch since 1689, was clearly drawing to its close. Already in February 1697 Peter's agent, Nefimonov, who had been sent to Vienna over a year earlier, had signed with the emperor and the Venetian Republic an agreement by which the three states undertook a three-year offensive alliance against the Turks and promised to concert their military efforts to that end. Three months after the tsar left Russia a new and more directly important international complication forced itself on his attention. The death of John Sobieski, the last great king of Poland, in June 1697, led inevitably to a struggle over the succession (since the Polish monarchy was elective) in which the rival candidates were supported by competing foreign powers. Should France succeed in establishing its nominee, the Prince de Conti, on the Polish throne and defeating the Elector Augustus of Saxony, who was backed by Russia and the Habsburgs, [a royal German family], this would be a very serious defeat for Russia. It would almost certainly mean the withdrawal of Poland from the anti-Turkish league and possibly a Polish-Turkish alliance.

The great journey to the west, in other words, was much more than a matter of the acquisition of technical knowledge. This element, so far as Peter was concerned, was very important; and he used to the full the opportunities of this kind which now presented themselves. In Holland he worked for over four months (September 1697–early January 1698) in the docks of the East India Company in Amsterdam. In England he spent almost as long (February to early May 1698) in the dockyard at Deptford. His curiosity about technical processes and even, to a limited extent, scientific discoveries was boundless. Detained for three weeks at Pillau in East Prussia in July 1697 by the need to observe events in Poland after the death of Sobieski, he occupied the time in a serious study of gunnery and won a certificate of progress from the chief engineer of the fortress. At Zaandam in Holland he made a sheet of paper with his own hands. A little later he became competent in another art in which the Dutch were pre-eminent—etching and engraving. He met the two greatest Dutch scientists of the age, the doctor Boerhaave and the microscopist Leeuwenhoek, though the real significance of their work largely escaped him. In London he visited the Tower, the arsenal at Woolwich, the Mint and the Royal Society. Everywhere museums, cabinets of curiosities, factories and even theatres attracted his attention and provoked his incessant questions.

Establishing Alliances

However the political aspects of the embassy, the need to win allies for Russia, to strengthen its international position and pave the way for its future expansion, were not neglected. A treaty of friendship with Prussia was signed at Königsberg early in July 1697. Though this had little significance in itself, Peter and the Elector Frederick probably gave each other, during the sea journey to Pillau which followed, verbal promises of support against all enemies. In Utrecht, the Netherlands, Peter had an interview with William III, whom he had long admired and with whom his personal relations became very cordial. (He was delighted by the present of William's best yacht, the newly built *Transport Royal*.) In Vienna he discussed international affairs at some length with the Imperial Chancellor, Count Kinsky. None of this political activity had much result. The promises exchanged with Frederick of Prussia were a long way from constituting a treaty; and Prussia's energies and attention were in any case soon to be absorbed once more by a renewed struggle with France after the outbreak in 1701–2 of the war of the Spanish Succession. The Dutch and English governments had not the slightest intention of becoming involved in a conflict with the Turks of the kind for which Peter still hoped. On the contrary, they were now secretly doing their best to mediate between the Ottoman empire and the Habsburgs in the negotiations which were to bear fruit in the peace treaty of Carlowitz in January 1699. Austria was increasingly preoccupied by the imminent death of Charles II of Spain and the crisis over the Spanish inheritance which was likely to follow, and correspondingly more inclined to a peace with the Turks which would free its hands for action in Italy and on the Rhine. The Habsburg government therefore proved unresponsive to Russian pleas or demands that it should continue the war with the sultan, as agreed in the Russo-Austro-Venetian treaty of February 1697, until the Porte agreed to

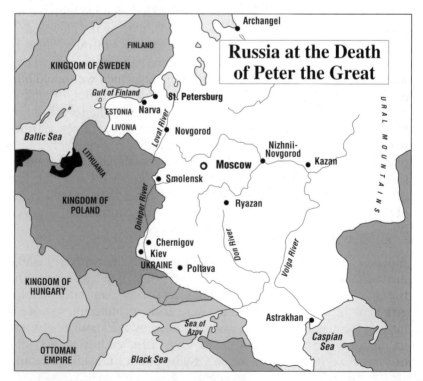

Russia at the Death of Peter the Great

cede Kerch to Russia. The whole configuration of international relations was, at least for the time being, unfavourable to Peter's hopes. This fact was strongly borne in upon him as his travels proceeded and his grasp of the situation improved.

The European Reaction

Reactions to the 'great embassy' and to Peter personally differed considerably. In the Swedish fortress-city of Riga (the first western city to be visited by the young tsar), through which the embassy passed to reach Prussian territory, his reception was polite and formally correct rather than warm. Peter's efforts to inspect the fortifications produced an incident trivial in itself but destined to have considerable consequences, when he was rudely ordered away by a sentry. Franz Lefort, as formal head of the embassy, admitted that the soldier had merely done his duty. But the insult rankled in the tsar's mind and the memory of it grew with the passage of time. More than three years later it was the only specific reason given for the Russian declaration of war against Sweden; and when the Russian siege of Riga began in 1709, Peter rejoiced that 'The Lord God has enabled us to see the beginning of our revenge on this accursed place.' Whatever his virtues, easy forgiveness of an injury, real or imagined, was not among them.

Nor did his passage through Prussian territory arouse great interest or enthusiasm in ruling circles. The official charged with the reception of the embassy in Königsberg was told by the elector that 'we should prefer it if he [Peter] wishes to pass through entirely incognito without speaking with us or coming to our court, so that we may remain free from the embarrassments which we should otherwise have with him.' In Holland and England the official attention paid to him was as much a matter of curiosity as the result of any feeling that this bizarre individual, a visitor almost from another world, was a figure of real political importance. In Vienna disputes over ceremonial meant a delay of over a month before the ambassadors could present their credentials to the Emperor Leopold I. The most active official interest taken in the tsar there was probably that of the papal nuncio, who hoped for his conversion, to be followed by that of his subjects, to Roman Catholicism.

If the 'great embassy' introduced Peter to Europe it also gave Europeans their first glimpse of a Russian ruler. Their reactions, like those of their governments, were mixed and often lukewarm. The tsar's energy and curiosity, together with his obvious native intelligence, aroused admiration. On the other hand, the uncouthness of his manners, his heavy drinking (striking even by the standards of that uncritical age) and the facial spasms that afflicted him at moments of strain (and were to do so for the rest of his life), all made him seem something of a savage, however powerful and interesting. 'The tsar is very tall, his features are fine, and his figure very noble,' wrote the widowed electress of Hanover after meeting him in Germany. 'He has great vivacity of mind and a ready and just repartee. But, with all the advantages with which nature has endowed him, it could be wished that his manners were a little less rustic.' She was amused when the Russians, in dancing, took the whale-bones of the German ladies' corsets for their ribs 'and the tsar showed his astonishment by saying that the German ladies had devilish hard bones.' In England the bishop of Salisbury thought Peter 'designed by nature rather to be a ship-carpenter, than a great prince', and went on to comment that 'after I had seen him often, and had conversed much with him, I could not but adore the depth of the providence of God, that had raised up such a furious man to so absolute an authority over so great a part of the world.' Hoffmann, the Austrian representative in London, reported to Vienna that 'They say that he intends to civilize his subjects in the manner of other nations. But from his acts here, one cannot find any other intention than to make them sailors; he has had intercourse almost exclusively with sailors, and has gone away as shy as he came.' Certainly it would be an error to imagine that this famous journey fundamentally changed Peter's ideas or even greatly widened his intellectual horizons. The science and political ideas of western Europe, even its forms of government and administrative methods, received little of his attention. But its wealth, its productive power, its military and still more naval strength had, by direct personal acquaintance, impressed themselves on his mind most forcibly. His determination, confused but unwavering, to win for Russia some of the same advantages by a programme of change imposed from above, was now stronger than ever.

Impressions of Peter the Great

Sophia Charlotte and her daughter

The following selection is a report on Peter the Great made by Sophia Charlotte, the wife of the elector of Brandenburg, Germany, and her daughter, who met Peter during his trip to Europe in 1697. Sophia reveals her observations of his manners, character, personality, and interests. For example, although she reports that his manners are "rustic," she found his company pleasant, describing him as an extraordinary man. Sophia's daughter enjoyed Peter's "natural, unconstrained air."

The Tsar is very tall, his features are fine, and his figure very noble. He has great vivacity of mind, and a ready and just repartee. But with all the advantages with which nature has endowed him, it could be wished that his manners were a little less rustic. We immediately sat down to table. Herr Koppenstein, who did the duty of marshal, presented the napkin to his Majesty, who was greatly embarrassed, for at Brandenburg, instead of a table napkin, they had given him an ewer and basin after the meal. He was very gay, very talkative, and we established a great friendship for each other, and he exchanged snuff boxes with my daughter. We stayed, in truth, a very long time at table, but we would gladly have remained there longer still without feeling a moment of ennui, for the Tsar was in

Excerpted from Sophia Charlotte, *Peter the Great* (New York: Scribner's, 1884), edited by Eugene Schuyler.

very good humor, and never ceased talking to us. My daughter had her Italians sing. Their song pleased him, though he confessed to us that he did not care much for music.

I asked him if he liked hunting. He replied that his father had been very fond of it, but that he himself, from his earliest youth, had had a real passion for the navigation of ships, showed us his hands, and made us touch the callous places that had been caused by work. He brought his musicians, and they played Russian dances, which he liked better than Polish ones.

Franz Lefort and his nephew dressed in French style, and had much wit. We did not speak to the other ambassadors. We regretted that he could not stay longer, so that we could see him again, for his society gave us much pleasure. He is a very extraordinary man. It is impossible to describe him, or even to give an idea of him, unless you have seen him. He has a very good heart, and remarkably noble sentiments. I must tell you, also, that he did not get drunk in our presence, but we had hardly left when the people of his suite made ample amends. . . .

I could embellish the tale of the journey of the illustrious Tsar, if I should tell you that he is sensible to the charms of beauty, but, to come to the bare fact, I found in him no disposition to gallantry. If we had not taken so many steps to see him, I believe that he would never have thought of us. In his country it is the custom for all women to paint, and rouge forms an essential part of their marriage presents. That is why Countess Platen singularly pleased the Muscovites; but in dancing, they took the whalebones of our corsets for our bones, and the Tsar showed his astonishment by saying that the German ladies had devilish hard bones.

They have four dwarfs. Two of them are very well-proportioned, and perfectly well-bred; sometimes he kissed, and sometimes he pinched the ear of his favorite dwarf. He took the head of our little princess (Sophia Dorothea) and kissed her twice. The ribbons of her hair suffered in consequence. He also kissed her brother (later George II of England). He is a prince at once very good and very *méchant*. He has quite the manners of his country. If he had received a better education, he would be an accomplished man, for he has many good qualities, and an infinite amount of natural wit. . . .

A Daughter's Impression

My mother and I began to pay him our compliments, but he made Mr. Lefort reply for him, for he seemed shy, hid his face in his hands, and said: "Ich kann nicht sprechen." But we tamed him a little, and then he sat down at the table between my mother and myself, and each of us talked to him in turn, and it was a strife who should have it. Sometimes he replied with the same promptitude, at others he made two interpreters talk, and assuredly he said nothing that was not to the point on all subjects that were suggested, for the vivacity of my mother put to him many questions, to which he replied with the same readiness, and I was astonished that he was not tired with the conversation, for I have been told that it is not much the habit in his country. As to his grimaces, I imagined them worse than I found them, and some are not in his power to correct. One can see also that he has had no one to teach him how to eat properly, but he has a natural, unconstrained air which pleases me.

The Manchu Dynasty Rules China

W. Scott Morton

In the following excerpt from his book *China: Its History and Culture,*
W. Scott Morton explains how the Manchu overcame the Ming dynasty
early in the seventeenth century. The Manchu tribes occupied the fertile northern region of China, and to protect China's northern border,
the Ming organized these tribes into separate Chinese military regiments. Until the rise of the Manchu tribal leader Nurhachi, these tribes
were divided and without power. However, Nurhachi slowly allied
these tribes and improved northern China's economic situation. According to Morton, Nurhachi organized the tribes into banners, military units distinguished by their flags, and slowly added Mongol and
Chinese banners, ultimately developing a military force that invaded
China. In 1618 Nurhachi attacked the Ming dynasty, and his son Abahi
took Peking in 1644. The Manchu or Qing dynasty eventually ruled all
of China when Taiwan was captured in 1683. In addition, Morton describes the emperor Kang Xi, who was not only a military ruler, but
also a scholar and moral leader of China. Kang Xi contributed to several publications of the seventeenth century, including the *Sacred Edict.*
Morton is a professor of Japanese and Chinese history at Seton Hall
University, in South Orange, New Jersey.

Excerpted from W. Scott Morton, *China: Its History and Culture.* Copyright © 1980, 1982, 1995,
W. Scott Morton. Reprinted with permission from The McGraw-Hill Companies.

The Chinese were past masters of the art of divide and rule. But when a Jürchen tribal leader of genius arose in Manchuria, the policy boomeranged and they lost their empire, only to gain it back again by making the tribesmen more Chinese than themselves. This extraordinary drama of the Qing dynasty [1644–1911] moved to its tragic climax when the empire, more generally cultured and apparently more powerful than it had ever been, suddenly crumbled in the face of internal rebellion and the external pressure of foreign powers.

The Origins of the Manchu

In order to understand the Qing dynastic period, its strengths and weaknesses, it is necessary to go back and look at the origins of the people known first as the Jürchen tribes and later as the Manzhou (Manchu). The country they inhabited has been called "the Canada of Asia." It is rich in natural resources, with wide, fertile plains, mineral deposits, and abundant timber in the mountains to the north and east. Today the plains produce soya beans, millet, and other hardy grains in great quantity. The southern region was under Chinese jurisdiction in Han times and was being increasingly settled in the Ming period by Chinese immigrant farmers coming by sea and land, mainly from Shandong province. The speech of the countryside still shows marked traces of the Shandong accent. This region, known as Liaodong, "east of the Liao River," was marked off from Mongolia and the warlike, nomadic hunting tribes to north and east by a "palisade" of earth and willow trees and was governed as a part of Shandong province.

In order to protect this valuable agricultural investment and to safeguard access to their ancient dependency of Korea, the Chinese had recourse to the same device of the commandery *(wei)* which had stood them in good stead on the Mongolian border. The commanderies consisted of local tribes enrolled as Chinese military regiments officered by their own leaders under a hereditary chieftain. The prestige of the Chinese empire was such that a number of these chiefs were glad to accept offices, titles, and seals from the emperor and to send tribute missions to Peking. By thus attaching them severally to himself, the emperor hoped to divide them from each other and to form a series of buffer states on his border. . . . The first Jürchen commandery was established at Jianzhou, northeast of Liaodong, in 1403, and others rapidly followed. In the next fifty years the Chinese had cause for anxiety, for there were movements of revolt and warfare from the Yi kingdom in Korea, from certain Mongol tribes, and especially from the Oirats. Although the Jürchen tribes took advantage of this unrest to plunder, the Chinese in the main retained control of the region.

The Rise of Nurhaci

The situation altered drastically, however, with the rise to power of a gifted Jürchen leader, Nurhaci (1559–1626). He moved slowly. Accepting confirmation by the Chinese as leader of his clan, he increased his power at home by disposing of enemies under the acceptable excuse of a blood feud. He cemented alliances with other tribes by marriage and erected a strong castle in the northeast as his base of operations. While maintaining good relations with the Ming court—he received the complimentary title of "Dragon-Tiger General"—Nurhaci over a thirty-year period succeeded in uniting the principal Jürchen tribes. He built at the same time an economic foundation for his nascent state by successful trading in minerals, furs, pearls, and especially ginseng, a root much in demand for restoring youth and increasing sexual powers.

Nurhaci is to be distinguished from other, less successful tribal chieftains by his notable achievements in military structure and in administration, by means of which he began the process of turning a loose coalition of tribes into an organized state. The army consisted of companies of 300 grouped in larger units called banners (qi), distinguished by the color of their flags. There were originally four Manzhou banners, then eight, followed by eight Mongol and eight Chinese banners, which formed an effective force of almost 170,000 men by the time the Manzhou invaded China. Although the name "banner" was applied to contingents in the earlier Chinese commanderies, Nurhaci introduced important changes when he evolved his own banner system. His leaders were not the hereditary chiefs but officers appointed by himself, and members of the banners did not hold land all in one region; nor did they fight as a unit. When an expeditionary force was required, it was made up of drafts from different banners. These provisions virtually eliminated the danger of tribal defections or disobedience.

Nurhaci and his successors were well aware of the advantages of Chinese administration. Advisers and even generals were chosen from among the large Chinese population of southern Manchuria. Nurhaci himself saw to the development of a system of writing using an adapted Mongolian script. Stone monuments and tablets erected after the full establishment of the Qing dynasty carry inscriptions in this Manzhou script as well as in Mongolian and Chinese. The possession of a script enabled Nurhaci not only to keep records and improve routine administration but also to have the Confucian classics translated as a basis for ordered government and social cohesion.

In 1618 Nurhaci moved into the open and attacked the Ming, capturing Fushun in Liaodong in that year and Liaoyang and Shenyang in 1621. Shenyang was renamed Mukden and made the capital of a new dynasty, to which Nurhaci had set up a claim some years earlier under the title Late Jin.

Taking Peking

When Nurhaci died in 1626 he was succeeded by his eighth son, Abahai (1592–1643), who instituted the standard Chinese Six Ministries for the government in Mukden and appointed as Grand Secretary a prominent Chinese official, Fan Wen cheng. Fan was a prize for the Manzhou. An ancestor of his had been a well-known statesman in the Song dynasty, and he himself had been captured by Nurhaci and had then collaborated with him. He was not atypical, for many Chinese of northern origin were quite prepared to work under the Manzhou. Abahai united the main area of Manchuria under his rule by 1642; the Amur region in the far north was brought in by 1644. Abahai's death in 1643 did not prove a setback to the mounting ambitions of the Manzhou, for his six-year-old son was fortunate in having as regent a loyal uncle, Dorgon, who carried on the tradition of the bold and determined yet wise and realistic rule of his immediate predecessors.

The Ming at this point were in no condition to offer strong resistance to any attempt to supplant them. Their finances were low, there was widespread disorder, and the armies in the north charged with defending Peking were demoralized. Even so, Dorgon might not have launched an attack but for one circumstance, for he knew that a child ruler made a poor rallying point for a people emerging from tribalism. The circumstance was that the Manzhou were invited into China by a Ming general, Wu Sangui, who was supposed to be defending the frontier. In the chaotic conditions prevailing at the end of the Ming period, as at the end of other dynasties, there was more than one rebellion afoot, and another general, Li Zicheng, was aiming at taking over power at the capital. Faced with this threat in 1644 the Ming emperor called upon Wu Sangui to help. Wu at this point felt that his own forces were not sufficient and secured valuable allies by opening the pass at Shanhaiguan to the vigorous "barbarians." He was too late to save the dynasty, for meanwhile time had run out for the emperor. Li entered Peking at the head of his troops and, as we have seen, found that the emperor had taken his own life.

Life Under the Manchu

It may have seemed that the Manzhou came to help Wu, but once in Peking they showed no disposition to depart and in fact stayed for nearly 300 years. Li was soon evicted from Peking and, after a long retreat, was ignominiously killed a year later by two peasants who offered his head to the pursuing general. The Manzhou from the first benefited in their political style from the fact that they had already become familiar in Manchuria with Chinese institutions. The offices in the main ministries at the capital were equally divided between Manzhou and Chinese, and the provinces were governed cooperatively by a Manzhou governor general and a Chinese governor.

The lower classes were not treated so well. Chinese men were compelled to wear the queue, or pigtail, and mixed marriages at all levels of society were forbidden. Manchuria was to be reserved as a special area sacred to Manzhou of pure blood, and Chinese were not allowed to settle there. During the early years of the new dynasty, Manzhou enclaves were set up in north China, where the farming was done by Chinese slaves, who could actually be bought and sold. But the experiment was seen by the Manzhou themselves to be unsuccessful. Production was scanty, and it was difficult to prevent slaves from absconding and becoming lost in the general population. The Manzhou found, as the Mongols before them in a different context had found, that you could do better by taxing free farmers. By 1685 no new enclosures were being made. And when it came to agrarian taxes, those levied by the Manzhou were lighter than the taxes demanded by most of the other dynasties.

Although the new dynasty, named the Qing, was ruling in north China, it was some decades before the south came fully under its control. Wu Sangui was collaborating with the Qing, and incidentally drawing considerable funds from Peking, but he was also pursuing his own ambitions. He drove the Ming supporters from one province to another and defeated a Ming prince in Burma in 1662. (The last Ming empress was converted to Christianity by the Jesuits.) Finally Wu, with his base in the southwest, made a bid for complete independence in 1673 and was joined by two other Chinese generals in the South in the Revolt of the Three Feudatories. It took the Qing forces until 1681 to suppress this rebellion. The last stronghold of Ming sympathizers was Taiwan (Formosa). Guo Xingye, the name Europeanized as Koxinga, was a power on the Fujian coast. Allied with the last of the Ming, he attempted unsuccessfully to secure Japanese help for them. He then seized Taiwan from the Dutch. From this base he revived the pirate menace to the south China coast and supported the Revolt of the Three Feudatories. The Dutch fleet, however, joined up with the Qing forces in the suppression. With this assistance Taiwan was captured from Guo Xingye in 1683 and became a part of Fujian province. The Qing emperors were at last established as the rulers of all China. The last phase of the conquest, however, was costly for the inhabitants of the seacoast, since they were forced to move ten miles inland and their coastal towns and villages were burned. The aim of the dynasty in this measure was, of course, to deny the rebels and pirates any support or supplies, but the anti-maritime frame of mind exhibited here by the central authorities rendered them less fitted than ever to cope with the overseas rivals from the West who would soon harass them.

The Reign of Kang Xi

The Qing dynasty thus took some time to establish itself, but, once established, it enjoyed a long middle period of stability and prosperity. This was due in part to the occurrence of two exceptionally long reigns in close succession, that of Kang Xi (1654–1722) who ruled for over sixty years, from 1661 until his death, and that of Qian Long, whose reign, from 1736 to 1795, was almost as long. Both emperors and their advisers devoted a great deal of attention to China's northern and western frontiers, and both reigns witnessed an expansion of the empire, until in Qian Long's time it reached proportions unknown before or since. Diplomatic and military means were employed by the Qing, and the religion of Lamaism also played a large part in the outcome. The chief example of the effect of Lamaism on the politics of the northern and western regions was the victory of the Yellow Sect, under the fifth Dalai Lama, over their Red Sect rivals. This Dalai Lama visited Peking in 1652, bearing tribute. He was well treated, exempted from the customary prostration before the emperor, and given the usual gold symbols of authority as a tributary ruler within the Chinese sphere.

This visit took place just before Kang Xi's time, but Kang Xi himself commanded a large Chinese force which penetrated as far as Urga in Outer Mongolia and defeated a powerful khan of the Western Mongols. The mounted nomads whose fighting skills had dominated the steppes for so long were now doomed to decline, for in this battle the Chinese employed artillery with deadly effect. . . .

Kang Xi by no means confined himself to the pursuit of military achievements. A brilliant ruler, a scholar and an all-around personality, he enjoyed hunting in the manner of his ancestors and built a summer palace for the purpose at Rehol, north of Peking. Hunting was more than a sport, since with a veritable army of beaters coordinating their efforts to round up the quarry, it served also as a war game and had been extensively so used by the Mongols. Kang Xi made it a point to go on inspection tours in south China, which had the double advantage of keeping him in touch with that reservoir of first-rate scholar officials and of enabling him to check on the conservancy of the Yellow and Huai rivers in the north and on the vital Grand Canal artery which brought tribute rice from the south. Most important of all, he had a genuine love of scholarship and succeeded in attracting to his side some of the best Chinese literati of the time. A small group was attached to his personal study, and they and wider committees of scholars collaborated in works to which he wrote prefaces. Thus there appeared under Kang Xi's patronage the great dictionary of some 40,000 characters, a collection devoted to calligraphy and painting, an extensive treatise of geography, and a complete edition of the works of Zhu Xi. The vast encyclopedia, *Tu Shu Ji Cheng,* begun in the seventeenth century, was published in 1728.

In his capacity as moral leader of the nation, Kang Xi published in 1670 the *Sacred Edict,* an amplification of earlier imperial maxims of the fourteenth century, which exhorted the people to be filial and thrifty, to value scholarship and avoid unorthodoxy, and to respect the law and pay their taxes. This edict was to be brought to the attention of the populace twice a month by the officials and gentry. The wording of the edict provides a good illustration of the division between the rulers and the ruled and of the lofty, paternalistic attitude of the Chinese government toward its people, which was based on a genuine moral concern but was before long to strike foreign governments as arrogant and anachronistic.

The Establishment of the Tokugawa Shogunate in Japan

Mikiso Hane

In the following excerpt from the book *Modern Japan: A Historical Survey,* historian Mikiso Hane explores the rise of the Tokugawa shogunate and the influence of Shogun Ieyasu on the culture of Japan in the seventeenth century. Hane explains how Ieyasu controlled the feudal lords (daimyo) by requiring that each lord spend every other year in the capital city of Edo (Tokyo) and forbidding marital alliances among different daimyo. Ieyasu encouraged Confucian values that focused on maintaining social and political relationships. For example, Confucianism demanded respect, loyalty, and obedience of a son toward his father, and the Tokugawa rulers expected the same allegiance to the samurai lords. In addition, Hane writes, during the Tokugawa period scholars stressed a return to original Japanese teaching before it was contaminated by Chinese and Christian influence.

In 1600 Tokugawa Ieyasu defeated his rivals and the supporters of the Toyotomi family in the Battle of Sekigahara. In 1603 the emperor designated him shōgun, and he made Edo (Tokyo) the seat of government. By 1615 he had eliminated the Toyotomi family, and he tightened his grip on the entire country by establishing a political and social order that brought all segments of the society under his firm control. He and the third shōgun, Iemitsu (1604–1651), adopted and implemented measures that would ensure the security of Tokugawa hegemony.

The Tokugawa Social Structure

Ieyasu froze the social order, adapting Confucian China's four-class system—that is, scholar-officials (samurai), peasants, artisans, and merchants. In his Testament to his descendants, he stated: "The samurai are the master of the four classes. Agriculturists, artisans and merchants may not behave in a rude manner towards samurai. . . . A samurai is not be interfered with in cutting down a fellow who has behaved to him in a manner other than is expected." In other words, the samurai were to be at the top of the social hierarchy, the peasants were to remain on the land, and the artisans and merchants were to keep their places and behave in a manner expected of humble people.

In order to control the feudal lords (daimyō), of whom there were 295 in the early seventeenth century and 276 at the end of the Tokugawa era, the Tokugawa rulers adopted the following measures. They classified the daimyō into three categories: members of the Tokugawa clan (*shimpan*), lords who had been followers of the Tokugawa family before the Battle of Sekigahara (*fudai,* or hereditory lords), and those who submitted to or joined the Tokugawa family later (*tozama,* or outside lords). The fudai lords' domains (*han*) were placed in strategic places, whereas the tozama lords were placed in outlying regions or between two fudai lords' domains. In 1635 Iemitsu issued the "Laws Governing the Military Households," which required that the feudal lords spend every other year in Edo and that their families remain in Edo (known as sankin kōtai); the feudal lords and their families were also forbidden to form marital ties with other daimyō families, or to build or repair castles without the Bakufu's [Shōgunate's] permission.

Of the 30 million *koku* (1 koku = 4.96 bushels) in rice, or rice equivalents, produced nationwide, the Bakufu's own holdings yielded 7 million koku. It also retained control over foreign relations, controlled coinage, and regulated inter-han transportation. The local lords were allowed to manage their own internal affairs and to retain their own vassals, who, in most instances, received stipends in rice rather than land allotments as fiefs.

The Persecution of Christians

In foreign relations Shōgun Iemitsu decided to virtually seal off the country from the outside world in order to prevent Christian influences from seeping into the country. Restrictions against Christians had started under Hideyoshi, who in 1587 ordered the missionaries to leave the country; but the edict was not stringently enforced until the last years of his life, when he crucified twenty-six missionaries and converts in 1597. Ieyasu initially pursued a policy of toleration, but in 1614 he issued an edict banning Christianity because he had come to believe that Christians were a threat to his plan to establish absolute control over the society. Thus commenced was a policy of ruthless persecution of Christians, who at that time numbered about 300,000. Iemitsu continued this policy with even less mercy than that shown by Ieyasu. In the years from 1614 to 1640, between 5,000 and 6,000 Christians were executed. In 1637–1638 a peasant rebellion against the local lord erupted in the Shimabara Peninsula and the Amakusa Islands. As the leadership was Christian, Iemitsu's distrust of Christians was reinforced. In 1639 he decided to virtually isolate Japan from the rest of the world. Only the Dutch and the Chinese were allowed to come to Nagasaki to trade in a limited fashion. The Koreans were permitted to trade through Iki Island off Honshu. In addition, books from the West were banned until 1720, when nonreligious works were allowed to enter Japan. . . .

Modern Japan cannot be comprehended without an understanding of the social, economic, political, intellectual, and cultural forces that emerged in the Tokugawa period. The hierarchical outlook and behavior, the emphasis on class order and social cohesion, the demand for obedience and submissiveness that the Tokugawa rulers insisted upon—all of these forces molded the values and attitudes of the people of the time and, in fact, have persisted to the present day. Specifically, it was during the Tokugawa period that the Confucian and samurai values and ideals became ingrained in the society.

The Rise of Confucianism

With the advent of Chinese civilization, Chinese classics, history, and poetry entered Japan. Confucianism, however, did not affect the cultural and intellectual life of Japan as quickly as Buddhism had done. Nevertheless, because the Tokugawa rulers encouraged the study and propagation of Confucian values, Confucianism became the predominant intellectual force in this era—even though the early Tokugawa rulers had used Shinto and Buddhist concepts as well to legitimize their hegemony.

Ieyasu wanted his vassals not only to be well trained in the martial arts but also, like the Chinese scholar-officials, to be steeped in Confucian learning. The Confucian school that received official backing was Confucianism, as interpreted by the Sung Confucian, Chu Hsi (1130–1200). As the pursuit of Confucian studies continued for two-and-a-half centuries, the Japanese intellectual frame of

reference came to be largely Confucian. Confucian values continued to be instilled in the society after the Meiji Restoration (1868)
because they were incorporated in the school textbooks until the end
of the Second World War.

Confucius and his followers were interested primarily in man's
relationship with his fellowmen and in maintaining social and political order, stability, and harmony. They believed there are five basic human relationships: those between lord and subject, father and
son, husband and wife, elder brother and younger brother, and friend
and friend. Of these, the relationship between father and son was the
most important, and filial piety was considered the cardinal virtue.

Like their Chinese counterparts, the Japanese Confucians emphasized filial piety; but the Tokugawa rulers made loyalty to the
lord equally or more important than filial piety. The two were linked
together as *chū-kō* (loyalty and filial piety). Social order was to be
maintained by means of a hierarchical order in which the relationship between superior and inferior persons was strictly preserved.
The superior person was expected to be benevolent and to set a
moral example to those below, while those below were to be respectful, deferential, and obedient toward the superior. . . .

The Way of the Warriors

During the years of Tokugawa peace, warrior-philosophers began to
formulate what they considered to be the ideal mode of conduct for
the samurai. Of course, even before the Tokugawa era, righteous and
unrighteous conduct had been defined, and the samurai was expected to live by the principles of duty, loyalty, integrity, honor, justice, fidelity, and courage. In the Kamakura period, the life of the
samurai was spoken of as *yumiya no michi,* the way of the bow and
arrow. The lord-vassal relationship that constituted the basis of the
feudal system rose out of familial relationships. A follower of the
lord was called *gokenin* (man of the house), or *ie-no-ko* (child of the
house). Hence the relationship between lord and vassal was akin to
that of father and son. Like the European medieval knight, the samurai pledged allegiance to his lord in a ritualistic ceremony. In return,
the lord was expected to reward the vassal with land, stipends, or the
right to collect taxes.

In relating tales of warriors who were engaged in the power struggles of the late Heian period and after, storytellers have often idealized the conduct of the warriors, who were depicted as being chival-
rous, selfless, and heroic. But, in reality, some samurai were motivated not by noble ideals but by self-interest. In times of strife the
principle that prevailed for such samurai was the law of the jungle.
What really counted were physical strength and martial skill. Expe-
diency and opportunism guided the actions of many warriors who

were ready to shift with the changing tide of fortune. For this reason, the period between 1337 and 1392, when the northern and southern imperial courts were in conflict, is referred to as the "great age of turncoats." The same situation prevailed during the years of the Warring States in the fifteenth and sixteenth centuries. The strong conquered the weak; the powerful destroyed the helpless. Given the opportunity, a vassal would likely turn against his master. Thus, in order to ensure his vassal's loyalty, the master had to reward him properly. The vassal then was obligated to him, he owed him *on*. Eventually the concept of *on* became a cardinal virtue in the Japanese value system. A person owed *on* to his feudal lord, parents, teachers, emperor, society, and so on.

The samurai's interests were closely bound to the interests of his family. If he died in battle he expected his family to be properly rewarded. But self-interest caused frequent conflicts among family members, conflicts in which sons turned against fathers and brothers fought brothers.

Zen influenced the life of the samurai during the Ashikaga period, for it disciplined the warrior to concentrate, control his emotions, and overcome the fear of death. One sixteenth-century warlord exhorted his retainers to "devote yourselves to the study of Zen. Zen has no secrets other than seriously thinking about birth and death." Unfortunately, this belief reinforced the samurai's rather cold-blooded attitude about killing people, despite the fact that, ideally, the samurai was expected to behave in a compassionate and magnanimous fashion. . . .

In the Tokugawa period seppuku was used to punish warriors who committed serious offenses. But it was regarded as an honorable way of dying; indeed, samurai of their own free will often committed ritual suicide to uphold their honor, to prove their sincerity, or to protest the unjust actions of their superiors. . . .

A possession of the samurai that distinguished them from the commoners was the sword—the samurai's symbol of superior status. (The common people were prohibited from bearing a sword.) The sword supposedly embodied the spirit of the samurai. It was the emblem of their power, honor, and status, but for the common people it was an instrument of terror because the samurai were given the right to cut down any commoner who offended them. Thus, it might be said that the courtesy, politeness, humility, and subservience of the common people were instilled in them at the edge of the sword.

The Scholars of National Learning

In the Tokugawa period, when the scholars of National Learning began to emphasize the unique nature of Japanese culture and religion, the nativistic aspects of Shinto were also emphasized. The scholars were influenced by the Confucian school of Ancient Learning, which, as noted, stressed the importance of going back to the original teachings of Confucius. In addition, Shinto scholars began to stress the need to return to the roots of Japanese culture and religion, to the time before Japan had become overwhelmed by Chinese culture and thought. Thus, the "native" texts of Japan, the *Man'yōshū* (*Collection of Ten Thousand Leaves*) and the *Kojiki* (*Records of Ancient Matters*) were extolled as true embodiments of the Japanese spirit because, according to these scholars, they were free of foreign contamination.

Among the pioneers of the scholars of National Learning was Kamono-Mabuchi (1697–1769). He rejected Confucianism for having made people "crafty" in contrast to the ancient Japanese who were simple, honest, sincere, and free from abstruse teachings. The scholar who came to be regarded as the sage of National Learning was Motoori Norinaga. Norinaga devoted his life to the study of the *Man'yōshū* and the *Kojiki*. The latter, he asserted, embodied "The Way of the Gods," and what was recorded in it were absolute truths. One such truth concerned the founding of Japan by the Sun Goddess, who was the Sun itself. Hence Japan, as a land favored by the gods, was believed to occupy a unique place in the world. Norinaga's followers then insisted that Japan was superior to the other nations of the world. . . .

Norinaga believed that, previous to the advent of Chinese civilization, the Japanese behaved in a natural and uninhibited fashion and that this natural way was distorted by Chinese thought and culture—especially Confucianism, with its artificial rules and regulations about decorum and propriety. It was important to allow one's true feelings to have free play, he insisted, for only in this way could one be fully sensitive to all facets of life.

Even though Norinaga spoke of the sacred origin of Japan and the imperial dynasty, he did not call for the restoration of political authority to the imperial court. Instead, he accepted the existing political order. This he justified by asserting that "great shōgun have ruled the land ever since Azumaterunokami [Ieyasu] founded the government in accordance with the designs of the Sun Goddess Amaterasu, and by the authority vested in him by the imperial court. . . . The rules and laws of the founder and succeeding shōgun are all rules and laws of the Sun Goddess Amaterasu." Hence "to obey the laws of the day is to follow the true way of the Gods." It was not until the later stages of the Tokugawa era that Shinto nationalists began to urge the restoration of authority to the emperor.

The Age of Discord in England

PREFACE

The seventeenth century was a tumultuous time in England. It was a time of political plots, revolution, and civil war. The nation was divided by religious and political factions that competed for power and influence. Those with little power sought freedom from persecution and hoped to gain protection for their basic rights. Those who supported the Anglican Church of England faced opposition from both the Puritans and the Roman Catholics, and the king who ruled by divine right faced opposition from a Parliament that wanted to curb royal power. Religious and political claims were often intertwined, making it difficult to determine whether disputes and their causes had religious or political origins.

The names of the competing factions varied during the century. The Royalists, or Cavaliers, supported the king while the Parliamentarians, or Roundheads, sought to curb, if not eliminate, royal rule. During the parliamentary rule of the interregnum, the conservative Presbyterians and the radical Levellers faced a new faction, the Agitators, who represented the New Model Army. Later in the century Parliament would be divided by Tories and Whigs, and although the influence of the Puritans waned, the Catholics continued to vie for power and protection.

English political history during the seventeenth century can be loosely divided into four periods: the succession of James Stuart to the throne of England in 1603, the English civil wars of 1640–1660, the Restoration of the Monarchy in 1660, and the Glorious Revolution of 1688. The clash between king and Parliament began with the succession of James IV of Scotland to the throne of England upon the death of Elizabeth I. James I claimed to rule by divine right while Parliament believed kings were to rule for the benefit of the people and were subject to the laws established by Parliament. James had the support of the Church of England, so those who sought religious freedom, the Puritans and the Catholics, gave their support to the Parliamentarians. Despite plots against James and his supporters, James continued to override the authority of Parliament.

After James died in 1625, Charles I succeeded to the throne. Although Charles was popular at his coronation, he offended his Protestant subjects with his marriage to the Catholic Henrietta Maria, sister of Louis XIII of France. In an attempt to curb royal power, Parliament passed the Grand Remonstrance, indicting his royal policies. When, in 1642, Charles attempted to arrest his opponents, support for the Parliamentarians poured into London and forced Charles to flee. The civil war between the Royalists and Parliamentarians had begun.

Both sides suffered victories and defeats. With the aid of Scotland, Parliament gained control of the north, but because the parliamentary armies had no united command, they could not follow up their victory. As a result, Parliament formed the controversial New Model Army and defeated the Royalists at Naseby in 1645, but the Parliamentarians were now divided as a result of the controversy. The Presbyterians opposed the New Model Army, and after Parliament tried to disband it, the army briefly occupied London. Adding to the internal conflict within Parliament, when trying to negotiate a constitution, the radical Levellers pushed for a more democratic constitution and a deadlock resulted. Oliver Cromwell, a general and an influential Puritan leader of the Parliamentarians, terminated constitutional discussion when, in 1648, Charles, hoping to take advantage of the division in Parliament, made a last attempt to take London. Charles was defeated, however, by forces led by Cromwell. A court was established to try the king, and Charles was executed for treason. Cromwell was elected lord protector, but he was unable to resolve internal squabbles between conservatives, radicals, and representatives of the New Model Army, which paved the way for the return of Charles II in 1660.

Royalist hopes for a return to the political climate that existed before the civil war were disappointed because Parliament was reluctant to relinquish its newfound power. Likewise, Protestants feared a new threat in Parliament: the growing influence of the Catholic Church. Both Charles II, and his successor James II, had close ties to Catholicism. Moreover, neither king seemed to have learned the lessons of his predecessors and began to again evade parliamentary law. Although the Tories supported the right of James II to rule by divine right, when threatened by James's overt Catholicism, the Tories joined with the Whigs, who opposed James. In the Glorious Revolution, a temporarily united Parliament brought the Protestant William of Orange, and his wife Mary, from the Dutch Republic to rule England. Shortly thereafter Parliament adopted a Bill of Rights.

Although it might appear that the end of the century saw no real resolution to the basic issues that divided England at the century's beginning, the discord that threatened to tear the nation apart actually laid the groundwork for a more peaceful transition to the republican form of government that emerged in the next century.

James I: The Beginning of Stuart Rule

S. Reed Brett

Elizabeth, the last of the Tudors, died on March 24, 1603, and James VI of Scotland was proclaimed James I of England, beginning the reign of the Stuart family. In the following excerpt, the late historian S. Reed Brett examines the early years of the reign of James I. Although James had considerable experience as a monarch and was educated in many areas, Brett writes that, to some, his devotion to peace appeared to be fear of battle. Moreover, Brett reveals, James inherited from Elizabeth the problem of religious discord: Both Puritans and Roman Catholics sought freedom to express their faith without fear of fines and punishment. However, Brett explains, James claimed to rule by divine right, and because the Puritans believed that the Bible, not the church hierarchy, should be the ultimate authority, religious freedom threatened this philosophy. As a result, some of those who opposed James plotted against him. The plots, led by embittered Roman Catholics, failed, which resulted not only in severe laws against Roman Catholics but also in intense persecution by the people. According to Brett, the growing discord was further agitated when James appealed to the courts to override Parliament, especially when he hoped to gain revenue to compensate for his personal spending.

Excerpted from S. Reed Brett, *The Stuart Century,* 1603–1714 (London: George G. Harrap & Co. Ltd, 1961).

The reigns of the first two Stuart Kings, James I and Charles I, form together a single, undivided historical period. The great political and religious issues of James' reign continued into, and came to a head during, the reign of Charles. Moreover, for some time before James' death, Prince Charles and his favourite, [George Villiers, the first duke of] Buckingham, had been the virtual rulers of England, so that they did little more than continue the same methods of ruling when the Prince became King. The distinguishing character of the two reigns was the resistance of the Parliaments to what they regarded as the excessive use of the royal prerogative.

Ruling by Divine Right

The clash between King and Parliament was provoked by the Stuarts' claim to rule by Divine Right. Their insistence upon the divine origin of their authority meant that the dispute became a religious one. Not the least influential of the King's supporters were the [Anglican] bishops; and this intensified the support which the Puritans gave to Parliament. Further, it was Archbishop [William] Laud who, by his Church reforms in England, and his attempted reforms in Scotland, finally precipitated hostilities. Thus, on account both of the fundamental principles involved and of the immediate cause of the dispute, the Civil War became, for most of those who engaged in it, a religious rather than a political conflict.

Nevertheless, though the dispute had religious causes, the issue itself went even deeper than that. It was concerned with nothing less than the possession of sovereignty in the State. The Stuarts claimed that sovereignty was theirs by Divine Right. Parliament claimed that whatever prerogative the King possessed was to be exercised for the welfare of his subjects and in accordance with the nation's rights established by charters, statutes, and precedents. For itself, as the representative body of the nation, Parliament claimed an essential part in the work of government.

At the outset we need to be clear that, to whatever extent the Stuarts were giving a new emphasis to royal supremacy, Parliament's claim to a directive share in government was at least equally without precedent. Both James I and Charles I committed some unpardonably foolish blunders; yet, according to the letter of the law at least, the King was in a sounder position than Parliament. Stuart Parliaments would need such experiences as their failure to substantiate their impeachment of [Thomas Wentworth, first earl of] Strafford before this fact was brought home to the average Member and even to many of the leaders.

James I's reign is divisible into two almost equal parts—namely, 1603–14, and 1614–25. The dividing-point was the Addled Parliament of 1614, which quarrelled with the King over irregular taxation and was dissolved after sitting for only two months. During the first half of the reign James' chief Minister was Sir Robert Cecil, who had been Secretary to Elizabeth. During the second half of the reign James allowed himself and the Kingdom to be ruled by personal favourites irrespective of their capacity to govern.

When James ascended his new throne he was not without certain advantages. To the problems that Elizabeth had bequeathed to him he brought considerable experience both as a man and as a monarch. Born in 1566 he had been crowned King of Scotland in the following year after the enforced abdication of his mother, Mary, following her defeat at Carberry Hill and her imprisonment in Lochleven Castle. Intellectually, too, he had gifts above the average. As a theologian he could hold his own with learned divines; and as a political philosopher he had few equals among contemporaries—witness his *True Law of Free Monarchies* published in 1598. Further, in an age when Court morals were commonly, almost unashamedly, lax, James' personal life was apparently untouched by such evils.

Yet with all his gifts, James lacked two which made the rest ineffective—namely, strength of will to carry out the truth he saw, and ability to judge the characters of other men. Highly susceptible to flattery, he was an easy prey to anyone with a smooth tongue and persuasive manner. In consequence he was vacillating in policy and the victim of unworthy favourites. He suffered the further disadvantage of being doctrinaire in disposition: even when his judgement was sound (as often it was) he rarely understood how or to what extent to apply his theory so as to achieve his purpose. Personally, also, he had some unattractive traits. Clear talking was made difficult for him by a tongue too large for his mouth, though in spite of this defect he was incorrigibly garrulous, using the broadest of Scots speech. His gait was an awkward shamble. The sight of a naked sword sent him into a nervous shiver. This last characteristic was perhaps a reflex of his sincere devotion to peace, but it was not likely to deepen the average seventeenth-century Englishman's respect for him. James I was as sharp a contrast to the kingly—and queenly—Tudors [the royal family that ruled England from 1485 to 1603] as could well be imagined.

Facing the Puritans

The importance which religion was to have during the new reign was plainly indicated by its opening events. James was still on his way to London when a petition was presented to him supposedly representing the views of one thousand Puritan clergy and hence known as the Millenary Petition. The terms of the petition were scrupulously respectful towards the monarch and moderate in their demands for reform. . . .

For James the petition was in the nature of a test-question. Inoffensive though many of its terms may have been to large numbers of English people, to grant them would have seemed to show that the new King was an active sympathizer with the Puritans. This would offend a numerous and influential section of the nation, and would be a disastrous opening of the new reign. Moreover, to give a direct answer to a question, especially to a religious question, was not in James' nature. He would much prefer a long debate in which he could adjudicate and air his own theological learning. He therefore ordered a conference to consider the petition and relevant ecclesiastical matters.

The Hampton Court Conference met in January 1604. The Archbishop of Canterbury and eight bishops headed the eighteen members representing the orthodox Church party, while the Puritans were limited to four. This sufficiently indicated the line that the proceedings were likely to take. During the opening deliberations, however, James held the balance fairly even. In the end Dr Reynolds, the Puritan leader, delivered himself into his enemies' hands by referring to the "Bishop and his Presbyters." At the word Presbyter James rose in anger that was half-frightened and half-indignant. To James, a Presbyter pointed in one direction— namely, to the Presbyterian Church in Scotland where the Church was supreme and the King subordinate. During the months since his coming into England James had tasted enough of the sweets of English Episcopacy, which recognized the monarch's pre-eminence, to make him determined never to return to the humiliations of Presbyterianism. "A Scottish

James I

Presbytery," he declared, "agreeth as well with a monarchy as God and the Devil." Thereupon he rated the Puritan divine roundly and even coarsely. The climax of the King's outburst was this ominous declaration: "If this be all your party hath to say, I will make them conform themselves, or else will harry them out of the Kingdom."

James' reasons for this attitude are easy to understand. He himself summed them up in the heat of the argument: "I thus apply it. . . . No bishop, no King." But it was a short-sighted policy. At the outset of his reign he had lost a never-to-be repeated opportunity to effect a reasonable compromise within the Church. Out of the parties which from that time grew more and more pronounced, there sprang the Civil War and much subsequent strife.

The one good result of the conference was the order for a new translation of the Bible. This arose from Dr Reynolds' plea that "there might be a new translation of the Bible because those which were allowed in the reign of Henry VIII and Edward VI were corrupt and not conformable to the truth of the original." The suggestion pleased James who, in spite of the grumble of [Richard] Bancroft, Bishop of London, that "if every man's humour should be followed, there would be no end of translating," ordered the work to proceed. Fifty of the most eminent Bible-scholars of the day, divided into six groups, laboured almost continuously until 1611 to produce the Authorized Version of the Bible whose influence, in providing a matchless example of English prose and in moulding the religion of generations of English people all over the world, is beyond calculation. . . .

Plotting Against the King

The Puritans were not the only people to suffer religious disabilities. The Roman Catholics also laboured under a sense of grievance, particularly because James continued to collect recusancy fines—that is, fines for non-attendance at English Church services. Nor were these the only reasons for general discontent. About the Court were many men disgruntled from various causes with the new regime. Sir Walter Ralegh [commonly known as Raleigh], for example, was the centre of a group angered by the new King's policy of peace with Spain. So uncompromising was Ralegh on this subject that James' accession had been followed almost at once by Ralegh's disgrace. He was deprived of all the offices he had held at Elizabeth's Court, and henceforward was a violent opponent of James and Cecil. Lord Cobham, who shared Ralegh's political views, had also a personal grievance in that James had refused to grant him an office promised by Elizabeth. Different groups of such malcontents toyed with ideas of how to obtain redress for their wrongs. Some of these ideas were foolish and slightly criminal; others were plainly treasonable. Cobham, for example, had a scheme to remove James and his Minister, Cecil, and to enthrone Arabella Stuart [first cousin of James]. Some attempt to sort out these various schemes resulted in two being known as the Bye Plot and Main Plot; but the plotters of them overlapped so bewilderingly that neither at the time nor since has anyone been able to make clear sense of the whole business. There is a strong suspicion that Cecil purposely confused the evidence so as to rid the Court of his opponents.

Not unnaturally, when Cecil heard of the plots, Ralegh and Cobham were among the arrested persons. Cobham, on trial, attempted to shuffle out of the affair by accusing Ralegh of leading him into the plot. Ralegh was even charged with plotting with Spaniards, which is enough to show the absurdity of the proceedings. Three of them were actually executed. Cobham and Ralegh were led out to execution but were reprieved and placed in the Tower, where they remained until 1619. Ralegh spent the thirteen years of his imprisonment in writing his *History of the World.*

What had been known as the Bye Plot of June 1603 was revealed to James by Jesuits. James, as a reward for the loyalty of his informers and of the mass of his Roman Catholic subjects, promised that the recusancy fines should not in future be collected. One effect of this was that large numbers of Roman Catholics who had hitherto disguised their faith came out in their true colours. The sudden revelation of the large numbers of Catholics in England took James so much by surprise, and caused him so much apprehension, that he went from one extreme to the other. In February 1604 all priests were ordered to leave the country, and in November the collection of recusancy fines was resumed. This change of policy embittered Roman Catholics, and a small band of them formed a desperate plan to cure their ills by violence: they would overthrow the Government that was persecuting them. Out of this resolve sprang the Gunpowder Plot.

The Gunpowder Plot

The arch-plotter was Robert Catesby, who conceived the idea of blowing up the King and his Ministers as they were assembled for the opening of Parliament, so making a clean sweep of the Protestant leaders. To take advantage of the resulting confusion, a rising of Roman Catholic gentry and their retainers was to be organized so as either to seize the Government or to obtain favourable terms for Roman Catholics. The scheme was hopelessly fantastic: the explosion-plot might or might not succeed in its immediate objective, but a rising of Catholics must inevitably be crushed, and the only effect would be heavier penalties than ever upon Catholics in general. Yet the men who planned and executed the scheme did not lack intelligence, good breeding, or experience. The depth of their folly was a measure of their desperation. Whatever our views on the justice or injustice of their cause, and however we may condemn their methods, we must admire their unquenchable bravery.

Catesby's closest associates were his cousin, Thomas Winter, and Thomas Percy, cousin of the Earl of Northumberland. Gradually certain others were brought into the plot. In May 1604 Percy hired a house next to the Parliament House, and mining operations were begun. These were carried out under the direction of Guy Fawkes, who had been brought up a Yorkshire gentleman, but who, a dozen years before the Plot, had sold his property and enlisted in the Spanish Army in Flanders. His combination of Roman Catholic zeal with expert knowledge of siege-tunnelling made him ideally suited for the work. The task of digging through a nine-foot wall was terrific, and progress was necessarily slow. Also, a long prorogation of Parliament, in July 1604, and other difficulties, caused various changes of plan.

The final plan was for Sir Everard Digby to hold a hunting-party at Dunchurch, near Rugby, on the appointed day; for Digby then to reveal to the assembled Roman Catholics the nature of the plot; and then, as soon as news of the explosion reached them from London, for them to raise a general rebellion. The day finally fixed for the opening of the new session of Parliament was November 5.

The Consequences of Failure

One of the men associated with Digby in organizing the rebellion was Francis Tresham. His brother-in-law was Lord Monteagle, for whose safety Tresham was deeply concerned. On the evening of October 26 Monteagle received a mysterious note urging him to find some excuse for absence from the opening of Parliament. "Think not slightly of this advertisement but retire yourself into the country, where you may expect the event in safety, for though there be no appearance of any stir, yet I say they shall receive a terrible blow this Parliament, and they shall not see who hurts them." Monteagle passed on the note to Cecil (lately created Earl of Salisbury) who thus gleaned his first information of the plot. Though the conspirators learned that Monteagle had received a letter, they gave themselves away in two respects. First, the dauntless Guy Fawkes insisted upon staying at his post hoping that he would be able to carry out the explosion before he was detected; and just before midnight of November 4 he was discovered and carried off. Second, Catesby and the other leaders decided to continue the other part of the plot. Setting out from London, they rode to Dunchurch but no one rallied to them. They became fugitives, and were rounded up at Holbeche House, in Staffordshire, where most of the ringleaders—including Catesby, Percy, and Wright—were shot dead during the attack. Fawkes, subject to long and horrible torture, gradually revealed the names of the conspirators. Those who remained alive were put on trial and executed early in 1606.

So ended what is perhaps the most famous plot in English history. It had disastrous effects on the Catholic cause. New and severe penal laws were enacted. The recusancy fines were enormously increased; recusants were forbidden to practise law or medicine and to hold any commission in the Army or Navy; and recusants could be required to take an oath that the Pope had no power to depose a King and that they would defend the King to the utmost of their ability. The last provision was an attempt to distinguish between those Catholics who were loyal to the King and the State and those who were disloyal. It was against the latter that the Penal Laws were to be enforced. This position continued until 1619 when James' anxiety for a marriage between Prince Charles and a Spanish princess necessitated some improvement in the lot of English Roman Catholics.

But the real effect of the plot was to be seen not so much in Parliamentary statutes as in the reaction of the mass of the people. A howl of execration against Roman Catholics went up on every side. The common folk did not stay to draw nice distinctions between different kinds and degrees of Catholics. In the eyes of the nation all Catholics were alike traitors. . . . These effects were confirmed and intensified by the Gunpowder Plot.

The Parliament which Catesby and his fellow-conspirators had intended to blow up had first met on March 19, 1604. . . . Influences had been at work during the closing years of the sixteenth century to produce a clash between Monarch and Parliament. Only Elizabeth's consummate statecraft and the nation's habitual loyalty to its great Queen had prevented the clash from coming in her lifetime. James I's accession brought this unstable equilibrium to an end. The Members of his first Parliament met under a sense of being on the verge of decisive events. The new King seemed to go out of his way to justify the sense of crisis. His insistence upon his Divine Right was a virtual challenge to his Parliaments to counter his claim by asserting their own rights and privileges.

Further, the persecution of the Puritan clergy, foreshadowed during the Hampton Court Conference, and the growing High Church influence at Court, provided Parliament with an active motive which sprang from the deepest convictions; for a large proportion of its Members were drawn from the middle classes, who were the strongest supporters of Puritanism. . . .

The opening session of James' first Parliament ended on July 7, 1604. The interest of the second session (1605–6) centred in the Gunpowder Plot. When on November 19, 1606, James opened the third session, he referred at some length to the relations between his two Kingdoms of England and Scotland. Ever since his accession in England James had cherished the hope that the two might be fully united. As early as April 1604 he had brought the subject to Parliament's notice, and twenty-eight commissioners (fourteen from the Lords and fourteen from the Commons) had then been appointed to discuss the subject with Scottish commissioners. Their report, presented to Parliament in November 1606, included the recommendations that there should be free trade between England and Scotland, and that Scots born after James' accession (and hence called *post-nati*) should be considered as naturalized Englishmen. But Parliament rejected the proposals. The traditional antagonism between the two nations was still strong; and the English, as the richer nation, were jealous lest the Scots should gain unfairly from the union.

Actually, the status of the *post-nati* was settled in a manner beyond Parliament's control. The test case of whether Robert Colvill, or Calvin, could own land in England was brought before the English judges. Though Colvill had been born in Edinburgh, in 1605, the judges ruled that, in accordance with English Common Law, he was a natural subject of the English King. Henceforward this rule would apply to all *post-nati*.

Overiding the Will of Parliament

The judges' verdict was sound in law, but the process of securing the royal will by appealing to the law-courts to override, or to evade, the will of Parliament was capable of serious abuse. The method was to be a favourite one of James and of the Stuarts generally in their disputes with Parliament. The judges' verdict in Colvill's case was not delivered until June 1608. Already two years earlier James had used a similar method to evade the Commons' control of finance.

The case in question had arisen indirectly from the dissolution of the Levant Company. This company, formed during the latter part of Elizabeth's reign, had secured for its members a monopoly of English trade with Venice and Turkey. The company had a varied and not very prosperous history, and in 1603 it surrendered its charter. As a consequence, the King would lose the annual payment of £4000 which the company had been paying to the Crown in return for its privileges. This was the more serious because James was spending considerably in excess of his income. Hence, though the Levant trade was thrown open, the King tried to compensate himself by levying a customs duty on imported currants, which were one of the most valuable elements in Levant trade.

Previous to the formation of the Levant Company, a similar duty had been levied; and for that reason the duty might be regarded as legitimate now that the company no longer existed. On the other hand, the duty was not part of the customary standing revenue of the Crown, nor was it granted by Parliament. Such a duty, imposed by the King's arbitrary power, was known as an "imposition."

One merchant, named John Bate, refused to pay the duty which the customs officers demanded on a cartload of currants. This challenge to the Crown's right to levy impositions could not be ignored, and Bate was tried before the Exchequer Court which gave judgement for the King. But the court was careful to make clear the legal reasons for its decision. It claimed that the King had the right to levy customs duties without Parliament's consent because such duties were a means of regulating foreign trade, and the direction of all foreign affairs was within the royal prerogative. Thus the verdict was far from allowing to the King indiscriminate authority to impose any kind of tax or duty irrespective of Parliament's wishes.

Nevertheless the effect of Bates case was to open the way for further arbitrary taxation that would not always keep within the limits of the Exchequer definition. The immediate effect was the issue in 1608 of a new *Book of Rates* sanctioning further impositions which were calculated to bring in £70,000 annually.

Even this addition to the revenue was not enough to meet all the King's expenses. In 1610 Salisbury—who two years earlier had become Lord Treasurer while retaining the Secretaryship—tried to make with Parliament a settlement, called the Great Contract, which would place the King's revenue on a sound basis. His scheme was that the King should renounce the income he derived from out-of-date feudal aids, and in return should receive from Parliament a fixed annual amount, which, when added to income derived from other sources, would assure to the King £600,000 annually, which with care would suffice for all his needs. Long discussions took place about the particular dues which the King should renounce and about the exact amount which Parliament was to grant in exchange. Finally, in July, agreement was reached on all points, and the Commons drew up a statement embodying the terms.

While discussing the Great Contract, Parliament had been calling attention to many grievances in matters of religion. These included the continued silencing of the Puritan ministers who had refused to conform to the Canons of 1604, and the pluralities and non-residence commonly practised by the clergy. By this time James and the Established Church were too closely wedded to make concessions. As a result, the breach between King and Parliament widened, and the Great Contract remained unconfirmed. Such an atmosphere of mutual distrust made the continuance of parliamentary business unprofitable, and in February 1611 James dissolved the first Parliament of his reign.

The Civil Wars of 1640–1660: An Overview

Christopher Hill

In the following excerpt, historian Christopher Hill provides an overview of the major events and influential leaders of the English civil wars. Hill explains the struggle for power between King Charles I and Parliament and the chain of events that forced Charles to flee London, beginning the civil wars. The author outlines the major military engagements between the parliamentary armies and the Royalists, who supported Charles. To create a unified force against the Royalists, Hill writes, Parliament formed the New Model Army and passed the Self-Denying Ordinance, which stripped many in Parliament of their military commissions. Although the army defeated the Royalists at Naseby in June 1645, Hill notes that a rift had developed between Parliament and the army that continued throughout the interregnum. Although some in Parliament feared the power of the New Model Army and the radical constitutional changes proposed by the Levellers, Hill claims that Parliament mistrusted Charles I more, and in 1649, set up a court to try the king, who was executed on January 30, effectively abolishing the monarchy. Hill also reviews the generals who led the civil wars, including Oliver Cromwell, whose political influence and military success against Royalist armies helped unify, for a time, the divided Parliament. In addition, Hill explores the conflicts that plagued the new military government during the early years of the interregnum and after the election of Cromwell as Lord Protector, including controversial grants of land forfeited by those who had supported the monarchy, attempts to subvert Cromwell's military rule, efforts to establish a more democratic constitution, and opposition to continued religious intolerance. These parliamentary conflicts between the army, the radical Levellers, and moderate Presbyterians escalated, paving the way for a Royalist revolt, and in 1660, the exiled Charles II promised Parliament indemnity from prosecution for those who had opposed Charles I, settlement of land disputes, payment of arrears to the army, and religious tolerance. After decades of disagreement and civil war, a weary Parliament asked Charles II to return to rule England. Former master of Balliol College, in Oxford, Christopher Hill is a well-known and respected historian.

W hen the Long Parliament met [in November 1640] the House of Commons at once impeached [Thomas Wentworth, first earl of] Strafford and [archbishop William] Laud. Other ministers fled from the country. Strafford was executed in May 1641, under an Act of Attainder which had been substituted for impeachment. A Triennial Act provided for regular meetings of Parliament, with an automatic procedure if the King failed to summon them. An Act was passed against dissolving this Parliament without its own consent. It thus for the first time became a permanent part of the constitution. This revolutionary innovation was necessary if loans were to be raised, since only Parliament could inspire confidence. Collection of tunnage and poundage was forbidden with consent of Parliament; the judgment against [John] Hampden [who had refused to pay these taxes] and the levying of Ship Money [taxes] were declared illegal, together with the other non-Parliamentary taxes of the eleven years of personal government. Prerogative courts—Star Chamber, council of the North and in Wales—and the High Commission were abolished. . . .Victims of the personal government were released and compensated.

In October 1641 a rebellion took place in Ireland, at last liberated from Strafford's iron hand. Many hundreds, probably many thousands, of Englishmen were killed. The opposition group in Parliament refused to trust a royal nominee with command of an army to reconquer Ireland. So the question of ultimate power in the state was raised. In the panic caused by news of the Irish rebellion the Grand Remonstrance was adopted, a comprehensive indictment of royal policy. It passed the Commons by only eleven votes. For by now parties had formed. [King] Charles [I] replied by bringing a body of armed men to the House in an attempt to arrest [John] Pym, [John] Hampden, and three other leaders of the opposition group. They took refuge in the City and resolutions in their support poured in from all over the country. Charles quitted London, of which he had lost control; the Five Members [that had led the opposition] returned in triumph. Almost the last act of the King was to agree to the exclusion of Bishops from the House of Lords (February 1642) and to a Bill for raising troops for Ireland. The conflict had now extended from Westminster to the country at large, and civil war became inevitable. Desultory negotiations took place as Charles roamed over the north of England. In April Sir John Hotham [who had at one time been replaced by an appointee of Charles] refused to admit him into Hull; and in August the King raised his standard at Nottingham. [Robert Devereux], the Earl of Essex, was appointed to command the Parliamentary armies.

The Early Battles

The first engagement of the Civil War was a drawn battle at Edgehill (23rd October). Charles advanced on London, but was faced by the trained bands at Turnham Green in November, and withdrew to Oxford. Meanwhile the Marquis of Newcastle secured the north of England for the King, and Sir Ralph Hopton the south-west. In 1643 an attempt was made to advance on London from these two centres and from Oxford. This was checked by the resistance of Hull, Plymouth, and Gloucester, and by the march of the London trained bands to relieve Gloucester. They fought another drawn battle at Newbury on their way back.

In September, in the hope of breaking the military deadlock, Parliament signed the Solemn League and Covenant with the Scots, and in January 1644 a Scottish army crossed the Border again. In July the battle of Marston Moor was won by the combined armies of Scotland, Yorkshire (Sir Thomas Fairfax) and the Eastern Association (the Earl of Manchester and Oliver Cromwell). Control of the north passed to Parliament. But Parliament, with no united command, did not follow up its victory. The Earl of Essex was cut off in the south-west, and his army surrendered at Lostwithiel in September. This and the indecisive second Battle of Newbury (25th October) strengthened the hands of those who had been calling for the elimination of half-hearted officers and for a unified command. The New Model Army was formed with Fairfax as general, and the Self-Denying Ordinance (April 1645) deprived all peers and members of Parliament of their commissions. The immediate result was the decisive rout of the Royalists [those who supported Charles I] at Naseby (14th June). The rest of the war was a series of mopping-up operations, culminating in the surrender of Oxford in June 1646 after Charles had given himself up to the Scots. The latter handed him over to the English Parliament on 30th January 1647. Meanwhile Archbishop Laud had been executed in January 1645 and episcopacy abolished in October 1646. The same ordinance offered Bishops' lands for sale.

The New Model Army

The controversies over the New Model Army and the Self-Denying Ordinance had seen the formation of two parties among the Parliamentarians. These we usually call Presbyterians and Independents, the conservatives and the radicals. Once the fighting had ended, the "Presbyterian" majority in Parliament, which had long disliked and feared the New Model Army, proposed to disband it, with its wages unpaid, offering the rank and file the chance of volunteering for service in Ireland. This led to a mutiny, and to the election of Agitators [a body of men appointed by the Army to look after their interests] by the regiments. After some hesitation, Cromwell and most of the officers threw in their lot with the men. Those who did not were deprived of their commissions. Cornet Joyce was sent to take the royal prisoner out of Parliament's control into that of the Army. A General Council of the Army was set up, composed of the Generals and representatives of other officers and of the rank and file. The newly united Army issued a manifesto declaring that it would not disband or separate until its grievances had been met. It called for a purge of Parliament, an early dissolution, and new elections. Impeaching eleven Presbyterian leaders, the Army occupied London and forced their withdrawal from the Commons (August 1647). But now divisions arose among the Independents. Negotiations took place between Charles and the Generals for the establishment of limited monarchy (the Heads of Proposals). These roused the suspicions of radicals in London (the Levellers) and in the Army who produced a rival, more democratic constitution, the Agreement of the People. The two constitutions were discussed in the Army Council at Putney in October, between spokesmen of the Generals and of the Agitators. Deadlock resulted, and finally Cromwell forcibly terminated the discussions. The Agitators were ordered back to their regiments (15th November). One of the Agitators was shot and the recalcitrant regiments subdued.

Cromwell was able to do this because on 11th November the King had escaped from the Army's custody and fled to the Isle of Wight. The Army had to reunite in face of imminent renewal of civil war. In December Charles signed an agreement with the Scottish commissioners in London, as a result of which a Scottish army entered England in July 1648. But it was an army led by [James] Hamilton and the nobility, not the disciplined army of the Covenant. It was easily defeated at Preston by Cromwell, who had previously disposed of a "Presbyterian"-Royalist revolt in South Wales, whilst Fairfax reduced a Royalist force in Colchester.

The Monarchy Is Abolished

The "Presbyterians" in Parliament had meanwhile entered into negotiations with the King (the Treaty of Newport). But by now the Generals felt that the King could not be trusted, and were determined to settle accounts with him. They revived their alliance with the Levellers. London was occupied once more, . . . and a court was set up to try the King. On 30th January 1649 he was executed as a traitor to the good people of England. Monarchy and the House of Lords were abolished. But there were no democratic reforms, and the republican government soon forfeited Leveller support. There were demonstrations against it, and in March the Leveller leaders were imprisoned. There were also mutinies in the Army, the most serious of which was put down at Burford in May. Henceforth the government had to face opposition from left as well as right.

Nevertheless, its achievements were considerable. The Irish revolt, which had dragged miserably on since 1641, was crushed in a whirlwind campaign by Cromwell, which started with the storming of Drogheda and the massacre of its garrison. An Act for the Settlement of Ireland (12th August 1652) provided for expropriation of the owners of some two-thirds of the land, and for transplantation of the bulk of the Irish population to Connaught. This was never fully carried out, but a great deal of Irish land passed to London merchants who had lent money to Parliament, and to soldiers in lieu of wages. In 1650 Scotland, where Charles II had been recognised, was invaded. Cromwell, succeeding Fairfax as Commander-in-Chief, won the Battle of Dunbar on 3rd September. Exactly a year later Charles and an invading Scottish army were routed at Worcester. Scotland, like Ireland, was united to England, and occupied by a military garrison. Meanwhile the Commonwealth's authority had been asserted over the colonies. Navigation Acts of October 1650 and October 1651 aimed at wresting the carrying trade from the Dutch. They led to the First Dutch War (1652–4).

The Lord Protector

The Rump of the Long Parliament was expelled by Cromwell in April 1653. It had sold crown and Dean and Chapter lands, and the lands of some 700 Royalists, but produced few domestic reforms. In July an assembly was summoned by Cromwell, composed of 140 men selected by the Army leaders, in part from nominees of the Independent congregations. It came to be known as the Barebones Parliament, a social sneer directed against Praise-God Barbon, one of its members, who was a leather-seller. Proposals for radical reform frightened the conservatives in this assembly, and in December they engineered its dissolution. Power was handed back to the Lord General—i.e. to the Army. The officers produced a new constitution, the Instrument of Government, probably drafted by Major-General [John] Lambert, under which Cromwell was given the position of Lord Protector. The franchise was redistributed. But when a Parliament met, in September 1654, it refused to accept the Army's ascendancy, and was preparing a new constitution when Cromwell dissolved it in January 1655. A minor Royalist rising followed in March, and the opportunity was seized to extend the machinery of military rule. England was divided into eleven regions and a Major-General was set over each, with wide powers, including command of the militia. A decimation tax on Royalists was introduced, which it was hoped would finance the new system; but it came nowhere near doing so. In November 1654 a merchant called Cony had challenged the Protector's right to collect taxation under the Instrument of Government. Cromwell managed to obtain a favourable verdict only after dismissing a judge and prosecuting Cony's counsel, in a way reminiscent of Charles I. Money was badly needed, and another Parliament was summoned for September 1656.

A Foreign Policy

One reason for calling a Parliament was the foreign situation. In 1654 Cromwell had made peace with the Netherlands on favourable terms. He had signed an agreement which opened the Portuguese empire to English trade, and had established friendly relations with Sweden. He had equipped an expedition to attack the Spanish West Indies. This failed to capture its main objective, Hispaniola, but occupied Jamaica. In 1655 a Spanish treasure fleet was intercepted and in 1657 another destroyed. In 1655 England came to an agreement with France, by which the exiled court of Charles Stuart was expelled from France. This broadened into a treaty in March 1657; the Protector agreed to help France to defeat Spain in Europe. Dunkirk was captured at the Battle of the Dunes (June 1658) and handed over to England.

The government had hoped to use war against the traditional Spanish enemy to rally support in the Parliament of 1656. Money was indeed voted for the war, but, even after many members of Parliament had been excluded, the House rejected a bill to continue the militia under the Major-Generals. The members showed their hostility to the government's policy of toleration by savage persecution of the Quaker James Nayler. Cromwell failed to intervene to save him; but after Nayler had been flogged, branded, and bored through the tongue, the Protector at once asked the House on what authority they had acted. This, together with the discussions which had no doubt been going on behind the scenes since the rejection of the Militia Bill in January 1657, led to a constitutional debate and to the framing of the Humble Petition and Advice. This was a revised version of the Parliamentary constitution of 1654–5. Cromwell was offered the crown, and control of the executive was transferred to Parliament, which was to consist of two Houses. The new franchise instituted under the Instrument of Government was dropped. The Petition was fiercely opposed by the Army leaders, and after long hesitations Cromwell finally refused the crown but accepted the rest of the constitution with modifications. Lambert, who had been losing influence for some time, was dismissed from all his offices. But when Parliament met again in January 1658 the hitherto excluded members were admitted on taking an oath to be faithful to the Protector. In consequence opponents of the constitution captured control of the Commons, and in February Cromwell dissolved Parliament. Seven months later he died. The Petition and Advice had authorised him to nominate his successor, and his eldest son Richard succeeded him.

Making Way for Charles II

Richard had none of his father's prestige with the Army. A Parliament (elected on the old franchise) met in January 1659 and recognised the new Protector. The Commons also accepted the Other House, though reserving the right of peers who had been faithful to Parliament to sit in it. But the republican malcontents revived their alliance with Army malcontents, and the latter now included many higher officers. In April 1659 Parliament tried to assert control over the Army; the Generals retorted by forcing the Protector to dissolve it. Power reverted to the Army. On 5th May the Generals restored the remnant of the Rump, and Richard retired into oblivion. A national "Presbyterian"-Royalist revolt, planned for August 1659, took place only in Cheshire, where it was defeated by Lambert. But relations between Rump and Army deteriorated as the former tried to subordinate the latter to its control, and in October the Parliament was expelled once more. But it proved impossible to levy taxes except by military violence. The City of London refused to co-operate with the military government; and General [George] Monck, commanding the army in Scotland, was authorised by some of the deposed Council of State to take military action on their behalf. He advanced towards the Border. An army under Lambert was sent to oppose him. As long as this was paid, there were more rank-and-file desertions from Monck to Lambert than from Lambert to Monck. But Monck had more money and Lambert's army gradually melted away. The Generals in London capitulated and recalled the Rump in December; but Monck crossed into England.

He was greeted on the way south with organised petitions for "a free Parliament," but kept his own counsel until he arrived in the capital (3rd February 1660). The first task Parliament gave him was to arrest leading members of London's government and to destroy its defensive gates and chains. Monck complied, but immediately thereafter retreated into the City and sent Parliament an ultimatum calling for a dissolution. Monck's surrender to the City ensured the downfall of the Rump. He opened the doors of Parliament to the members excluded in 1648, and they carried out a pledge to Monck by dissolving themselves on 16th March, after providing for elections to a new Parliament. This met on 25th April. It was "Presbyterian"-Royalist in composition. The House of Lords was restored (though Royalist peers were still excluded), and Parliament accepted the Declaration which Charles II had issued from Breda on 4th April. By this he offered an indemnity, settlement of disputes about land sales, payment of arrears to the Army, and liberty of conscience—all subject to confirmation by Parliament. On 25th May Charles II returned to England.

The Trial and Execution of Charles Stuart

Parliament, King Charles I, and the Tribunal

The execution of King Charles I by Parliament on January 30, 1649, shocked and terrified many of Charles's subjects and had repercussions throughout Europe. The following documents—the ordinance establishing a tribunal to try Charles I, the proclamation by Charles I denying the legality of the tribunal, and the sentence of the tribunal—reveal the tensions between the Parliamentarians, who challenged the power of the king, and the Royalists, who supported Charles I and his divine right to rule. The legal procedures used to assemble the tribunal and try the king were without precedent, and the king's reasoning in opposing the tribunal was sound in both law and history, which was to haunt England for centuries.

Ordinance Establishing a Tribunal to Try the King, January 6, 1649

Whereas it is notorious that Charles Stuart, the now King of England, not content with the many encroachments which his predecessors had made upon the people in their rights and freedom, hath had a wicked design totally to subvert the ancient and fundamental laws and liberties of this nation, and in their place to introduce an ar-

Excerpted from John Rushworth, *Historical Collections*, 2nd edition, vol. 7, 1721.

bitrary and tyrannical government, and that besides all other evil ways and means to bring his design to pass, he hath prosecuted it with fire and sword, levied and maintained a civil war in the land, against the Parliament and kingdom; whereby this country hath been miserably wasted, the public treasure exhausted, trade decayed, thousands of people murdered, and infinite other mischiefs committed; for all which high and treasonable offences the said Charles Stuart might long since have justly been brought to exemplary and condign punishment: whereas also the Parliament, well hoping that the restraint and imprisonment of his person, after it had pleased God to deliver him into their hands, would have quieted the distempers of the kingdom, did forbear to proceed judicially against him, but found, by sad experience, that such their remissness served only to encourage him and his accomplices in the continuance of their evil practices, and in raising new commotions, rebellions and invasions: for prevention therefore of the like or greater inconveniences, and to the end no Chief Officer or Magistrate whatsoever may hereafter presume, traitorously and maliciously, to imagine or contrive the enslaving or destroying of the English nation, and to expect impunity for so doing, be it enacted and ordained by the (Lords and) Commons in Parliament assembled, and it is hereby enacted and ordained by the authority thereof, that the Earls of Kent, Nottingham, Pembroke, Denbigh and Mulgrave, the Lord Grey of Wark, Lord Chief Justice Rolle of the King's Bench, Lord Chief Justice St. John of the Common Pleas, and Lord Chief Baron Wylde, the Lord Fairfax, Lieutenant-General Cromwell, and others [in all about 136], shall be and are hereby appointed and required to be Commissioners and judges for the hearing, trying and judging of the said Charles Stuart; and the said Commissioners, or any twenty or more of them, shall be, and are hereby authorised and constituted an High Court of justice, to meet and sit at such convenient times and place as by the said Commissioners, or the major part, or twenty or more of them, under their hands and seals, shall be appointed and notified by proclamation in the Great Hall or Palace-Yard of Westminster; and to adjourn from time to time, and from place to place, as the said High Court, or the major part thereof, at meeting shall hold fit; and to take order for the charging of him, the said Charles Stuart, with the crimes and treasons above mentioned, and for receiving his personal answer thereunto, and for examination of witnesses upon oath (which the Court hath hereby authority to administer) or otherwise, and taking any other evidence concerning the same; and thereupon, or in default of such answer, to proceed to final sentence according to justice and the merit of the cause; and such final sentence to execute, or cause to be executed, speedily and impartially.

And the said Court is hereby authorised and required to choose and appoint all such officers, attendants and other circumstances as they, or the major part of them, shall in any sort judge necessary or useful for the orderly and good managing of the premises; and Thomas Lord Fairfax the General, and all officers and soldiers under his command, and all officers of justice and other well-affected persons, are hereby authorised and required to be aiding and assisting unto the said Court in the due execution of the trust hereby committed unto them; provided that this Act, and the authority hereby granted, do continue in force for the space of one month from the date of the making thereof, and no longer.

The King Denies the Tribunal's Legality and Jurisdiction, January 23, 1649

Having already made my protestations, not only against the illegality of this pretended Court, but also, that no earthly power can justly call me (who am your King) in question as a delinquent, I would not any more open my mouth upon this occasion, more than to refer myself to what I have spoken, were I in this case alone concerned: but the duty I owe to God in the preservation of the true liberty of my people will not suffer me at this time to be silent: for, how can any free-born subject of England call life or anything he possesseth his own, if power without right daily make new, and abrogate the old fundamental laws of the land which I now take to be the present case? Wherefore when I came hither, I expected that you would have endeavoured to have satisfied me concerning these grounds which hinder me to answer to your pretended impeachment. But since I see that nothing I can say will move you to it (though negatives are not so naturally proved as affirmatives) yet I will show you the reason why I am confident you cannot judge me, nor indeed the meanest man in England: for I will not (like you) without showing a reason, seek to impose a belief upon my subjects.

There is no proceeding just against any man, but what is warranted, either by God's laws or the municipal laws of the country where he lives. Now I am most confident this day's proceeding cannot be warranted by God's laws; for, on the contrary, the authority of obedience unto Kings is clearly warranted, and strictly commanded in both the Old and New Testament, which, if denied, I am ready instantly to prove.

And for the question now in hand, there it is said, that "where the word of a King is, there is power; and who may say unto him, what dost thou?" Eccles., viii. 4. Then for the law of this land, I am no less confident, that no learned lawyer will affirm that an impeachment can lie against the King, they all going in his name: and one of their maxims is, that the King can do no wrong. Besides, the law upon which you ground your proceedings, must either be old or new: if old, show it; if new, tell what authority, warranted by the fundamental laws of the land, hath made it, and when. But how the House of Commons can erect a Court of Judicature, which was never one itself (as is well known to all lawyers) I leave to God and the world to judge. And it were full as strange, that they should pretend to make laws without King or Lords' House, to any that have heard speak of the laws of England.

And admitting, but not granting, that the people of England's commission could grant your pretended power, I see nothing you can show for that; for certainly you never asked the question of the tenth man in the kingdom, and in this way you manifestly wrong even the poorest ploughman, if you demand not his free consent; nor can you pretend any colour for this your pretended commission, without the consent at least of the major part of every man in England of whatsoever quality or condition, which I am sure you never went about to seek, so far are you from having it. Thus you see that I speak not for my own right alone, as I am your King, but also for the true liberty of all my subjects, which consists, not in the power of government, but in living under such laws, such a government, as may give themselves the best assurance of their lives, and property of their goods; nor in this must or do I forget the privileges of both Houses of Parliament, which this day's proceedings do not only

King Charles I defends himself before the tribunal.

violate, but likewise occasion the greatest breach of their public faith that (I believe) ever was heard of, with which I am far from charging the two Houses; for all the pretended crimes laid against me bear date long before this Treaty at Newport, in which I having concluded as much as in me lay, and hopefully expecting the Houses' agreement thereunto, I was suddenly surprised and hurried from thence as a prisoner; upon which account I am against my will brought hither, where since I am come, I cannot but to my power defend the ancient laws and liberties of this kingdom, together with my own just right. Then for anything I can see, the higher House is totally excluded; and for the House of Commons, it is too well known that the major part of them are detained or deterred from sitting; so as if I had no other, this were sufficient for me to protest against the lawfulness of your pretended Court. Besides all this, the peace of the kingdom is not the least in my thoughts; and what hope of settlement is there, so long as power reigns without rule or law, changing the whole frame of that government under which this kingdom hath flourished for many hundred years? (nor will I say what will fall out in case this lawless, unjust proceeding against me do go on) and believe it, the Commons of England will not thank you for this change; for they will remember how happy they have been of late years under the reigns of Queen Elizabeth, the King my father [James I], and myself, until the beginning of these unhappy troubles, and will have cause to doubt, that they shall never be so happy under any new: and by this time it will be too sensibly evident that the arms I took up were only to defend the fundamental laws of this kingdom against those who have supposed my power hath totally changed the ancient government.

Thus, having showed you briefly the reasons why I cannot submit to your pretended authority, without violating the trust which I have from God for the welfare and liberty of my people, I expect from you either clear reasons to convince my judgment, showing me that I am in an error (and then truly I will answer) or that you will withdraw your proceedings

This I intended to speak in Westminster Hall on Monday, January 22, but against reason was hindered to show my reasons.

The Tribunal Sentences Charles Stuart, January 27, 1649

Whereas the Commons of England assembled in Parliament, have by their late Act intituled [titled] an Act of the Commons of England assembled in Parliament, for erecting an High Court of justice for the trying and judging of Charles Stuart, King of England, authorised and constituted us an High Court of justice for the trying and judging of the said Charles Stuart for the crimes and treasons in the said

Act mentioned; by virtue whereof the said Charles Stuart hath been several times convented before this High Court, where the first day, being Saturday, the 20th of January instant, in pursuance of the said Act, a charge of high treason and other high crimes was, in the behalf of the people of England, exhibited against him and read openly unto him, wherein he was charged, that he, the said Charles Stuart, being admitted King of England, and therein trusted with a limited power to govern by, and according to the law of the land, and not otherwise; and by his trust, oath, and office, being obliged to use the power committed to him for the good and benefit of the people, and for the preservation of their rights and liberties; yet, nevertheless, out of a wicked design to erect and uphold in himself an unlimited and tyrannical power to rule according to his will, and to overthrow the rights and liberties of the people, and to take away and make void the foundations thereof, and of all redress and remedy of misgovernment, which by the fundamental constitutions of this kingdom were reserved on the people's behalf in the right and power of frequent and successive Parliaments, or national meetings in Council; he, the said Charles Stuart, for accomplishment of such his designs, and for the protecting of himself and his adherents in his and their wicked practices, to the same end hath traitorously and maliciously levied war against the present Parliament, and people therein represented, as with the circumstances of time and place is in the said charge more particularly set forth; and that he hath thereby caused and procured many thousands of the free people of this nation to be slain. . . .

[He is author of the] unnatural, cruel, and bloody wars, and therein guilty of high treason, and of the murders, rapines, burnings, spoils, desolations, damage, and mischief to this nation acted and committed in the said war, and occasioned thereby. For all which treasons and crimes this Court doth adjudge that he, the said Charles Stuart, as a tyrant, traitor, murderer, and public enemy to the good people of this nation, shall be put to death by the severing of his head from his body.

[After the sentence was read], His Majesty then said, Will you hear me a word, Sir?

PRESIDENT OF THE COURT. Sir, you are not to be heard after the sentence.

HIS MAJESTY. No, Sir?

PRESIDENT. No, Sir, by your favour, Sir. Guards, withdraw your prisoner.

HIS MAJESTY. I may speak after sentence, by your favour, Sir, I may speak after sentence, ever. By your favour, hold—the sentence, Sir —I say, Sir, I do—I am not suffered to speak, expect what justice other people may have.

The Restoration of the Monarchy in 1660

J.P. Kenyon

According to historian J.P. Kenyon, the Restoration, which began with
the return of Charles II to the throne of England, marked the beginning
of a new age in England. Although in 1660, most seventeenth-century
English longed for a return to life as it had been during the reign of
Charles I, Kenyon explores some of the philosophical changes that prevented such a return. Kenyon points out that despite fading Puritanism,
the driving force opposing the monarchy before and during the civil
war, the Anglican church that supported monarchy was now losing its
power to developing interest in natural science, a result of discoveries
by scientists like Isaac Newton. These discoveries focused on the power
of the individual, eroding the power of hierarchical religion that had
dominated life before the civil war. Although the political theories of
the philosopher Thomas Hobbes supported absolute monarchy, Hobbes
used science, not religion, to explain his philosophy. Furthermore, despite Hobbes's philosophical support and the support on his return by
much of the nation, Charles II failed to strengthen the monarchy, weakening his authority by delegating responsibility and overspending. The
late J.P. Kenyon was Distinguished Professor Emeritus at the University of Kansas; a fellow of Christ's College, Cambridge; and a professor of modern history at the University of St. Andrews, in Fife, Scotland, and the University of Hull, in England.

In retrospect it is clear that the Restoration marked the beginning of a new age, though contemporaries avoided seeing this. It is idle to pretend that the reigns of Charles II and James II were simply an interlude between two revolutions, 1649 and 1688. In the furnace of the Civil Wars England had forged a new military and commercial machine, and her presence in Europe was enormously enhanced. Charles II's interventions in Europe were botched and bungled, but they were taken much more seriously than his father's. The fact that the upper classes had dabbled with revolution, then abandoned it, enhanced the monarchy's strength and prestige, but its authority was now defined and confined, and many issues which had been crucial to Charles I and his parliaments were dead under Charles II; extra-parliamentary taxation was virtually unthinkable, freedom of speech in Parliament was taken for granted, and an efficient system of taxation centred on the excise was now accepted as a fact of life. Not far in the future lay a style of adversarial politics not envisaged before the Great Rebellion, in which political allegiance was not necessarily associated with government, for or against.

Returning to the Status Quo

Nevertheless, in 1660 there was a general urge to return to the *status quo ante bellum*, or something near it. By simply overriding any act or ordinance which had not received the royal assent, the Convention Parliament of 1660 turned back the clock to the spring of 1641. This left the Act of 1642 excluding the bishops from the House of Lords, which was repealed by the Cavalier Parliament [that supported Charles I] in 1661. It was thus a decisively negative settlement, and the only important positive enactment, the Militia Act of 1661, which placed the command of the armed forces unambiguously in the King, only confirmed the general desire to return to the *status quo*.

There had been a shift in the balance of power, but no one would acknowledge it. The only advance in the power of Parliament—as distinct from restrictions imposed on the King—was the Triennial Act of 1641, which on the dissolution of the Long Parliament at last took effect. This was a muddled measure—it was never clear whether it was intended to secure regular general elections or regular sessions of Parliament—but in any case it was decisively amended in 1664 so as to make it permissive, not mandatory. The fact that since 1642 Parliament had defeated the King's father twice, executed him, abolished the upper house, routed the present king, conquered Ireland and Scotland and lorded it over Western Europe, was simply ignored. True, these stirring events had much less effect on the composition or attitude of Parliament than might have been expected, but surely they could not be ignored altogether?

The Fall of Puritanism

But the failure of Parliament to assert itself in 1660 was just one aspect of a general trend which still defies analysis—the collapse of Puritanism. This vital intellectual and spiritual force, credited with the downfall of the monarchy (and not only by nineteenth- and twentieth-century historians but also by acute contemporaries like Thomas Hobbes), abruptly faded away in 1660, and with it the "Good Old Cause," and all those other dreams of a restricted monarchy, general toleration, a New Deal and a New Age.

In fact . . . the power and cohesion of Puritanism was much exaggerated, not least by the royalists. In terms of influence on government it reached its apogee in 1648, then it was betrayed by a bitter quarrel between the right-wing Puritans, or "Presbyterians," bent on the imposition of their own ecclesiastical discipline, and a triumphant army committed to universal toleration. In the mêlée men took sides on a class basis, and the concept of a New Millennium just around the corner, which had gained many converts amongst the upper classes in the early days of the Long Parliament, now subsided into a working-class delusion with dangerous radical undertones. Thereafter the notoriety of the Levellers [a radical Puritan sect that advocated religious and political equality] and the excesses of the independent Sects, which it is safe to say never constituted more than a small minority of the population, strengthened the conservatism of the "Presbyterians" and encouraged the drift towards a conventional church establishment. At the same time the *laissez-faire* attitude of the Interregnum [the time between the reign of Charles I and his successor Charles II] governments gave the Anglicans [of the Church of England] a considerable measure of *de facto* toleration, as it did the Roman Catholics. The precipitate circumstances of the Restoration, and the fatal association of Puritanism with regicide in the public mind, did the rest. . . .

The Influence of Natural Science

As Puritanism fell, so the Church of England rose, but it only rose towards an Indian summer. In common with all other hierarchical churches, including the Roman Catholic, its power over men's minds was being eroded. The scientific spirit and the rationalist approach were the dragon's teeth of Puritanism. The nature and extent of Puritanism's contribution to the new natural science is still fiercely debated. No question but that the Puritan pursuit of natural learning was inchoate, over-confident and intellectually disorderly; but the savants who flourished in the general breakdown of educational and intellectual supervision in the 1640s and 1650s came to realize that there was now a natural science, quite distinct from religion. Taking their inspiration from [Francis] Bacon's *Novum Organum* (1620), a book whose posthumous influence was incalculable, they proposed the thorough reform of education and the law and the wholesale encouragement of technology and invention by the State, in the confident expectation that through what Bacon called "The Great Instauration" perfectibility was attainable now, in a world in which intelligence was set free from the trammels of the imagination. This may seem a strange doctrine for the Puritans to embrace, but stranger things arose in the ferment of the Interregnum: divorce was seriously discussed, and strongly advocated by [poet John] Milton, who had an unhappy marriage behind him; civil marriage was instituted by the Little Parliament of 1653; and there was even talk of raising the inferior social status of women.

Unfortunately, all such schemes were woefully unsuccessful. Plans for a new technology never left the drawing board, the campaign for a new system of education foundered on the indifference of government—for the Interregnum governments proved no more liberal than their predecessors. [Oliver] Cromwell bowed to public pressure for law reform, but even he was defeated by the inertia of the legal profession, and the example set by his Chancery ordinance of 1654 was ignored in 1660. (Legal reform had to wait until the 1870s.)

A New Focus on the Individual

But it was not all in vain; the spirit of rational inquiry could not easily be exorcized. The Puritan emphasis on the confrontation between the individual and God was soon deflected towards a preoccupation with the individual alone, and in this they, or their successors, were fortified by [René] Descartes, to whom the universe was an objective, uncaring machine. The Royal Society "for improving natural knowledge" came under the patronage of Charles II, that great improviser, in 1662, but it had grown out of the meetings of various groups of savants in London and Oxford in the previous decade. In fact, William Harvey, whose discovery of the circulation of the blood (in *De Motu Cordis et Sanguinis*, 1628) and the fundamentals of reproduction (in *De Gentratione Animalium*, 1653), flourished originally under Charles I, and Robert Boyle, the father both of physics and chemistry, began his life's work in the 1650s (his most famous work, *The Sceptical Chemist,* appeared in 1661). But the tide rolled on, and [Isaac] Newton's epoch-making work on optics, physics and astronomy (the *Principia Mathematica,* 1686) was published in the reign of James II, not usually regarded as the most enlightened of rulers, and under the auspices, as President of the Royal Society, of Samuel Pepys. John Locke, in *An Essay Concerning Human Understanding* (1690), completed the ruin of previous philosophical and moral systems by rejecting totally the theory of innate ideas and arguing instead that human personality owed everything to upbringing and education. None of these men—all of them devout Christians—willed the end, but they used the means by which reason supplanted faith, and before their attack organized, hierarchical religion continued to crumble all over Europe, not least in England, where the confidence of Anglican churchmen was further undermined by their failure to eliminate Dissent and their failure to accommodate to the latest fluctuations in the doctrine of political obligation.

For among the most famous children of the new scientific age was Thomas Hobbes, who reacted to the Great Rebellion by propounding a theory of political obligation based on the unchanging laws of geometry and the constitution of the human body. The result, in *Leviathan* (1651), was a theory of life and politics which was based entirely on fear, not love, force, not persuasion, which had no place in it for man's higher nature, and reduced religion to a matter of superstition. Moreover, it posited a theory of absolute despotism which drove the theory of the Divine Right of Kings to its utmost logical conclusion and beyond. It would have been better if Hobbes's critics could have ignored him, as they ignored the agrarian republican theories of James Harrington (*Oceana,* 1656), another spawn of the Interregnum. But it was a tribute to Hobbes that his enemies could never leave off publicizing and propagating his views by opposing them; and though he did not find in Charles II the platonic philosopher-king who would put his theories into practice, the bases of political obligation were never the same again after *Leviathan.*

The Economic Climate

The economic parameters of society were changing, too. The landed classes as a whole had stood up remarkably well to the penal fines and high taxation imposed on them by the Interregnum governments. Few royalists had to sell their lands to pay fines, and those whose estates were confiscated received them back after the Restoration; the immediate social effects of the Interregnum were surprisingly muted. But a dragging burden of debt lasting over generations, the return of high taxation, especially after the Revolution of 1688, and a sharp fall in agricultural prices at the end of the century forced many small landed families "out of business," a concealed, long-term effect of the Civil Wars. The larger the estate the more economical it was to manage, the easier it was to pay non-graduated taxation, and the easier it was to find the capital for agricultural improvement; manuring, marling, draining, planting root crops to feed winter cattle and improving the breed of stock. The preservation of such estates from the depredations of improvident heirs or the temptation to sell was also facilitated during Charles II's reign by the introduction of a new system of entail known as the "strict settlement.". . . .

The rise of a wealthy career aristocracy was just one symptom of England's increasing prosperity. The slumps and depressions which had been a feature of the first half of the century recurred in the second half, but their effect was muted; for instance, England withstood the disastrous harvests of 1697–8 with ease, while financing a major war on an unprecedented scale; earlier she withstood the enormous dislocation of the Great Plague of 1665 and the Great Fire of 1666 in successive years (again during a major war) with much greater case than she thought she had. . . .

The Appeal of Charles II

Charles II seemed the very man to take advantage of the prevailing trends—for there was no reason why the monarchy should stand in opposition to the general national development. He was thirty when he came back to England, mature and wise, with an abundance of political experience behind him. He was shrewd and accommodating, and much more resilient politically than any other member of

his family; he had learned to ride humiliation and survive with his identity intact, and when he wanted to be he was a master of political timing. Lord [Charles Montagu] Halifax said of him, "As a sword is sooner broken upon a feather bed than upon a table, so his pliantness broke the power of a present mischief much better than a more immediate resistance." A child of the new age, a friend of Hobbes, a patron of science and technology, witty and convivial, he appealed at once to a new generation of courtiers alienated from the "puritanism" of their fathers (whether it was spelled with a small "p" or a large). To

King Charles II

them his cynicism, his sexual athleticism, his worldly wisdom were more attractive than otherwise, and to them he offered leadership, or at least "spokesmanship."

At the same time he was not at odds with the older generation. He had a personal appeal for men like [Edward Hyde, first Earl of] Clarendon, the veteran Earl of Southampton and the Duke of Ormonde, which offset their disapproval of much that he did and said. Whatever his character, he was also a symbol of national unity after the disorder and social instability of the previous twenty years. The Church, shorn of much of its power and prestige, was for that very reason more dependent on the monarchy than ever and willing to exalt its moral authority. The new cult of monarchy found expression in the near-deification of Charles I. In the new order of service for 30 January, reserved by Parliament as a day of fasting, repentance and self-abasement in perpetuity, the late king appeared as a saint-like figure of overpowering sweetness, moderation and humility, tormented and destroyed by cruel and bloody men. Masochistic preachers did not hesitate to draw the obvious comparison between him and the Saviour of the World, a comparison the more apt in that Charles I was now held to have offered himself as a sacrifice to expiate the sins of his people. The anniversary of Charles II's return, 29 May, was also celebrated with ecstatic pomp. Then, and on 30 January, and on any and every occasion, the pulpits of the Anglican Church rang with exhortations to perfect obedience.

Nor were such exhortations entirely necessary. Charles II had been recalled with the general approval of the great majority of the nation, and the enthusiastic support of many. He had no visible enemies, nor serious critics. The new government he formed under Edward Hyde, Earl of Clarendon, embraced all significant political interests and groupings, ex-parliamentarian as well as royalist. The Act of Oblivion, passed by the Convention in 1660 with strong royal support, was a constructive and statesmanlike attempt to wipe out the animosities, enmities and prejudices of the previous twenty years, and to a great extent it succeeded. . . .

The Failings of Charles II

As it was, in the first few vital years of the Restoration, Charles squandered all his chances. He was not a lazy man, but he lacked concentration, his interests were too diversified, and he did not apply himself to the business of governing. He had a knack of managing men which his father conspicuously lacked, but he relied too much on it. By leaving much of the responsibility to Clarendon, he ignored his father's last advice, which was to beware of putting too much trust in a single minister; then he undermined Clarendon's authority by permitting the "young bloods" at Court . . . to oppose him publicly. When Clarendon went hard on the rocks in 1667 it was too late for Charles to jump clear. But whenever he had a chief minister . . . he could not resist tampering with his power in this way; otherwise he favoured loose ministerial coalitions like the Cabal, whose jarring internal disputes he viewed with complacency, though they weakened his own authority and made continuity of policy difficult.

He was glad of any opportunity to enhance the power of the monarchy, but unlike his brother James he gave no continuous thought to it. In any case, though he was a supremely able tactician he was a poor strategist, and it is to be doubted if he had a long-term policy at any stage. He announced in 1660 that he did not intend to go on his travels again; this was understandable in the beginning, but throughout his reign the concept of survival too much dominated his thinking. In addition, he had the usual Stuart failings: he did not understand finance, and when he chose good finance ministers it was by accident, or as a by-product of other intrigues. His over-spending on the Court and on his own pleasures was perhaps not so spectacular as James I's, but it was just as heavy, and it kept him poor even when his income was rising, as it was for the second half of his reign. He was a very bad public speaker, and just as incompetent at dealing with Parliament as his father and grandfather, though the fact is disguised by his agility in avoiding direct confrontation and his willingness to compromise when hard pressed. All in all, it is not so surprising that the affairs of the monarchy should remain at a standstill during his reign: what *is* surprising is that, until the closing stages, they went backwards.

Leviathan: An Artificial Man

Thomas Hobbes

Thomas Hobbes was a political philosopher who supported King Charles I of England and the divine right of kings. In 1646 while a mathematics tutor to Charles II, Prince of Wales, at the exiled English court in Paris, he began to write his masterpiece of political philosophy, *Leviathan,* from which the following excerpts are taken. Although Hobbes supported the British monarchy, he also maintained that a subject had the right to abandon a ruler who could no longer protect him, and for this reason Hobbes was barred from the exiled court. In 1652, Hobbes returned to England, submitted to the rule of Oliver Cromwell, and settled in London. After being introduced to Euclidian geometry, Hobbes extended its method into a comprehensive science of man and society. In *Leviathan,* Hobbes argues that because all men are generally equal in mind and body, they compete for the fruits of their labor and, as a result of this competition, man's natural state is war. According to Hobbes, only by fear of punishment and the threat of force will men avoid the state of war. For this reason, Hobbes explains, men submit their will by consent to one person who represents the common will. Hobbes characterized this commonwealth of men under a sovereign as an "artificial" man who represents all men, and, therefore, to do injury to the sovereign is to do injury to oneself. Moreover, Hobbes explains that because men institute a sovereign by consent, the sovereign is entitled to certain rights, including the right to obedience.

Excerpted from Thomas Hobbes, *Leviathan* (Oxford: Clarendon, 1651).

Nature (the Art whereby God hath made and governes the World) is by the *Art* of man, as in many other things, so in this also imitated, that it can make an Artificial Animal. For seeing life is but a motion of Limbs, the begining whereof is in some principall part within; why may we not say, that all *Automata* (Engines that move themselves by springs and wheeles as doth a watch) have an artificiall life? For what is the *Heart* but a *Spring;* and the *Nerves,* but so many *Strings;* and the *Joynts,* but so many *Wheeles,* giving motion to the whole Body, such as was intended by the Artificer? *Art* goes yet further, imitating that Rationall and most excellent worke of Nature, *Man.* For by Art is created that great LEVIATHAN called a COMMON-WEALTH, or STATE, (in latine CIVITAS) which is but an Artificiall Man; though of greater stature and strength than the Naturall, for whose protection and defence it was intended; and in which, the *Soveraignty* is an Artificiall *Soul,* as giving life and motion to the whole body; The *Magistrates,* and other *Officers* of judicature and Execution, artificiall *Joynts; Reward* and *Punishment* (by which fastned to the seate of the Soveraignty, every joynt and member is moved to performe his duty) are the *Nerves,* that do the same in the Body Naturall; The *Wealth* and *Riches* of all the particular members, are the *Strength; Salus Populi* (the *peoples safety*) its *Businesse; Counsellors,* by whom all things needfull for it to know, are suggested unto it, are the *Memory; Equity* and *Lawes,* an artificiall *Reason* and *Will; Concord, Health; Sedition, Sicknesse;* and *Civill war, Death.* Lastly, the *Pacts* and *Covenants,* by which the parts of this Body Politique were at first made, set together, and united, resemble that *Fiat,* or the *Let us make man,* pronounced by God in the Creation. . . .

Of the Naturall Condition of Mankind

Nature hath made men so equall, in the faculties of body, and mind; as that though there bee found one man sometimes manifestly stronger in body, or of quicker mind then another; yet when all is reckoned together, the difference between man, and man, is not so considerable, as that one man can thereupon claim to himselfe, any benefit, to which another may not pretend, as well as he. For as to the strength of body, the weakest has strength enough to kill the strongest, either by secret machination, or by confederacy with others, that are in the same danger with himselfe.

And as to the faculties of the mind, (setting aside the arts grounded upon words, and especially that skill of proceeding upon generall, and infallible rules, called Science; which very few have, and but in few things; as being not a native faculty, born with us; nor attained, (as Prudence) while we look after somewhat els,) I find yet a greater equality amongst men, than that of strength. For Prudence, is but Experience; which equall time, equally bestowes on all men, in those things they equally apply themselves unto. That which may perhaps make such equality incredible, is but a vain conceipt of ones owne wisdome, which almost all men think they have in a greater degree, than the Vulgar; that is, than all men but themselves, and a few others, whom by Fame, or for concurring with themselves, they approve. For such is the nature of men, that howsoever they may acknowledge many others to be more witty, or more eloquent, or more learned; Yet they will hardly believe there be many so wise as themselves: For they see their own wit at hand, and other mens at a distance. But this proveth rather that men are in that point equall, than unequall. For there is not ordinarily a greater signe of the equall distribution of any thing, than that every man is contented with his share.

From this equality of ability, ariseth equality of hope in the attaining of our Ends. And therefore if any two men desire the same thing, which neverthelesse they cannot both enjoy, they become enemies; and in the way to their End, (which is principally their owne conservation, and sometimes their delectation only,) endeavour to destroy, or subdue one an other. And from hence it comes to passe, that where an Invader hath no more to feare, than an other mans single power; if one plant, sow, build, or possesse a convenient Seat, others may probably be expected to come prepared with forces united, to dispossesse, and deprive him, not only of the fruit of his labour, but also of his life, or liberty. And the Invader again is in the like danger of another. . . .

Of the Definition of a Common-Wealth

The finall Cause, End, or Designe of men, (who naturally love Liberty, and Dominion over others,) in the introduction of that restraint upon themselves, (in which wee see them live in Common-wealths,) is the foresight of their own preservation, and of a more contented life thereby; that is to say, of getting themselves out from that miserable condition of Warre, which is necessarily consequent (as hath been shewn) to the naturall Passions of men, when there is no visible Power to keep them in awe, and tye them by feare of punishment to the performance of their Covenants, and observation of those Lawes of Nature. . . .

The only way to erect such a Common Power, as may be able to defend them from the invasion of Forraigners [foreigners], and the injuries of one another, and thereby to secure them in such sort, as that by their owne industrie, and by the fruites of the Earth, they may nourish themselves and live contentedly; is, to conferre all their power and strength upon one Man, or upon one Assembly of men, that may reduce all their Wills, by plurality of voices, unto one Will: which is as much as to say, to appoint one Man, or Assembly of men, to beare their Person; and every one to owne, and acknowledge himselfe to be Author of whatsoever he that so beareth their Person, shall Act, or cause to be Acted, in those things which concerne the Common Peace and Safetie; and therein to submit their Wills, every one to his Will, and their Judgements, to his Judgment. This is more than Consent, or Concord; it is a reall Unitie of them all, in one and the same Person, made by Covenant of every man with every man, in such manner, as if every man should say to every man, *I Authorise and give up my Right of Governing my selfe, to this Man, or to this Assembly of men, on this condition, that thou give up thy Right to him, and Authorise all his Actions in like manner.* This done, the Multitude so united in one Person, is called a COMMON-WEALTH, in latine CIVITAS. This is the Generation of that great LEVIATHAN, or rather (to speake more reverently) of that *Mortall God,* to which wee owe under the *Immortall God,* our peace and defence. For by this Authoritie, given him by every particular man in the Common-Wealth, he hath the use of so much Power and Strength conferred on him, that by terror thereof, he is inabled to forme the wills of them all, to Peace at home, and mutuall ayd against their enemies abroad. And in him consisteth the Essence of the Common-wealth; which (to define it) is *One Person, of whose Acts a great Multitude, by mutuall Covenants one with another, have made themselves every one the Author, to the end he may use the strength and means of them all, as he shall think expedient, for their Peace and Common Defence.*

And he that carryeth this Person, is called SOVERAIGNE, and said to have *Soveraigne Power;* and every one besides, his SUBJECT.

The attaining to this Soveraigne Power, is by two wayes. One, by Naturall force; as when a man maketh his children, to submit themselves, and their children to his government, as being able to destroy them if they refuse; or by Warre subdueth his enemies to his will, giving them their lives on that condition. The other, is when men agree amongst themselves, to submit to some Man, or Assembly of men, voluntarily, on confidence to be protected by him against all others. This later, may be called a Politicall wealth, or Common-wealth by *Institution;* and the former, a Common-wealth by *Acquisition.* And first, I shall speak of a Common-wealth by Institution.

Of the Rights of Soveraignes by Institution

. . . From this Institution of a Common-wealth are derived all the *Rights,* and *Facultyes* of him, or them, on whom the Soveraigne Power is conferred by the consent of the People assembled.

First, because they Covenant, it is to be understood, they are not obliged by former Covenant to any thing repugnant hereunto. And Consequently they that have already Instituted a Common-wealth, being thereby bound by Covenant, to own the Actions, and Judgements of one, cannot lawfully make a new Covenant, amongst themselves, to be obedient to any other, in any thing whatsoever, without his permission. And therefore, they that are subjects to a Monarch, cannot without his leave cast off Monarchy, and return to the confusion of a disunited Multitude; nor transferre their Person from him that beareth it, to another Man, or other Assembly of men: for they are bound, every man to every man, to Own, and be reputed Author of all, that he that already is their Soveraigne, shall do, and judge fit to be done: so that any one man dissenting, all the rest should break their Covenant made to that man, which is injustice: and they have also every man given the Soveraignty to him that beareth their Person; and therefore if they depose him, they take from him that which is his own, and so again it is injustice. Besides, if he that attempteth to depose his Soveraign, be killed, or punished by him for such attempt he is author of his own punishment, as being by the Institution, Author of all his Soveraign shall do: And because it is injustice for a man to do any thing, for which he may be punished by his own authority, he is also upon that title, unjust. And whereas some men have pretended for their disobedience to their Soveraign, a new Covenant, made, not with men, but with God; this also is unjust: for there is no Covenant with God, but by mediation of some body that representeth Gods Person; which none doth but Gods Lieutenant, who hath the Soveraignty under God. But this pretence of Covenant with God, is so evident a lye, even in the pretenders own consciences, that it is not onely an act of an unjust, but also of a vile, and unmanly disposition.

Secondly, Because the Right of bearing the Person of them all, is given to him they make Soveraigne, by Covenant onely of one to another, and not of him to any of them; there can happen no breach of Covenant on the part of the Soveraigne; and consequently none of his Subjects, by any pretence of forfeiture, can be freed from his Subjection. That he which is made Soveraigne maketh no Covenant with his Subjects before-hand, is manifest; because either he must make it with the whole multitude, as one party to the Covenant; or he must make a severall Covenant with every man. With the whole, as one party, it is impossible; because as yet they are not one Person: and if he make so many severall Covenants as there be men, those Covenants after he hath the Soveraity are voyd, because what act soever can be pretended by any one of them for breach thereof, is the act both of himselfe, and of all the rest, because done in the Person, and by the Right of every one of them in particular. . . .

Thirdly, because the major part hath by consenting voices declared a Soveraigne; he that disssented must now consent with the rest; that is, be contented to avow all the actions he shall do, or else justly be destroyed by the rest. For if he voluntarily entered into the Congregation of them that were assembled, he sufficiently declared thereby his will (and therefore tacitely covenanted) to stand to what the major part should ordayne. . . .

Fourthly, because every Subject is by this Institution Author of all the Actions, and Judgments of the Soveraigne Instituted; it followes, that whatsoever he doth, it can be no injury to any of his Subjects; nor ought he to be by any of them accused of Injustice. For he that doth any thing by authority from another, doth therein no injury to him by whose authority he acteth: But by this Institution of a Common-wealth, every particular man is Author of all the Soveraigne doth; and consequently he that complaineth of injury from his Soveraigne, complaineth of that whereof he himselfe is Author; and therefore ought not to accuse any man but himselfe; no nor himselfe of injury; because to do injury to ones selfe, is impossible. It is true that they that have Soveraigne power, may commit Iniquity; but not Injustice, or Injury in the proper signification.

Fiftly, and consequently to that which was sayd last, no man that hath Soveraigne power can justly be put to death, or otherwise in any manner by his Subjects punished. For seeing every Subject is Author of the actions of his Soveraigne; he punisheth another, for the actions committed by himselfe.

And because the End of this Institution, is the Peace and Defence of them all; and whosoever has right to the End, has right to the Means; it belongeth of Right, to whatsoever Man, or Assembly that hath the Soverainty, to be Judge both of the meanes of Peace and Defence; and also of the hindrances, and disturbances of the same; and to do whatsoever he shall think necessary to be done, both before hand, for the preserving of Peace and Security, by prevention of Discord at home, and Hostility from abroad; and, when Peace and Security are lost, for the recovery of the same.

The Glorious Revolution of 1688

Hugh Trevor-Roper

In the following excerpt, historian Hugh Trevor-Roper explores the motives and alliances that led to the Glorious Revolution of 1688, wherein James II was replaced by his Protestant daughter Mary and her Dutch husband, William. Those who led the revolution feared both the rise of Catholic power and absolute monarchy. Not only did James alienate Parliament by suspending its laws, but he was an overt Catholic, who repealed the laws against the dissenters who opposed the Anglican Church of England. After the birth in 1688 of a Catholic prince who would succeed to the throne, seven eminent Englishmen wrote to the Protestant William of Orange, asking him to come to England with an army to oust James. William of Orange agreed, hoping with this alliance to protect the Dutch Republic from the threat of invasion and domination by the French. When William landed, he advanced slowly on London as James's support and troops deserted him. Unlike his father Charles I, whose refusal to yield led to a bloody civil war, James offered little resistance and fled England for France and, therefore, the revolution is also called the "Bloodless" Revolution. Parliament concluded in January 1689 that James's flight represented an abdication and offered the crown to William and Mary jointly. The Bill of Rights that emerged as a result of the revolution redefined English monarchy. It barred Catholics from the throne, therefore eliminating rule according to the doctrine of divine right; abolished the king's power to suspend laws; and required frequent parliaments and free elections, lending support to John Locke's contention that government was a social contract between the king and his people. Trevor-Roper was Regius professor of modern history at Oxford University and master of Peterhouse College, Cambridge.

Excerpted from Hugh Trevor-Roper, *From Counter-Reformation to Glorious Revolution.* Copyright © 1992 Hugh Trevor-Roper. Reprinted with permission from The University of Chicago Press and PFD on behalf of Hugh Trevor-Roper.

The Glorious Revolution of 1688–9 was made by an alliance of three parties, or at least of three political or ideological groups: Whigs [opponents of the succession of James II], who provided its necessary motive force; Tories [supporters of ecclesiastical uniformity and the doctrine of the divine right of kings], who provided its necessary parliamentary majority; and radicals who sought to provide its philosophy. Without the Whigs it would never have got up the necessary steam; without the Tories it would never have been carried through; without the radicals it would have lacked a continuing philosophical appeal. These three parties, united against James II, preserved their uneasy unity so long as there was a possibility that he, or his male descendants, being Roman Catholic, might be restored to the throne. They continued to preserve it long afterwards on ritual occasions. And yet on each such occasion their internal differences would break through, adding a nice flavour of controversy—a sign of its continuing significance—to the interpretation of the Revolution. . . .

The Risks of Revolution

All the historians of the Revolution agree that, whether treacherous or glorious, superficial or profound, it was a decisive act. Men did not blunder into it unwillingly, as they had blundered into the Civil War of 1642. They took firm decisions, knowing full well the probable consequences. They knew that their action demanded great political skill, careful planning, strong nerves, and that it entailed enormous risks: risks of disaster through disunity, delay, mere ill luck. How could they not know? Their whole lives had been spent in the shadow of the civil wars, the Republic, the usurpation. All those disasters had stemmed from a well-prepared programme of reform which had gone wrong. And then there were their own fierce internal divisions. . . . Nevertheless, laying aside these divisions, they were now drawn together in a perilous adventure by a conviction of overwhelming imminent danger. In their secret invitation to William of Orange they urged him to come without delay, to save the liberties of England "before it be too late."

William did indeed come speedily. But he came for his own reasons, not theirs, to save the liberty not of England but of his own country, the Dutch Republic, which, he believed, was in similar peril, and whose peril meant much more to him than any threat to the liberties or privileges of Englishmen. He too took an enormous risk. He left the Netherlands exposed to foreign attack and sailed, with his invading force, the whole length of the Channel, past that strong English fleet on which James II had bestowed such care. There was no comforting precedent for success either in such an invasion or in such a rebellion. Monmouth [the illegitimate son of Charles II] had failed. [Archibald Campbell, ninth Earl of] Argyll had failed. He was attempting what Philip II of Spain had attempted exactly a hundred years ago; and Philip II had failed too. Even if his army, unlike that of Philip, should succeed in landing, what guarantee had he of success? James II's standing army—it was one of the charges against him—was very different from the militia of Elizabeth. And how could he rely on the cohesion of his English allies? He knew, only too well, the fickleness, the treachery of the English, including, especially, the English Whigs. He too was well aware that the last aristocratic rebellion against the Stuarts had led to a decade of "blood and confusion." Short of a quick and complete success (and how could he, or anyone, be sure of that?), he might well, as Louis XIV hoped, and indeed expected, be entangled for years in that incalculable island.

A Unifying Fear

We know that in fact this did not happen. But who could have predicted the accidents which prevented it: the winds which bottled James's fleet in port and carried William's to land; the nervous collapse of James, who had always hitherto shown such resolution; his flight from London, which enabled his Whig and Tory opponents to sink their ideological differences in the imperatives of the hour? And if we cannot assume this, then we have to ask what force, what conviction, impelled the conspirators to take this fearful risk? Why did they believe—both the Englishmen for their reasons and the Dutchman for his—that they all stood on the razor's edge, that they must act decisively together, that it was now or never? I do not believe that the answer to such a question is to be sought in "high politics," in personal "petulance" or "treachery," or in economic interest. Such slender motives cannot carry men through so huge a risk. The only force which can unite men of different, even opposite interests in desperate common action is overriding common fear. The men who acted together in 1688 believed that they were facing a fearful threat: that they were threatened—to use their own words—with "popery [Roman Catholicism] and slavery."

Popery and slavery are abstract terms. What, in 1688, did they mean? If we are to answer this question, we must, I believe, look at the Revolution, as they did, in a large context, in both time and space: in time, because men do not live in one moment only, their philosophy is formed by the accumulated experience of their lives and of those of their generation; in space, because England was not, except in a geographical sense, an island. It was, is, always has been, part of Europe.

The Threat of Royal Power

Most of the Englishmen who took an active part in the Revolution of 1688 were middle-aged. Their minds had been formed in the middle years of the century: troubled years in Europe as in England. They were conscious that, throughout Europe, royal power was becoming "absolute"—not absolute in a literal sense, not arbitrary, tyrannical (though they sometimes used these adjectives), but centralized, authoritarian, its authority buttressed by a subservient law. This process they ascribed not to the objective momentum of politics but to the machiavellian policy of power-hungry rulers. They also observed that those rulers who were most successful in building up and preserving such power were Roman Catholics: indeed, that Counter-Reformation Catholicism was a kind of magic ointment, warranted to preserve such a monarchy, once established, against disintegration or reform. This view was held by monarchs too. It was indeed a truism of the time.

One of those who held it was the Catholic Queen of Charles I, Henrietta Maria. She considered that her husband had made a great mistake in seeking to set an authoritarian monarchy on the fragile basis of the Anglican Church, which, not being a true Church, lacked the essential preservative ingredients and, in consequence, had both failed him and itself dissolved in ruin. Why could he not have learned the lesson that her father, Henri IV, had so usefully learned? These views she pressed, in her widowed exile in the 1650s, on her two sons, who found them plausible, and who both, after the Restoration, in their different ways—the one indolent and astute, the other a conscientious bigot—sought to realize them. The opportunity to do so came after 1667, with the fall of [Edward Hyden, first Earl of] Clarendon, who had made the Restoration on the old Anglican base. It was then that Charles II, for the first time, felt that he was really King. Being really King, he could embark on a personal policy, and in his astute, indolent way, he did.

A Secret Treaty with Louis XIV

The crucial years were 1670–2. In 1670, by the secret Treaty of Dover, Charles II promised Louis XIV, against payment of £200,000 to be made at a convenient time, to declare himself a Roman Catholic and to import a French army to assist in the conversion of England. In 1672 he prepared the way by publishing, on his own authority, a "Declaration of Indulgence," i.e. a general toleration for Dissenters from the established Church. Such a toleration would have many practical advantages. It would weaken the established Church and engage the support of the Protestant Dissenters. It would also remove the disabilities of the Roman Catholic Dissenters and enable them, with the help of royal patronage and the 6,000 French troops, to play their part in the great design.

This personal policy of 1670–2 had its foreign dimension, for by the same Treaty of Dover Charles II also committed himself to a war against the Netherlands in collusion with Louis XIV. Such a war would not necessarily be unpopular in England. If successful, it would be profitable to English mercantile interests, which would thus be won over, and their increased profits would in turn, through the increased revenue from customs, improve the finances, and therefore the independence, of the Crown. Meanwhile the French subsidy would help. So a coherent policy was devised: toleration of Dissent, Catholic as well as Protestant; mercantile support; royal affluence. This much was avowed. The other element in the plan, the catholicization of England, was secret.

The Emergence of William of Orange

This coherent personal policy of Charles II soon foundered, and it foundered first of all in the Netherlands. When the French armies invaded the Netherlands, a popular revolt swept the old "appeasing" rulers aside and brought the young William of Orange to the power from which he had hitherto been carefully excluded. Thanks to him, the invasion was halted. In that great national crisis, when the Dutch Republic was nearly extinguished by French power, William's life acquired its purpose. The Republic, he resolved, must never again be exposed to such peril. European coalitions must be organized to protect its independence, not now from Spain—that danger was over—but from France. Above all, England must not fall into dependence on France. That combination could be fatal to the Netherlands—as it would have been, had the policy of Louis XIV and Charles II succeeded. In fact, on this occasion, thanks to the Orangist *coup d'état* of 1672, it had not succeeded. The Netherlands had been saved. With the failure of the French attack, and the prolongation of the war, Charles II's coherent policy began to crumble. England pulled out of an expensive and indecisive war. The policy of religious toleration failed too. The Anglican Church, having so narrowly survived, would not so easily jettison its protective monopoly. Charles II found himself obliged to withdraw the Declaration of Indulgence. Finally, his secret treaty became less secret. Instead of granting toleration to Roman Catholics, he was forced to accept a Test Act excluding them from office, and his cabinet—half accomplices, half dupes—disintegrated in disarray. He did not declare himself a Catholic. He never would.

Thus already in 1670–2 we see, as it were, a dress-rehearsal for the drama of 1687–8. Some of the actors would change in the interim, but one, William of Orange, would not. Nor would the plot of the play. Weaving his coalitions from The Hague, William, himself half-English, and from 1677 married to the heiress presumptive to the English Crown, watched its progress. Charles II had indeed been forced to draw back from his great design; but was that design abandoned, or merely suspended? In particular, would it be revived if or when the King's Catholic brother should succeed him? In the later 1670s the men who would be called Whigs were convinced that it would, and so they mounted a determined attempt to exclude that brother from the succession, unscrupulously exploiting for their purpose the canard of the

Popish Plot. That attempt ultimately failed, broken on the resistance of the "Tories" who, whatever their apprehensions, clung to that lifeline of the monarchy, divine hereditary right. When it had failed, Charles II, exploiting its failure, resumed his old policy. But after those traumatic experiences he resumed it more cautiously. Whatever his own religious preferences, he would not now meddle with popery. That was too dangerous a subject for public policy: a powder-keg which had nearly blown him up. Instead, he would build up his power with the aid of the new Tory party which had proved its worth and strength in the days of crisis, and he would rest it, ideologically, at least for the time being, as his father had done, on the Anglican Church, now greatly strengthened, since [the times of Archbishop William Laud], by lay support. Half a loaf was better than no bread. Louis XIV would understand, and pay. Perhaps, when royal power had been secured, Charles II could use it to complete the policy which, in 1672, he had been forced to suspend.

Finding a Place for Catholicism

Perhaps, perhaps not: or at least not yet. In his last years, when he had dismissed his last Parliament, broken the organization of his enemies, and remodelled the institutions which they had used against him, Charles II felt that he was as absolute a King as any of his predecessors. He had also learned an important lesson. Popery might be the preservative of monarchy, but only if carefully and correctly applied by a qualified physician. The dose had to be adjusted to the patient, for it could encounter dangerous allergies or cause dangerous side-effects. England, he knew, was a difficult patient. He also knew that his brother was not a careful physician. Might he, if he were put in charge, apply the medicine too rashly and risk disaster? In his last days, when he realized that his brother would in fact be put in charge, Charles II seems to have had doubts and to have contemplated a complete reversal of recent policy, or at least tactics. He would declare his own Protestant son, the Duke of Monmouth, legitimate and thus disinherit his Catholic brother. But death forestalled him. "Ah, cruel Fate!" Monmouth wrote in his diary on hearing that his hopes, so recently raised, had been so suddenly dashed. If the report was true, it means that Charles II believed that the time for an open Catholic policy had not yet come; that the monarchy needed to be still further strengthened on its present Anglican base before the perilous leap could be risked; that meanwhile it was essential to move slowly; and that his brother could not be trusted to go slow. If so, he was dead right. . . .

The politicians who opposed the Stuart kings were convinced that Roman Catholicism, though allowable as a personal religion, was, in politics, inseparable from the absolutism which they feared. Therefore it could be tolerated only in private. This view was held by most literate Protestant Englishmen. [Poet John] Milton, who advocated universal toleration of all forms of Christianity, excepted Roman Catholics—although he had good personal relations with his own Catholic kinsmen—on the ground that Catholicism was not Christian at all. Archbishop [James] Ussher, Oliver Cromwell, [poet and politician] Andrew Marvell were equally ambivalent. John Locke, who wrote explicitly in favour of the natural right to toleration of all religions, equally explicitly denied that right to Catholics, on the same grounds. For this rational and limited political anti-popery of the educated classes there was ample justification in contemporary Europe. It did not provide a reason for persecuting papists, only for excluding them from political activity.

The irrational anti-popery of the common people was quite different. It was, I suggest, a form of popular hysteria comparable with the persecution of supposed witches at that time or with antisemitism at all times. Like them, it had a rationalized justification, but it was essentially irrational, an expression of popular psychology. . . . Moreover, having once been formulated and used for public purposes, it had acquired a momentum of its own: a dangerous momentum which was both increased and prolonged by periodic deliberate exploitation: for in certain circumstances it was a means, perhaps the only means, of mobilizing popular violence, if that were judged necessary, against a government which had a monopoly of legitimate, organized force. In 1641 it had been exploited against Charles I and Archbishop Laud. Since both men were firm Anglicans, it was then rationally indefensible, but it was used unscrupulously and defended cynically as a political necessity. Its use during the Exclusion crisis, in the agitation against the "Popish Plot," was rationally more defensible in that there were some shreds of evidence for such a plot and the heir to the throne who was to be excluded was an avowed Catholic. In 1688 it needed no justification.

The Tories' Reluctant Support

Of course the high Tories, the Jacobites, the non-jurors denied this. They persuaded themselves that James II, when he offered toleration to Roman Catholics, intended no more than he said: that he was simply seeking equal rights for all his subjects. He would be a Catholic King of a Protestant country, just as the Elector of Brandenburg was a Calvinist ruler of a Lutheran country. No doubt this would bring some incidental advantage to his fellow-Catholics, but it would not alter the constitution of Church or State. This argument was of course necessary to Protestant Jacobites, as the only solution of the dilemma in which they found themselves: how else could they defend their double loyalty, to Church and King? . . . Forced to decide whether to be consistent with their own past actions—their resolute and successful championship of James's inalienable right to succeed—or to face the unmistakeable implications of his present policy, their minds were marvellously concentrated. They swallowed their pride and, with some face-saving formulae, joined their former adversaries and kicked him out.

Indeed, it was their kick which was decisive. The point is important and needs to be emphasized. Without Tory support in the country and in Parliament, neither the Revolution nor the subsequent settlement would have been achieved, at least in its actual form, and some respect is due to the men who were prepared, in effect, to admit that their hard-fought battle, so fresh in memory, had been a mistake and their hard-won victory vain, for their opponents had been right. It cannot have been an easy admission. Naturally enough, they did what they could to save their faces, and their former adversaries helped them to do so. Thus the abuses of power which were cited to justify William's invasion, and which would be set out in the Bill of Rights, did not include those practised in the last years of Charles II, when the victorious Tories had been in power. The whole burden of guilt was laid upon James II. This concentration of blame narrowed the context and abridged the pedigree of the Revolution. Historically it was inexact. But it served its immediate practical purpose: it enabled the Tories to make common front with the Whigs rather than be caught in the dilemma, or resort to the weak arguments, of the non-jurors and Protestant Jacobites.

Questioning the Policies of James II

It is difficult to argue that they were wrong. William Penn, the Quaker, like some other Dissenters, swallowed the bait of the Declaration of Indulgence. From an opponent of Charles II he became an election agent of James II, an active supporter of his policies. He evidently believed that, thanks to his personal influence with the King, the Quakers would be safe, and he preferred the promise of Catholic protection to the reality of Anglican persecution. But what if that personal link were snapped, as ultimately it must be? Could Quakers, or their Continental equivalents—Mennonites, Bohemian Brethren, Moravians—be found flourishing under any Catholic monarchy? And what of the Huguenots of France, granted legal toleration in 1598 and now, after their legal immunities had been withdrawn, their aristocratic protectors seduced by the court, and their numbers diminished by constant harassment, summarily ordered to conform or to be expelled from their country? This example of the King of France was quickly followed by his satellite, the Duke of Savoy. No doubt, once Roman Catholicism had become firmly entrenched in the English court, and the assets and the patronage of the established Church had been taken over (for that, clearly, was the end of the process of which the attack on the universities was the beginning), the same pressure and the same seduction would have been

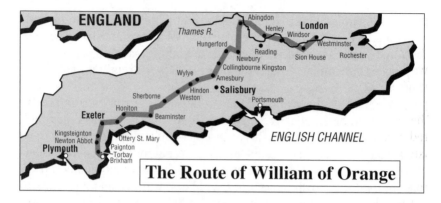

The Route of William of Orange

applied in England; and perhaps, in the end, the same force. So long as James II had no male heir, that argument could be countered, for the heir presumptive was his Protestant daughter, the wife of William of Orange himself. But the birth of the Prince of Wales changed all that. No wonder his adversaries decided that the time had come for desperate measures: to play the anti-popish card. The myth of the warming-pan, [in which many believed that the son of James II was an imposter who was slipped into the Queen's bed in a warming pan in order to provide a Catholic successor], was the new version of the Popish Plot: factually false, unscrupulously used, but, in a desperate situation, judged to be politically necessary. . . .

Thus all the evidence, available then or now, in England or in Holland, political or personal, historical or analogical, suggests that James II's personal professions of moderation could not and should not have been taken literally. Even if he himself had sought to abide by them, the nature of political Catholicism would have made it impossible for him to do so; and his Catholic successors would anyway not have been bound by them. And what then would have been the consequences? In Europe, of course, they would have been immense. Louis XIV, guaranteed against English intervention, would have had a good chance to divide and destroy any coalition against him. Whether he would have succeeded, we cannot say: we cannot press history so hard; it is enough to state the probability.

The Effects of the Revolution

But what of the consequences in England? The astonishing speed and completeness of the Revolution, which constituted part of its "glory," ensured that, socially, its effects were limited. The great risk, once William had safely landed and thus survived the first hazard, was of civil war. If James II had not lost his nerve and fled, if he had stood firm until the cracks in the alliance had opened up, who can say that civil war would not have broken out? That, after all, was what had happened in the reign of his father, in the great crisis of 1641–2 which was ever

present in men's minds. At that time future royalists . . . and future parliamentarians . . . had worked together, just as Whigs and Tories would
do in 1688–9: it was Charles I's refusal to yield, his conviction that God
was on his side and that there were men who would fight his battles—
if not in England, then in Scotland and Ireland—which broke up the
parliamentary coalition and led to the long struggle for sovereignty. In
the course of that struggle, which no one had wanted, radical ideas and
radical social forces had emerged. In 1688–9 all these possibilities existed; but the collapse of James II and the presence of an agreed heir
enabled a still undivided political nation to settle for a quick compromise. The compromise, in the circumstances, was bound to be conservative. Civil war was confined to Ireland and Scotland, and there isolated. The radicals, the heirs of the Levellers, the Republicans, the Com-
monwealthmen of the 1640s and 1650s, were given no chance to
emerge. The Revolution was therefore, in their eyes, incomplete. . . .

The political system—if it can be so called—established by the Revolution did last. That indeed is its great merit. Some of it is with us still.
Since it was essentially defensive, the product of determined resistance
to innovation, it too was necessarily conservative. The framers of the
Bill of Rights insisted that they were defending an ancient constitution:
the institution of Parliament, the regularity of parliaments, the parliamentary control of finance, the independence of the judges, the rights
of the established national Church. But even a conservative revolution
can incidentally liberate new forces, and many of the consequences of
the Revolution of 1688 were incidental, not intended. For every revolution must be defended against counter-revolution. The Revolution of
1688 was quickly over in England, but its defence involved it, as it had
involved the more protracted and bloody revolution of the 1640s, in
war in Scotland and Ireland, ending in an oppressive reconquest of Ireland and a parliamentary union with Scotland: here, as in other respects,
the completion of the Cromwellian settlement, at less cost, and more
durably, but without its radical social content. It also led to a foreign
war, which in turn entailed a financial revolution: the founding of the
Bank of England, the creation of the National Debt. At the same time
it brought continued discrimination against Roman Catholic and indeed—in theory at least—Protestant Dissenters for another 150 years.
William III, who has become the tribal hero of the most intolerant sec-
tarianism in the British Isles, would have relieved both Catholics and
Protestants, but was prevented. The disastrous attempt of James II to
impose both "popery and slavery" on his country, and even, after his
failure, to set up a separate kingdom of Ireland under French protection, rebounded terribly on those whom he had claimed to serve. But
what, we must ask, would have been the consequences of his victory:
if William's fleet had been destroyed at sea or if his enterprise had
foundered in civil war? At once we are lost in vain speculation. One

thing we can perhaps venture to say. If James had succeeded in his plans, the English Parliament would not have survived in a recognizably continuous form and thus a vital organ of peaceful change would have been reduced to impotence. Whatever modifications we may make to the classical Whig interpretation, in the end it is difficult to contest . . . that the English Revolution of 1688 saved England from a different kind of revolution a century later.

An Essay Concerning the True End of Civil Government

John Locke

John Locke defends the Glorious Revolution of 1688, attacks the philosophy of his contemporary, Thomas Hobbes, and provides a foundation for the defense of individual rights and liberty in the following excerpts from his *Second Treatise: An Essay Concerning the True Original, Extent, and End of Civil Government* (1689). Locke had lived in exile in Holland as a result of his opposition to James II and did not return until after the Whig families, who opposed royal power and feared Catholic rule, replaced James with William of Orange, the king of the Dutch Republic and husband of James's Protestant daughter Mary. According to Locke, men who are equal in a state of nature establish a community or government to better secure their natural rights of life, liberty, and property. Locke argues that the government is the product of a voluntary contract among men, that those who govern hold their authority in trust, and that when such trust is violated by tyranny, a people may rightfully revolt. Much of the liberal social, economic, and ethical theory of the next century was rooted in Locke's social-contract theories. Leaders of both the French and American Revolutions found support in Locke's doctrine that revolution in some circumstances is not only a right but an obligation. Locke's argument for broad religious

Excerpted from John Locke, *Of Civil Government, Second Treatise* (Chicago: Henry Regenery, 1955).

freedom and his policy of checks and balances can be seen in the U.S. Constitution. One of the major influences on modern philosophical and political thought, Locke represented the next century's faith in the middle class, the new science, and human goodness.

It having been shown in the foregoing discourse [a refutation of political writer Sir Robert Filmer's arguments for absolute monarchy]:

That Adam had not, either by natural right of fatherhood or by positive donation from God, any such authority over his children, nor dominion over the world, as is pretended.

That if he had, his heirs yet had no right to it.

That if his heirs had, there being no law of nature nor positive law of God that determines which is the right heir in all cases that may arise, the right of succession, and consequently of bearing rule, could not have been certainly determined.

That if even that had been determined, yet the knowledge of which is the eldest line of Adam's posterity, being so long since utterly lost, that in the races of mankind and families of the world there remains not to one above another the least pretence to be the eldest house, and to have the right of inheritance.

All these premises having, as I think, been clearly made out, it is impossible that the rulers now on earth should make any benefit, or derive any the least shadow of authority from that which is held to be the foundation of all power, Adam's private dominion and paternal jurisdiction; so that he that will not give just occasion to think that all government in the world is the product only of force and violence, and that men live together by no other rules but that of beasts, where the strongest carries it, and so lay a foundation for perpetual disorder and mischief, tumult, sedition, and rebellion (things that the followers of that hypothesis so loudly cry out against), must of necessity find out another rise of government, another original of political power, and another way of designing and knowing the persons that have it, than what Sir Robert Filmer hath taught us.

To this purpose, I think it may not be amiss to set down what I take to be political power; that the power of a magistrate over a subject may be distinguished from that of a father over his children, a master over his servant, a husband over his wife, and a lord over his slave. All which distinct powers happening sometime together in the same man, if he be considered under these different relations, it may help us to distinguish these powers one from another, and show the difference betwixt a ruler of a commonwealth, a father of a family, and a captain of a galley.

Political power, then, I take to be a right of making laws with penalties of death, and consequently all less penalties, for the regulating and preserving of property, and of employing the force of the community in the execution of such laws, and in the defence of the commonwealth from foreign injury, and all this only for the public good.

To understand political power aright, and derive it from its original, we must consider what state all men are naturally in, and that is a state of perfect freedom to order their actions and dispose of their possessions and persons as they think fit, within the bounds of the law of nature, without asking leave, or depending upon the will of any other man.

A state also of equality, wherein all the power and jurisdiction is reciprocal, no one having more than another; there being nothing more evident than that creatures of the same species and rank, promiscuously born to all the same advantages of nature, and the use of the same faculties, should also be equal one amongst another without subordination or subjection, unless the Lord and Master of them all should by any manifest declaration of His will set one above another, and confer on him by an evident and clear appointment an undoubted right to dominion and sovereignty. . . .

But though this be a state of liberty, yet it is not a state of licence; though man in that state [has] an uncontrollable liberty to dispose of his person or possessions, yet he has not liberty to destroy himself, or so much as any creature in his possession, but where some nobler use than its bare preservation calls for it. The state of nature has a law of nature to govern it, which obliges every one; and reason, which is that law, teaches all mankind who will but consult it, that, being all equal and independent, no one ought to harm another in his life, health, liberty, or possessions. For men being all the workmanship of one omnipotent and infinitely wise Maker—all the servants of one sovereign Master, sent into the world by His order, and about His business—they are His property, whose workmanship they are, made to last during His, not one another's pleasure; and being furnished with like faculties, sharing all in one community of nature, there cannot be supposed any such subordination among us, that may authorise us to destroy one another, as if we were made for one another's uses, as the inferior ranks of creatures are for ours. Every one, as he is bound to preserve himself, and not to quit his station wilfully, so, by the like reason, when his own preservation comes not in competition, ought he, as much as he can, to preserve the rest of mankind, and not, unless it be to do justice on an offender, take away or impair the life, or what tends to the preservation of the life, the liberty, health, limb, or goods of another.

And that all men may be restrained from invading others' rights, and from doing hurt to one another, and the law of nature be observed, which willeth the peace and preservation of all mankind, the execution of the law of nature is in that state put into every man's hand, whereby every one has a right to punish the transgressors of that law to such a degree as may hinder its violation. For the law of nature would, as all other laws that concern men in this world, be in vain if there were nobody that, in the state of nature, had a power to execute that law, and thereby preserve the innocent and restrain offenders. And if any one in the state of nature may punish another for any evil he has done, every one may do so. For in that state of perfect equality, where naturally there is no superiority or jurisdiction of one over another, what any may do in prosecution of that law, every one must needs have a right to do.

And thus in the state of nature one man comes by a power over another; but yet no absolute or arbitrary power, to use a criminal, when he has got him in his hands, according to the passionate heats or boundless extravagance of his own will; but only to retribute to him so far as calm reason and conscience dictate what is proportionate to his transgression, which is so much as may serve for reparation and restraint. For these two are the only reasons why one man may lawfully do harm to another, which is that we call punishment. In transgressing the law of nature, the offender declares himself to live by another rule than that of common reason and equity, which is that measure God has set to the actions of men, for their mutual security; and so he becomes dangerous to mankind, the tie which is to secure them from injury and violence being slighted and broken by him. Which, being a trespass against the whole species, and the peace and safety of it, provided for by the law of nature, every man upon this score, by the right he hath to preserve mankind in general, may restrain, or, where it is necessary, destroy things noxious to them, and so may bring such evil on any one who hath transgressed that law, as may make him repent the doing of it, and thereby deter him, and by his example others, from doing the like mischief. And in this case, and upon this ground, every man hath a right to punish the offender, and be executioner of the law of nature.

I doubt not but this will seem a very strange doctrine to some men: but before they condemn it, I desire them to resolve me by what right any prince or State can put to death or punish an alien, for any crime he commits in their country. 'Tis certain their laws, by virtue of any sanction they receive from the promulgated will of the legislative, reach not a stranger: they speak not to him, nor, if they did, is he bound to hearken to them. The legislative authority, by which they are in force over the subjects of that commonwealth, hath no power over him. Those who have the supreme power of making laws in England, France, or Holland, are to an Indian but like the rest of the world—men without authority. And, therefore, if by the law of nature every man hath not a power to punish offences against it, as he soberly judges the case to require, I see not how the magistrates of any community can punish an alien of another country; since in reference to him they can have no more power than what every man naturally may have over another.

Besides the crime which consists in violating the law, and varying from the right rule of reason, whereby a man so far becomes degenerate, and declares himself to quit the principles of human nature, and to be a noxious creature, there is commonly injury done, and some person or other, some other man receives damage by his transgression, in which case he who hath received any damage, has, besides the right of punishment common to him with other men, a particular right to seek reparation from him that has done it. And any other person who finds it just, may also join with him that is injured, and assist him in recovering from the offender so much as may make satisfaction for the harm he has suffered.

From these two distinct rights—the one of punishing the crime, for restraint and preventing the like offence, which right of punishing is in everybody; the other of taking reparation, which belongs only to the injured party—comes it to pass that the magistrate, who by being magistrate hath the common right of punishing put into his hands, can often, where the public good demands not the execution of the law, remit the punishment of criminal offences by his own authority, but yet cannot remit the satisfaction due to any private man for the damage he has received. That he who has suffered the damage has a right to demand in his own name, and he alone can remit. The damnified person has this power of appropriating to himself the goods or service of the offender, by right of self-preservation, as every man has a power to punish the crime, to prevent its being committed again, by the right he has of preserving all mankind, and doing all reasonable things he can in order to that end. And thus it is that every man in the state of nature has a power to kill a murderer, both to deter others from doing the like injury, which no reparation can compensate, by the example of the punishment that attends it from everybody, and also to secure men from the attempts of a criminal who having renounced reason, the common rule and measure God hath given to mankind, hath by the unjust violence and slaughter he hath committed upon one, declared war against all mankind, and therefore may be destroyed as a lion or a tiger, one of those wild savage beasts with whom men can have no society nor security. And upon this is grounded that great law of nature. "Whoso sheddeth man's blood, by man shall his blood be shed." And Cain was so fully convinced that every one had a right to destroy such a criminal, that after the murder of his brother he cries out, "Every one that findeth me shall slay me"; so plain was it writ in the hearts of mankind.

By the same reason may a man in the state of nature punish the lesser breaches of that law. It will perhaps be demanded, With death? I answer, each transgression may be punished to that degree, and with so much severity, as will suffice to make it an ill bargain to the offender, give him cause to repent, and terrify others from doing the like. Every offence that can be committed in the state of nature, may in the state of nature be also punished equally, and as far forth as it may, in a commonwealth. . . .

To this strange doctrine—viz., That in the state of nature every one has the executive power of the law of nature—I doubt not but it will be objected that it is unreasonable for men to be judges in their own cases, that self-love will make men partial to themselves and their friends. And on the other side, that ill-nature, passion, and revenge will carry them too far in punishing others; and hence nothing but confusion and disorder will follow; and that therefore God hath certainly appointed government to restrain the partiality and violence of men. I easily grant that civil government is the proper remedy for the inconveniences of the state of nature, which must certainly be great where men may be judges in their own case, since 'tis easy to be imagined that he who was so unjust as to do his brother an injury, will scarce be so just as to condemn himself for it. But I shall desire those who make this objection, to remember that absolute monarchs are but men, and if government is to be the remedy of those evils which necessarily follow from men's being judges in their own cases, and the state of nature is therefore not to be endured, I desire to know what kind of government that is, and how much better it is than the state of nature, where one man commanding a multitude, has the liberty to be judge in his own case, and may do to all his subjects whatever he pleases, without the least question or control of those who execute his pleasure; and in whatsoever he doth, whether led by reason, mistake, or passion, must be submitted to which men in the state of nature are not bound to do one to another? And if he that judges, judges amiss in his own or in any other case, he is answerable for it to the rest of mankind.

The Changing Face of Europe

PREFACE

In the Middle Ages, the countries of Europe were not political entities but rather items of inheritance. In the sixteenth century, for example, Charles V, the Holy Roman Emperor, inherited Austria, Spain, and the Netherlands. Territories within inherited empires were only superficially united under a prince. However, the notion of a personal empire was already changing, and in the seventeenth century the "new" monarchy and the nation-state emerged.

To achieve the role of absolute monarch, a prince had to control the feudal units of medieval society, the estates. All the countries of western Europe had assemblies of estates, and the achievement of absolute power was dependent on control of these estates and the nobles who inherited them. This was more easily accomplished in states that had an emerging middle class that could aid the sovereign in opposing the nobles. In Holland, developments in Dutch commerce created wealthy merchants who became powerful enough to gain an effective authority within the state. In France, bourgeois merchants wanted to rise to the aristocracy, and the monarchy took advantage of their ambition, allowing bourgeois money to pay for official posts and thereby fund the monarchy.

In Germany, the growing power of the princes within their states often brought them into conflict with the local diet—that is, representatives of the Holy Roman Empire. The diet claimed the right to share with the prince at least the imposition of taxes and some legislation. Political conflict with the empire escalated while the rise of Protestantism further divided the empire. Many of the German princes were Protestant. Since they had no middle class to support them in their fight for independence from the emperor, they sought alliances with other Protestant states.

By the seventeenth century, the division of the countries of western Europe between the Catholic and Protestant faiths was practically completed. Conflicts between Catholic and Protestant states, however, were not simply questions of religion. Catholic France, which sought to increase its power in Europe, often allied itself with Protestant nations such as Denmark to defeat the Catholic Holy Roman Emperor, and the Protestant Dutch, who sought to increase their commercial influence, allied themselves with France to oppose Catholic Spain.

The most significant event in seventeenth-century Europe that reflects the complexity of the struggle of emerging nation-states and the new monarchy was the Thirty Years' War. When, in 1618, Protestant

Bohemian nobles deposed King Ferdinand, the Catholic Holy Roman Emperor, the Thirty Years' War began. Under the leadership of Christian IV, Protestant Denmark invaded Germany to aid the Protestant princes but was defeated by the imperial armies, and Christian was forced to cede northern territory in a treaty with the emperor. Fearing the proximity of the empire, Gustavus II Adolph of Sweden entered the war, and although he was killed at Lützen, Sweden was successful against the imperialist forces. By 1634 Germany was in ruin, and the warring princes of the empire hoped for peace. However, the ambitious first minister of France, Cardinal Richelieu, hoping to install the king of France as emperor, brought France into the war, which finally ended with the Peace of Westphalia in 1648. The settlement marked the end of the influence of the Holy Roman Empire and inaugurated the nation-state system. Having won important territories, Sweden increased its influence, but France emerged as the dominant European power.

The French monarchy's influence was felt throughout Europe in the later seventeenth century. Monarchs of other countries consciously lived and ruled as Louis XIV. Under his finance minister, Jean-Baptiste Colbert, Louis expanded industry and commerce, and with the guidance of his war minister, François-Michel Le Tellier, he laid the foundations of French military greatness. The king was a patron of writers and artists, and he built a lavish palace at Versailles. Because of the brilliance of his court, Louis is often called the "Sun King."

The once powerful Ottoman Empire, on the other hand, had lost its influence in Europe in the seventeenth century. The corrupt Turkish court was a place of constant power struggles, and assassination and fratricide were common. However, in 1683, the Turks made one last advance on Vienna. Having surprised the Austrians, they nearly succeeded, but Kara Mustafa Pasa, the Turkish vizier, was not a skilled tactician, and with the aid of Poland, Vienna was liberated.

To maintain the emerging nation-state, the new monarch of the seventeenth century had a vested interest in promoting the economic welfare of the state. A system of direction, regulation, and encouragement, which had been generally termed *mercantilism,* was necessary to increase national wealth. The state encouraged production and protected commercial interests from foreign competition. Mercantilism, therefore, envisaged trade in terms of competition or even warfare between states. During the sixteenth century, Spain and Portugal dominated trade; however, during the seventeenth century other nations, led by the Dutch, began to displace their dominance. The Dutch built up a vast merchant fleet and combined private ventures into a monopoly known as the Dutch East India Company chartered by the government and governed by wealthy merchants.

To make their place in an expanding world, many European princes and kings united their territories into nation-states. Some gained control with the help of an emerging middle class; others sought the aid of political and religious allies. By the end of the century, Sweden emerged as a new power, France solidified its place in Europe culturally and politically, the Dutch expanded their commercial empire, and the Turks made their last stand, all forever changing the face of Europe.

The Thirty Years' War: An Overview

Gerhard Rempel

At the beginning of the seventeenth century, supporters of the Catholic Reformation were hoping to curb the rise of Protestantism in Europe while restoring the power of the Holy Roman Emperor against constitutional reform. Many European states, such as France and Spain, were often at war with one another, and allegiances within the empire often shifted. These religious, political, and constitutional conflicts embroiled Europe in war for thirty years. In the following excerpt from his lectures on Western civilization, history professor Gerhard Rempel provides an overview of the politics and personalities of those who participated in the Thirty Years' War. For example, Rempel explains that after the Protestant uprising in Bohemia, Holy Roman Emperor Ferdinand II turned to Bavaria and Spain for assistance in retaking Bohemia. The French, who opposed control by the Catholic Habsburg family, and the Dutch, who feared the ousting of the Protestant princes, marched with the Danes into Germany. Rempel also explores the motives of Bohemian general Albrecht von Wallenstein, who defeated the Danish troops, and Gustavus Adolph [referred to here as Adolphus], the Swedish king whose successful military tactics made Sweden a formidable foe. Peace negotiations concluded with the Treaty of Westphalia, which divided Catholic and Protestant Germany, established France as the greatest power in Europe, and recognized the independence of European states. Rempel is a professor of European history at Western New England College in Springfield, Massachusetts.

Excerpted from Gerhard Rempel, "The Thirty Years' War," available at http://mars.wnec.edu/~grempel/courses/wc2/lectures/30yearswar.htm. Reprinted with permission from Gerhard Rempel.

Europe had expected that the struggle between Catholic and Protestant would be renewed in 1621, when the truce between Spain and the northern provinces of the Netherlands came to an end. But it began in the [Holy Roman] Empire several years earlier and gradually most of Europe became involved. Since Charles V [Holy Roman Emperor from 1519–1556], backed by the power of Spain, had been unable either to strengthen his authority at the expense of the territorial princes or to wipe out Protestantism, it was natural that his immediate successors preferred to leave the constitutional and religious issues alone. Ferdinand I (1556–1564) and Maximilian II (1564–1576) devoted most of their energy to fighting the Turks, while Rudolf II (1576–1612) preferred to dabble in astrology and to search for the philosopher's stone to turn base metals into gold. During their reigns, however, the Catholic revival was gathering momentum, and it remained only for Ferdinand II (1619–1637) to put the new Catholic fervor into action.

The Dilemma of Ferdinand II

The red-haired, red-faced, good-natured Ferdinand was not a great man, but he possessed more virtues than most kings. He was both a devoted husband and father and a conscientious ruler interested in the welfare of his people. It was said with exaggeration no doubt that when he was Duke of Styria, he knew the names of all his subjects and that he provided free legal service for the poorest of their number. Above all else, however, he was a Habsburg [a member of the royal German family who ruled Europe from the late Middle Ages to the twentieth century]: he was dedicated to the twofold task of restoring the authority of the emperor in the Empire and of reestablishing Catholicism in central Europe.

In his desire to restore the authority of the emperor, he could count on the support of Spain. Spain was only awaiting the end of a twelve-year truce made in 1609 to renew its efforts to reconquer the rebellious provinces in the Netherlands. Because of Dutch naval strength, the Spanish would have to send their troops to the Netherlands by way of Italy, the Alpine passes, and the Rhine River Valley. A strong emperor meant greater imperial authority in the Rhineland and with it more ease in moving troops. Indeed, Ferdinand had already promised Alsace to his Spanish cousins in return for supporting his candidacy to the imperial throne, and he was to promise more in return for military assistance.

Ferdinand could rely on the forces of the Catholic Reformation in his efforts to roll back the tide of Protestantism. The Catholic revival had already recouped a few losses in southern Germany, and Ferdinand himself had stamped out Protestantism in his duchies. Unfortunately, his allies were at cross purposes. The Spanish emphasized the need to increase imperial authority because it was essential to their reconquest of the Netherlands, but the German Catholic princes were only willing to help Ferdinand against the Protestants and strongly opposed any increase in imperial power that might curb their own independence.

More serious still was the interest of foreign powers in Germany. Would France permit Spain to take Alsace, the rest of the Rhineland, and the Netherlands, thereby drawing a tight net around its borders? Would Denmark and Sweden sit quietly by while the Habsburgs extended their power to the Baltic Sea and suppressed their fellow Lutherans? Or would they intervene to maintain their security and, perhaps, to add to their lands in northern Germany? Germany was in central Europe, and the German problem could not be settled without the intervention of surrounding states. It was not enough for Ferdinand to win the allies necessary to defeat the German Protestant princes. He ought to have been less ambitious or else prepared to fight both France and the leading Protestant states. It was not, however, left to him to decide to break the peace. The first step was taken by his rebellious subjects in Bohemia. Gradually and inevitably, the struggle spread to the rest of Germany and then to Europe.

Rebellion in Bohemia

The majority of the inhabitants of Bohemia were Lutheran, Calvinist, or members of one of the Hussite sects, although the Catholic minority supported by the Habsburgs was growing in strength. In addition, the Bohemian nobles were opposed to the encroachment by Habsburg officials on their power. This dissatisfaction with the religious and political policies of the Habsburgs, taken with the certainty that Ferdinand would push them further when he came to power, led to the revolt. On May 23, 1618, a year before Ferdinand was named emperor, the Bohemian leaders unceremoniously threw two imperial officials out of a window in the palace at Prague. They fell seventy feet, but escaped with their lives, either because of the intercession of the Virgin Mary, as Catholic propagandists confidently asserted, or because they landed in a dung hill, as Protestants claimed. In any case, civil war was now inevitable and a European conflict almost certain.

The rebels quickly seized control of Bohemia, won assistance from Transylvania, elected as king the Calvinist Elector Frederick of the Palatinate [now southern Germany], and marched on Vienna. Ferdinand had neither money nor troops, but he had to regain Bohemia. That wealthy country furnished half the imperial revenue, and its king held one of the seven electoral votes that determined who would be emperor. Since three votes already belonged to Protestant princes, the loss of Bohemia might mean the choice of a Protestant instead of a Catholic Habsburg in an imperial election.

Ferdinand turned to Maximilian (1597–1651) of Bavaria and Spain for assistance. Maximilian was an able prince who had consolidated his hold over his duchy and had organized a Catholic League. Furthermore, he had the rare good fortune to have an army under an able, loyal commander. To him, Ferdinand promised the upper Palatinate and Frederick's title of elector. To Spain, he offered the control of Frederick's Rhineland possessions. With these allies, Ferdinand quickly reconquered Bohemia. Catholicism and imperial authority were ruthlessly restored. The once elective monarchy was made an hereditary Habsburg dominion. By 1623, Ferdinand and his Catholic allies had also occupied Frederick's hereditary lands. Southern Germany was theirs, but the Protestant princes in northern Germany had become alarmed, and foreign powers determined to intervene before the Habsburgs could consolidate their position. France took steps to cut the Spanish supply route through the Alps, and the Danes, financed in part by the English, the Dutch, and the French, marched into Germany with 30,000 men.

The Power of Wallenstein

However, Ferdinand had come to realize that he could not achieve his objectives if he had to depend solely on allies. He therefore accepted the offer of a Bohemian nobleman named Albrecht von Wallenstein (1583–1634) to raise an imperial army. Born a Lutheran, Wallenstein had become a Catholic to qualify for imperial favor. Certainly religion was not the motivating force in this tall, thin, forbidding man. It was to the stars that he turned for guidance when he doubted the conclusions reached by his own brilliant but undisciplined mind. He was born under the conjunction of Saturn and Jupiter. The great astronomer [Johannes] Kepler informed him when he cast his horoscope that he had "a restless, exacting mind, impatient of old methods and forever striving for the new and the untried, secretive, melancholy, suspicious, contemptuous of his fellow men and their conventions. He would be avaricious, deceitful, greedy for power, loving no one and by no one beloved, changeable in his humours, quarrelsome, friendless and cruel." Seldom have the stars spoken more truly.

The first step the wily Wallenstein took toward greatness was to marry a wealthy widow who conveniently died soon thereafter, leaving him her estates and the freedom to espouse the daughter of one of Ferdinand's councillors. To wealth and influence he added a businessman's instinct for organization and profit. He managed his estates so well that he came to control a quarter of the land in Bohemia and was able to offer to raise, quarter, and provision 50,000 men at his own expense, leaving to Ferdinand only the responsibility of their pay. The emperor recognized the danger of giving too much power to this powerful subject but the alternative was continued dependence on the Spanish and Bavarians. He therefore accepted Wallenstein's offer and was rewarded with quick victories by the Bavarian and imperial forces over the Danes. Much of northern Germany was occupied, and the ascendant Wallenstein was given Mecklenburg as a reward for his services, the former ruler of this Baltic duchy having made the mistake of siding with the Danes. Internal developments caused France and England to withdraw, and by the end of 1626 it looked as though the war might come to an end.

The fate of Germany rested upon Ferdinand's next step. He could accept Wallenstein's advice and use his great power to create a more centralized Germany, or he could satisfy the Catholic Reformation's demand for the restoration of the Church lands seized by the Protestants since the Peace of Augsburg in 1555. To choose the former course would alienate Maximilian and other Catholic princes who were opposed to any increase in imperial power. To choose the latter would frighten the remaining Protestant princes, some of whom had thus far been neutral. Ferdinand lacked the strength to take both courses simultaneously. He hesitated but finally chose Catholicism and political disunity. By the Edict of Restitution in 1629, he ordered the restoration of the former ecclesiastical territories to the Catholics, and to placate Maximilian, he dismissed Wallenstein. By placing his reliance on Maximilian and the Catholic League, Ferdinand had condemned Germany to more than two centuries of political disunity.

The Influence of Gustavus Adolphus

The folly of his choice was soon revealed. On July 4, 1630, Gustavus Adolphus (1611–1632) landed in Germany with a well-trained, well-disciplined army. The Swedish king was a tall, broad-shouldered man with a big appetite but simple tastes. From childhood he had been trained to be a king. When he was six, he began to accompany the army on campaigns; when he was ten, he began to sit at the council table and give his opinions; and when he was in his teens, he received ambassadors unaided. Now thirty-six, Gustavus had already given evidence of being one of the greatest men of his age. In his nineteen years as king, he had proved himself to be as able an administrator as Maximilian of Bavaria and as careful a military organizer as Wallenstein. He was now about to show that he was a gifted diplomat, a devout Protestant, and at the same time one of the greatest field commanders of his age.

His tactics deserve special comment. He abandoned the current emphasis on mass battle formations in order to achieve greater mobility and firepower. Cavalry and infantry were deployed in a series of alternating small squares so that they could turn easily in any direction. Light artillery was substituted for heavy artillery because it could be advanced rapidly, fired from the front lines in battle, and withdrawn quickly if necessary. Musketeers were organized in files five deep. The first file was taught to fire and step back to reload. Then the second file fired and stepped back to reload, and then the third and the fourth and the fifth, by which time the first file was ready to fire again. Thus, continuous fire emerged from the Swedish lines.

The one important advantage that Gustavus Adolphus lacked was money, for Sweden was a poor country. When the French offered financial assistance, he therefore accepted but was careful never to let French wishes interfere with his policy. During his brief, glorious career in Germany, he was clearly his own master.

The Swedish Intervention

Many considerations led Gustavus Adolphus to enter the war. First, he dared not permit the Habsburgs to consolidate their hold on the southern shores of the Baltic Sea. Sooner or later, they were sure to use the ports of this area as a jumping off place to attack Sweden. Their ally, the Catholic Sigismund of Poland, had a good claim to the Swedish throne. All he needed was imperial assistance to seek to depose Gustavus Adolphus and re-establish Catholicism in the northern kingdom. But if Sweden seized the southern shores of the Baltic, no invasion was possible. "It is better," the Swedish estates declared when they learned of the situation, "that we tether our horses to the enemy's fence, than he to ours." Second, the Swedes had long desired to turn the Baltic into a Swedish lake, and northern Germany would have to become theirs to make this dream a reality. Already a large part of the royal revenue came from Baltic commerce. Third, Gustavus Adolphus, a sincere Lutheran, was genuinely distressed to see the plight of his coreligionists in Germany.

The Swedish invasion completely altered the situation in the Empire. After a great victory in the battle of Breitenfeld, Gustavus Adolphus was free to march where he pleased. Ferdinand had no choice but to recall Wallenstein. The two generals fought an indecisive battle at Nuremberg, and Gustavus Adolphus withdrew to the north. Once more they clashed at Lützen, and this time the Swedes were victorious, but at the cost of their king's life.

The death of Gustavus Adolphus gave the Catholics new hope, but the rivalry between Maximilian and Wallenstein weakened their cause. The Bohemian, who had never forgiven Maximilian and Ferdinand for his first dismissal, plotted with the Swedes and French. Some think that he wanted to create a great middle European empire in which Catholic and Protestant could live in peace. Others see him as a Czech patriot who sought to revive the Bohemian state with himself as king. More probably he was motivated only by his selfish, restless ambition. Whatever Wallenstein's plans, Ferdinand knew that he could not be trusted. He was declared guilty of treason and was murdered, defenseless in his bedroom, by a disloyal contingent of his own troops.

Ferdinand was freed from one peril, and in September, 1634, six months later, he was relieved of another. The imperial forces defeated the Swedes at Nördlingen. The northern kingdom was no longer a serious threat, and one by one the German Protestant princes made peace in return for the abandonment of the Edict of Restitution. Ferdinand kept the gains he had made before 1627, and he now had the united support of the German princes. Their support was an important asset, because nine days before the terms of the peace were published, France had declared war in order to check the power of Spain.

The Treaty of Westphalia

The conflict entered a new phase. Spain, Austria, and the other German states were pitted against the French, the Dutch, and what was left of the Swedes. Religion had become a secondary issue, and the old struggle between the Habsburgs and the French, now ruled by the Bourbons rather than the Valois, held the center of the stage. There were no decisive battles, with the possible exception of Rocroi in 1643 where the young Duke of Enghein—later Prince of Conde—won a victory over the Spanish.

Peace negotiations were begun in 1643, but they proceeded slowly. Not until 1648 was the Treaty of Westphalia signed by most of the conflicting powers, France and Spain alone continuing the struggle. Finally, with the Treaty of Pyrenees in 1659, even this conflict was brought to an end. The Habsburgs had lost the first round of their struggle with the Bourbons.

The results of the war and the two peace treaties were highly significant. France replaced Spain as the greatest power in Europe. With Sweden, France had blocked the Habsburg efforts to strengthen their authority in the Empire. At Westphalia, the right of the individual states within the Empire to make war and conclude alliances was recognized. In theory as well as in fact, the most important of these states became virtually autonomous, and German unity was postponed for more than two centuries. The Empire was further dismembered by the recognition of the independence of Switzerland and the seven northern provinces of the Netherlands. Two new powers emerged in northern Germany. Sweden received part of Pomerania and the bishoprics of Bremen and Verden; Brandenburg-Prussia added the rest of Pomerania and several secularized bishoprics to its possessions. In southern Germany, the Bavarian rulers were permitted to keep the upper Palatinate and the title of elector, but the Lower Palatinate was restored to Frederick's son and an eighth electorate was created for him. France received most of Alsace by the Treaty of Westphalia, and by the Treaty of Pyrenees parts of Flanders and Artois in the Spanish Netherlands and lands in the Pyrenees.

The religious settlement at Westphalia confirmed the predominance of Catholicism in southern Germany and of Protestantism in northern Germany. The principle accepted by the Peace of Augsburg of 1555 that Catholic and Lutheran princes could determine the religion practiced in their territory was maintained, and this privilege was extended to include the Calvinists as well.

The Austrian Habsburgs had failed in their efforts to increase their authority in the Empire and to eradicate Protestantism, but they emerged from the war stronger than before. In Bohemia, they had stamped out Protestantism, broken the power of the old nobility, and declared the crown hereditary in the male line of their family. With Bohemia now firmly in their grasp and with their large group of adjoining territories, they were ready to expand to the east in the Balkans, to the south in Italy, or to interfere once more in the Empire.

The real losers in the war were the German people. Over 300,000 had been killed in battle. Millions of civilians had died of malnutrition and disease, and wandering, undisciplined troops had robbed, burned, and looted almost at will. Most authorities believe that the population of the Empire dropped from about 21,000,000 to 13,500,000 between 1618 and 1648. Even if they exaggerate, the Thirty Years War remains one of the most terrible in history.

The Rise of Swedish Influence

P.J. Helm

During the seventeenth century, Sweden emerged as a European power under King Gustavus Adolph [often called Gustavus Adolphus] and his chancellor, Axel Oxenstierna. In the following excerpt, P.J. Helm describes the role of Gustavus and Oxenstierna in the rise of Swedish influence in Europe. Gustavus, Helm explains, was well trained by his father to rule. He was educated, spoke several languages, and was particularly interested in modern forms of warfare, which he used to oppose the Catholic Habsburg power that threatened Sweden once the Holy Roman Empire gained control of Denmark. In addition, Helm writes, during the early years of his rule, Gustavus developed Sweden's economy and implemented some constitutional reform. According to Helm, Gustavus was victorious at Breitenfeld in one of the few great battles of the Thirty Years' War. Gustavus was killed, however, at Lützen, but he left behind his six-year-old daughter, Christina, and Oxenstierna was able to carry on the king's policies after Gustavus's death. As a result of the influence of these two men, Sweden obtained north German ports at the Peace of Westphalia, which gave Sweden representation within the empire. Helm is author of several books on sixteenth- and seventeenth-century history.

The new king [of Sweden], Gustavus Adolphus (1611–32), was seventeen. He had been trained by his father to rule: when he was nine he had attended meetings of the *Råd* (Council, roughly

Excerpted from P.J. Helm, *History of Europe, 1450–1660* (London: G. Bell and Sons, Ltd., 1961).

equivalent to the Tudor Privy Council); by the time he was thirteen he was receiving ambassadors; at fifteen he had been created Duke of Våstmanland and became for all practical purposes co-ruler with his father.

The Reign of Gustavus Adolphus

Gustavus had been given a good education. While not a scholar, he was full of curiosity, and an excellent linguist. As well as Swedish he spoke German (which he had learnt from his mother) like a native; Latin, Dutch, French and Italian "as if born to them"; and understood something of Spanish, English, Polish and Russian! He had studied history, law, rhetoric, arithmetic, geometry—and the new methods of fighting which were being developed by his idol, Maurice of Nassau. Like his father he was a sincere Calvinist in a mainly Lutheran country. He was a huge man, with broad shoulders, golden hair and tawny beard—in later life his Italian mercenaries called him *il re d'oro* or "the golden lion."

Gustavus began his reign by securing peace at home and abroad. In 1612 he accepted the Charter by which he undertook to give the nobles their share of the great offices of state, and to consult the *Råd* and the *Riksdag* [the primary legislative body] on all matters of law-making and of foreign affairs—a guarantee against royal misgovernment which it was not necessary to enforce. In 1613 he brought the recently-begun Danish war to an end by the Treaty of Knäred. Each country gave up its conquests; the Swedes were promised free passage through the Sound; the Danes were guaranteed freedom of trade with Courland and Livonia in the eastern Baltic. They were also left in control of the west coast of Sweden as security for the payment of an indemnity of one million *dalers* by the Swedes.

In thus buying off the nobles and the Danes Gustavus had secured his western flank, and was able to concentrate on securing concessions from Russia. That country was torn by civil war, and both Sweden and Poland, led by the rival branches of the house of Vasa, hoped to profit from the breakdown of the power which had seemed so menacing under Ivan the Terrible. Gustavus's policy proved successful. In 1617 the new Tsar, Michael Romanoff, acknowledged Sweden's rule in Karelia and Ingria by the Treaty of Stolbova. Sweden thus controlled both coasts of the Gulf of Finland, and Gustavus burst out: "I trust to God it shall hereafter be hard for the Russians to cross or leap over that stream."

At War with Poland

From 1617 to 1629 Gustavus was intermittently at war with the second of his adversaries, Poland. The war is episodic and confusing, but the causes are clear enough. The struggle can be regarded as in many ways a northern extension of the Thirty Years' War [the series of wars (1618–1648) initially involving German Protestants and Catholics]. Poland was Catholic, Sigismund was connected by marriage with the Austrian Habsburgs, the country was a centre of the militant Counter-Reformation and was encouraged by the Jesuits to go crusading against schismatic Russia and heretic Scandinavia. Both countries were ambitious to control the north German Baltic coast, but until the power of Denmark had been completely destroyed (as it was by [Bohemian general Albrecht von] Wallenstein in 1628) Gustavus dare not commit himself to full-scale intervention in Germany, for fear of a "stab in the heel," but was eager for a limited war. "What have we to expect of King Sigismund," he declared to the *Riksdag*, "who is not only evil himself, but allows himself to be governed by that Devil's party the Jesuits, the authors of the grievous tyranny in Spain, France, and elsewhere."

Meanwhile, with an army of 19,000 men and a fleet of about 160 ships, Gustavus landed in Livonia and captured Riga in 1621. He was unable to over-run the country though, and next year signed a three-years' truce with the Poles. When the truce expired in 1625 Gustavus renewed the war, and in January 1626 won a great victory at Wallhof against odds of five to one. It marked Sweden's rise to the rank of a great military power—a rank that they held until 1709. Gustavus left Livonia, and later in the year occupied Prussia and the coast as far south and west as Danzig. This was a critical step. He was moving towards Germany.

[Cardinal] Richelieu [the first minister of France], who knew of Gustavus's plans to start an offensive war against the Emperor and who was himself alarmed at the latter's success, encouraged the Poles and Swedes to reach an agreement, in order that the Swedish King might have his hands free to intervene in Germany. As a result, peace was made in 1629 (the Truce of Altmark), by which Sweden obtained Livonia and ports on the Prussian coast, together with customs dues—500,000 *dalers* in 1629—which would help to finance a German campaign.

The Political Framework

Gustavus was now poised for the invasion of Germany. What, meanwhile, had he achieved at home in constitutional and economic matters? He developed and used both the *Råd* and *Riksdag*. From the former he chose a small committee the members of which were appointed for life and, instructed by Gustavus, governed while the King was abroad. In 1626 the nobility was limited to those who then held the tide and they were expected to work for the good of the kingdom, a hall being built in Stockholm in which they could meet.

Between 1614 and 1634 the central administration was organized in five *Collegia* (departments) headed by five ministers of state; the Steward (justice, 1614), the Treasurer and the Chancellor (1618), the Marshal and the Admiral (1634). Of these, the Chancery rapidly became the most important organ of government, thanks to the activities of the Chancellor, Axel Oxenstierna, who worked in all things with Gustavus and carried on his plans unchanged for sixteen years after the King's death. . . . Eleven years older than the king, Oxenstierna was calmer and perhaps more civilized. When Gustavus once remarked "If we were all as cold as you, we should freeze," the Chancellor replied, "And if we were all as hot as Your Majesty we should burn." The combination of phlegm and choler made a good partnership.

The main legislative organ, the *Riksdag,* although still not further developed than the English parliament in the fourteenth century, was used by Gustavus to get popular opinion, particularly that of the free peasants, on his side, and was encouraged to discuss, in a secret committee, foreign affairs (1627). . . .

An attempt to give the Church a more centralized organization in 1623 was rejected by the clergy themselves. The following year local government was reformed, in a manner reminiscent of the Tudors. The country was divided into twenty-three districts, with a representative of the king in each—"viceroys" Oxenstierna called them—who was intended to act as a link between central and local government.

Economic Policies

Peace at home and war abroad, both demanded an active enlightened economic policy, for Sweden was under-populated even by seventeenth century standards, with less than one and a half million people, and no towns of any size. Fifteen new towns were started by Gustavus, a system of free schools (*gymnasia*) begun and great endowments made to the existing university at Uppsala. Göteborg, situated at the one point where Sweden's territory touched the North Sea coast, was enlarged in 1619. The country's economic strength lay in its mineral resources and, after the conquest of the south Baltic coast, in tolls and profits from the Baltic sea trade. The early seventeenth century was a time of metal starvation. Copper, of which Sweden had a virtual monopoly, was in great demand; Spain had adopted a copper coinage in 1596, and the metal was essential for the development of cannon—as was iron, with which Sweden was also well-supplied. Copper exports increased from 100 tons in 1548 to 2,600 tons in 1650, iron exports during the same period rose from 1,600 tons to 20,000 tons. When Gustavus visited the copper mines at Falun he exclaimed: "What potentate has a palace like to that in which we now stand?" And a modern economic historian has commented, "Without copper, presumably, Sweden's part in the Thirty Years' War would not have been feasible."

The aim of all seventeenth century governments was to control trade and manufactures in the interests of the state, and Sweden was no exception. Oxenstierna said, "The King's Majesty controls and steers mines, commerce, manufactures, and customs just as a steersman steers his ship." Gustavus was particularly anxious to make industry and commerce equip and pay for the new army he was creating and the ships he was building. Regulation made taxation easier; trade with foreigners was confined to thirteen towns, and internal trade to market towns. Industrial standards were supervised by reorganized guilds. Chartered companies were given a monopoly of foreign trade in copper, iron, corn and salt. Dutch and French traders and technicians—notably Louis de Geer, a Liègois Calvinist from Amsterdam—were responsible for most of the progress made and for a time the Dutch really controlled the economic life of the country.

These measures were so successful that when Gustavus left to take part in the Thirty Years' War in 1630 the army he took with him had been completely fitted out from Swedish sources. On the other hand, he was no more able to balance his budget in time of war than any other statesman. The main sources of revenue available to Gustavus were the traditional taxes such as market and mill tolls and excise; the alienation of crown lands; tax-farming; the establishment of monopolies; and tolls from the conquered Baltic ports. The last provided at least 10 per cent of his income. Mercenaries however were expensive, and though the revenue trebled (1623: 2,550,000 *dalers;* 1632: 6,500,000 *dalers*) the King's debt in 1629 was 7,000,000 *dalers*.

The Swedish Army

Gustavus's army consisted of about 70,000 men, of which 40,000 were active troops while the remainder were used on garrison duty and to guard the rather vulnerable lines of communication. In general, the cavalry and artillery were Swedish (there was conscription from fifteen to fifty), while the bulk of the infantry were mercenaries, including many Scots and some English who were able later to apply in the English Civil War the lessons they had learnt under Gustavus. For the King taught the seventeenth century how to fight.

Military ideas were in a state of flux, and Gustavus adopted or adapted all the most valuable innovations. . . . The object of his changes was to make the army flexible and mobile. Much attention was paid to artillery; the guns were made lighter, and the King introduced a light regimental gun, a three-pounder that could be moved by three men or one horse. Instead of a great block of pikemen, surrounded by an unwieldy collection of musketeers, Gustavus organized his army in two or three lines, each line not more than six deep.

The lines were broken into a "chessboard" formation of small alternate blocks of pikemen and musketeers, with gaps between through which the cavalry could operate. Musketeers were also attached to the cavalry, who were ordered to advance slowly, gallop the last fifty yards, and then use their swords. The musketeers were armed with matchlocks in place of arquebuses and were arranged in ranks so that while one rank was firing the rest were preparing to fire or reloading. In this way a relatively continuous rate of fire could be kept up; alternatively, the ranks could fire a salvo simultaneously. All this demanded strict training, good discipline and reliable equipment.

The list of lesser innovations is endless: field-chaplains; some attempt at uniform (blue and yellow, or blue with red facings); charge wired to the shot; and so on. In the second half of the century the Swedish methods—linear order, training, combination of arms, light regimental artillery—were adopted all over Europe, and their immediate influence . . . was great.

Challenging the Empire

While Sweden had been fighting Poland in the eastern Baltic, the Imperial general Wallenstein had gained control of the western shores from Denmark to Stralsund. By 1628 Denmark was decisively defeated, and the Catholic Habsburg power faced Sweden across the Baltic Sea. It was no coincidence that Sweden's first direct intervention in the Thirty Years' War was to raise the siege of Stralsund in 1628. "We must go and find the Emperor at Stralsund, or he will come and find us at Kalmar," said Gustavus, speaking to the *Riksdag,* ". . . Pomerania and the Baltic coast are the outworks of Sweden."

War was declared in October 1629, and in June 1630 Gustavus began to disembark his troops at Peenemünde. Although he styled himself *Restitutor Germaniae* and wrote to Oxenstierna that he hoped ". . . to touch off a rocket of universal rebellion throughout Germany," he got little help at first from the Germans and none at all from the Protestant Electors of Saxony and Brandenburg. The invasion proceeded slowly therefore, and by January 1631 the Swedes had occupied only the Baltic coastal states of Pomerania and Mecklenburg. Then Sweden and France concluded the Treaty of Bärwalde, by which Gustavus was to keep an army of 36,000 in the field until 1636, for which Richelieu would pay an annual subsidy of 400,000 *dalers.* The sack of Magdeburg and the pressure of Gustavus at last persuaded the Protestant Electors to support him, and he began to move south.

On September 17 one of the few great battles of the war took place at Breitenfeld, a few miles north of Leipzig. Gustavus had about 17,000 foot, 7,500 horse and 60 guns, together with a Saxon army of 18,000 under the Elector. The army of the League and the Emperor, under [Graf von] Tilly, consisted of 23,000 foot, 12,000 horse and 30 guns. When the battle had been going on for two hours the Saxons, on the left wing, broke and fled; but Gustavus's flexible formation enabled the Swedes not only to turn and face an encircling movement on their own right wing, but also to check the Imperial forces on their broken left. Late in the afternoon, the wind and the sun having moved round behind him, Gustavus in his turn launched his attack, cutting off the Imperial cavalry from their own infantry, recapturing the Saxon guns and finally driving the broken army back along the Leipzig road. The Swedes lost 2,100 men, the Imperial losses were 7,600 dead on the field and 6,000 prisoners. The battle was a triumph for the King, and for the new style of fighting.

The Last Battles of Gustavus

Gustavus now had a choice of plans: he could drive southeast to Vienna, or turn southwest through Franconia to the middle Rhineland. To seize imperial Vienna would be spectacular, but it would not be a safe base and the long lines of communication would be exposed to Catholic states, to the doubtful Elector of Saxony, to hostile Poland. Gustavus marched southwest instead. In this direction the land to the north was in friendly hands, he was able to link up with the Protestant Rhineland and to be in close touch with France—too close for Richelieu, who protested when the Swedes occupied territory on the left bank of the Rhine. Gustavus set up his winter quarters at Mainz.

In 1632 Tilly was wounded to death and the army of the Catholic League defeated at the battle of the Lech, and Gustavus, marching through Bavaria towards Vienna, occupied Munich in May. The Emperor had meanwhile recalled Wallenstein, and Gustavus failed to drive him from Nuremberg, where the Imperial forces lay encamped. Then word came that Wallenstein was moving north to Saxony, to conquer, or perhaps to negotiate with, the lukewarm Elector. Gustavus, his communications seriously threatened, moved north also. On November 16 the two armies met at Lützen, very close to the earlier battlefield of Breitenfeld. After a fierce struggle the Swedes were victorious. But Gustavus had been killed early in the battle, cut off in an isolated cavalry movement by the November mist and hanging battle-smoke. He was thirty-seven. . . .

For sixteen years Gustavus in a way ruled Sweden from his grave. He left behind a girl of six, Christina, and Oxenstierna was able to carry on his policy unchanged, so that the Peace of Westphalia is the logical conclusion of Gustavus's work. The Chancellor united Sweden and the Protestant princes of western and central Germany in the League of Heilbronn, under the command of Bernard of Saxe-

Weimar, who had taken charge at Lützen when Gustavus was killed. At first the League was successful, but in 1634 Spain entered the war, large bodies of troops were moved north through the Valtelline, and the Swedes were decisively defeated at Nördlingen. As a result Richelieu was forced to intervene directly, and Sweden ceased to play an important part in the war. At the Peace of Westphalia Gustavus obtained his posthumous reward: Western Pomerania; Bremen and Verden; and the port of Wismar in Mecklenburg; territories which gave Sweden the right to be represented in the German Diet. The Swedes now held all the important north German ports except Hamburg and Danzig.

The Peace of Westphalia

S.H. Steinberg

The Peace of Westphalia was signed in 1648, ending the Thirty Years' War and readjusting the religious and political affairs of Europe. The main participants were France and Sweden and their opponents, Spain and the Holy Roman Empire. In the following excerpt, historian S.H. Steinberg explores the politics and personalities that contributed to the peace treaty and also details of the treaty's territorial, constitutional, and religious provisions. Steinberg explains that at the war's end, new personalities had assumed power in Europe: Emperor Ferdinand III was more realistic and less dogmatic than his devout father, first minister Cardinal Mazarin had a narrower vision for France than the longsighted Cardinal Richelieu, and Christina of Sweden preferred peace and prosperity for her people to the profits of war. To protect the Austrian Habsburgs, Ferdinand was willing to recognize the sovereignty of the European states despite the threat to his power and the unity of the empire. France and Sweden determined the numerous territorial provisions of the treaty, which resulted in a political reorganization that left France as the chief power on the continent. The treaty also prohibited all religious persecution in Germany, allowing each prince to decide the religion of the state.

A ll the major and minor wars that since 1609 had flared up in one part or another of central and eastern Europe were terminated by treaties of truce or peace. To call to mind this series, from the

Excerpted from S.H. Steinberg, *The Thirty Years War and the Conflict for European Hegemony, 1600–1660.* Copyright © 1966 S.H. Steinberg. Reprinted with permission from W.W. Norton & Company, Inc.

Spanish-Dutch truce of 1609 to the Swedish-Danish peace of 1645 is in itself sufficient to discredit the lingering con-concept of a single "Thirty Years War."

However, these earlier peace treaties were essentially *ad hoc* arrangements. They largely ignored the European character of all these conflicts and therefore left unsolved almost as many problems as they tried to settle. Consequently the peace of Westphalia, which ended the war between the French-Swedish-Dutch alliance and the Spanish-Austrian bloc, aimed at a comprehensive composition of all outstanding points at issue. Hence the long duration of the peace congress and the slow and tortuous progress of its deliberations, caused by the intertwining and overlapping problems on its agenda.

Shifting Leadership

Several changes among the leading personalities in the years around 1640 either speeded or retarded the peace negotiations. In 1637 the Emperor Ferdinand II died. His eldest son, Ferdinand III, had in the previous year at last been elected king of the Romans (though still against the opposition of Bavaria and the Curia) and now succeeded him, with none of the Electors dissenting. Unlike his father, the new Emperor was always prepared to abandon positions which his realistic mind recognized as untenable. In order to maintain and strengthen his absolute power in the hereditary crown lands of the house of Austria, he felt few if any qualms in bartering away what had been dearest to his father's heart: the unity of the church, the integrity of the Empire and the interests of the Spanish Habsburgs.

The accession to power of Cardinal Mazarin on the death of Richelieu (1642) gave a new turn, or at least a different emphasis, to French policy. During the minority of the new king, Louis XIV, Mazarin was the sole director of French affairs until his death (1661). Contrary to Richelieu's far-sighted concepts of the concert of Europe, the Italian-born Mazarin took a narrowly French view of European problems. This attitude soon roused the suspicion of the Dutch statesmen who began to see the greater danger in an aggressive France rather than a decaying Spain. . . .

The coming of age of [Swedish king] Gustavus Adolphus's daughter, Christina, in 1644 shook the exclusive rule of the high aristocracy in Sweden. The young queen took an active part in the deliberations of the council of state. In opposition to the civilian and military noblemen who regarded the war as a profitable business to fill their own pockets, Christina worked for peace—at almost any price. The sacrifices in blood and money which the mass of the population had to bear made her attitude very popular. In Adler Salvius, a man of low birth, Christina found a skilful and determined advocate of her policy, capable of holding his own against the bellicose and selfish nobility.

Among the German princes, the assumption of the regency in Hesse-Cassel by the landgravine [a woman who has jurisdiction over a large German territory] Amalia (1637) and the accession of Frederick William in Brandenburg (1640) brought to the fore two energetic Calvinist princes who completely overshadowed John George of Saxony, who still pursued his equivocal policy of appeasement. In the Catholic camp, the vacillations of Maximilian of Bavaria during the years 1646–48 showed that the ageing Elector was losing his firm grasp, although in the end he returned to the French allegiance.

On the other hand, France lost a valuable ally when Pope Urban VIII died in 1644. He had been an unswerving opponent of the Habsburgs, but the growing preponderance of France in the affairs of Italy made a determined minority of the cardinals anxious to restore the equilibrium. They defeated the pro-French majority in a long-drawn ballot and their victorious candidate Innocent X (1644–55) reversed his predecessor's policy in favour of Spain.

The Early Negotiations

The first steps towards the peace which was eventually concluded in 1648 were taken in 1638. The Hamburg treaty, signed on 6 March by the Count d'Avaux for France and by Adler Salvius for Sweden, bound the signatories to make peace only in common. The congress was to meet in two places, France and Sweden respectively presiding; the originally proposed cities of Cologne and Hamburg were later, in 1641, replaced by Catholic Münster and Protestant Osnabrück which recommended themselves because of their proximity. The aims were the restitution of the political, constitutional and religious status of 1618, a general amnesty, and the "satisfaction" of the "two crowns" of France and Sweden. At the same time Ferdinand III sounded the possibility of a separate peace with Sweden. But the Swedish council of state flatly rejected the Emperor's proposals and indeed any separate negotiations with him.

At a meeting of the Emperor with the Electors in Nürnberg (1640), Ferdinand realized that the Electors were willing to fall in with the basic demands of France and Sweden. As a counterstroke he summoned the imperial diet which had not met for nearly thirty years. Ferdinand hoped to mobilize the lesser princes against the Electors, but the diet expressed its longing for peace in declarations which corresponded completely with the wishes of the two crowns.

After three more years of half-hearted and inconclusive discussions and correspondence between all parties, the tireless exertions of the landgravine Amalia played a decisive part in overcoming the hesitancy of some, the obstinacy of others, and the backstairs intrigues of all. The final invitations, issued by France and Sweden to all Estates of the Empire in September–October 1644, were accepted, last of all by the Emperor. While the ambassadors of the Estates were gradually assembling in Münster and Osnabrück, the Emperor conceded that a general amnesty was to be promulgated, and all Estates should be admitted as fully qualified representatives of the Empire and as independent members of the society of European states.

The congress as a whole and its two sections at Münster and Osnabrück were never formally opened or constituted, but from the middle of 1645 the negotiations were in full swing. In December 1645 the Swedes and French for the first time made known their demands which were to underpin the "restitution of the German liberty" as they continued to describe their war-aim. Some of their demands were clearly meant only to be used for bargaining purposes. . . .

Breaking Away from the Empire

It was taken for granted by every participant of the congress that the German Empire was to square the reckoning in full. Two territories which were still nominally member states of the Empire, the Netherlands and Switzerland, therefore made haste to dissociate themselves formally from the Empire. The recognition in international law of Dutch independence was at once admitted by the Spaniards, as soon as the representatives of the United Provinces declared their willingness to abandon the French alliance and to conclude a separate peace with Spain. The inevitable consent of the Emperor and Empire was cloaked in the meaningless proviso that the ultimate fate of the "Burgundian circle" should be left in suspense until a Spanish-French peace be signed. In fact, the conclusion of the Dutch-Spanish peace on 30 January 1648 ended the Eighty Years War and separated the Netherlands for good from the German Empire.

The Swiss Confederation had come through the wars of the past forty years without being involved in any of them. The Grisons, it must be remembered, repeatedly the theatre of war, was a loose ally but not a member of the League. Swiss neutrality was as much the result of prudent statesmanship as of the impossibility of devising a consistent policy out of the discordant political, religious and economic interests of the thirteen cantons. The Confederation was therefore not invited to the peace congress, and its exclusion was accepted almost gratefully by the Roman Catholic cantons which were unwilling to side with or against Austria, Spain or France. However, when the annexionist plans of France became known, the city of Basel took alarm; for it would have been almost encircled by a series of French fortresses. The Roman Catholic cantons still objected to attending the peace congress, but the Protestant cantons sent the Basel burgomaster Johann Rudolf Wettstein as their plenipotentiary to Münster. Wettstein achieved his aim. A clause in the peace treaty formally "exempted" "the city of Basel and the other Swiss cantons" from their obligations towards the Empire.

Protecting Austria

The aversion to becoming implicated in the dismemberment of the Empire was also uppermost in the thoughts of the Emperor, who ought to have acted as the principal spokesman of its interest. Ferdinand III and his advisers were determined that whoever was to lose territory, to abandon principles, to pay indemnities, it should not be the house of Austria. In order to prevent the Electors and the other Estates from signing the peace without the Emperor, Ferdinand abandoned the Spanish alliance and accepted the religious compromises on which the Protestant and Catholic Estates had agreed. In order to keep Silesia and to exclude the Protestants of the Austrian crownlands from the religious toleration accorded to their coreligionists in the Empire, Ferdinand sacrificed Pomerania and the north German bishoprics to the Swedes and their German partisans. In order to keep the Breisgau and the upper Rhenish fortresses of Laufenburg and Rheinfelden, he offered France Upper and Lower Alsace and the imperial cities and bishoprics of Metz, Toul and Verdun. The fortress of Breisach was the only direct loss Austria suffered, for the Emperors feudal rights in Alsace and Lorraine were so nugatory that Ferdinand gave up little. From the French point of view, two main advantages resulted from these acquisitions: Alsace and Lorraine were sure to fall sooner or later under French dominion; and the garrisoning of Breisach and Philippsburg laid south Germany open to French invasion. France owed its success not least to the pressure which Maximilian of Bavaria exerted upon the Emperor on behalf of his French allies. He therefore benefited to the extent that he was confirmed in his electoral dignity and allowed to keep the Upper Palatinate. Moreover he saved Paderborn for his brother Ferdinand and Osnabrück for Ferdinand's bastard Wartenberg: Hesse-Cassel had wanted to annex the one bishopric, the Guelphs the other.

The Swedes had to abandon some of the extreme demands of the war party. Above all, the acquisition of the whole of Pomerania proved impossible in the face of the determined opposition of Frederick William of Brandenburg. His hereditary rights to the duchy would have availed him nothing; but Denmark, Poland and the Netherlands did not wish to see the entire Baltic coast in Swedish hands and therefore supported Brandenburg. In the end, Pomerania was divided: Sweden obtained the more valuable Western Pomerania with Stralsund, Greifswald, Stettin, the islands of Rügen, Usedom and Wollin, and a tract on the right bank of the river Oder; whereas Brandenburg received Eastern Pomerania with the bishopric of Kammin, which included Kolberg as the only port of any significance. This compromise was offset by the gains of both elsewhere: Sweden acquired the Mecklenburg port of Wismar and the bishoprics of Bremen and Verden, comprising the whole country between the lower Elbe and lower Weser; the mouths of the rivers Oder, Elbe and Weser, controlling the German commerce towards the Baltic and North Seas, were firmly in Swedish hands. Brandenburg received large compensations: the archbishopric of Magdeburg was to go to Brandenburg after the death of the present administrator, a Saxon prince; the bishoprics of Halberstadt and Minden and two Hartz counties nearly filled the gap between the Electorate and its Rhenish-Westphalian territories acquired from the Jülich inheritance. Brandenburg was definitely outstripping Saxony which only kept Lusatia (ceded by the peace of Prague) but obtained nothing further.

Two other adherents of Sweden, Brunswick-Lüneburg and Hesse-Cassel, were put off with minor gains that fell short of their expectations. Their disappointment was due mainly to the opposition of France and Bavaria, which did not wish to see powerful Protestant countries straddling north-west and west-central Germany.

All these gains and losses—including numerous minor adjustments—were determined entirely by the interests of the principal powers, France and Sweden. The genuine desire for peace, as well as the selfish ambitions of their respective partisans, gave the two crowns ample scope to harmonize their own, often seemingly insoluble differences at somebody else's expense, to reward the obedient or potentially useful, and to make the recalcitrant or negligible bear the cost of the final settlement.

Settling Constitutional and Religious Problems

However, the territorial acquisitions and cessions were not the only concern of the peace congress, or even the sole preoccupation of the two crowns and the Emperor. The peace of Westphalia finally settled the constitutional and religious problems which had for centuries beset the German Empire; and it settled them within a European framework.

The struggle between the monarchical and centralistic aspirations of the Emperor and the oligarchic and federalistic tendencies of the Estates was decided in favour of the latter. The edict of restitution and the peace of Prague—the highwater marks of imperial ascendancy—were repealed. The Estates were granted full sovereignty, including the right to conclude alliances among themselves and with foreign powers, limited only by the futile clause that such alliances must not be directed against the Emperor and Empire. The "electoral pre-eminence" was eliminated; all Estates were regarded as equal— but France and Sweden saw to it that their supporters were more equal than the rest. The Emperor had to cede to the imperial diet the *jus pacis et belli*, i.e. the declaration of war, conclusion of peace, levying and quartering of troops, building and garrisoning of fortresses. The chief imperial institutions were henceforth to be composed on a footing of religious equality—the supreme court, for instance, was to consist of two Protestant and two Catholic presidents and 26 Catholic and 24 Protestant judges. Religious disputes brought before the imperial diet were no longer to be decided by majority vote, but by amicable settlement between the Corpus Catholicorum and the Corpus Evangelicorum, each formed *ad hoc* by the respective Estates whenever religious issues came under consideration. . . .

Henceforth the conversion of the ruler did not automatically oblige his subjects to accept his new creed; and dissident subjects were allowed private worship and the right to emigrate, again with the exception of the Habsburg dominions. The Protestant administrators of the reformed north-German bishoprics were at last admitted to the imperial diet with full voting rights.

Although all the religious clauses were hedged in on every side by conditions, reservations and exceptions, they marked a definite step towards the separation of politics and religion. Politics became secularized, religion was to be left to the conscience of the individual. . . .

The Final Details

One of the most difficult questions to be settled was the financial "satisfaction" of the Swedish army. In this respect Oxenstierna was not a free agent, as the generals put forth their and the soldiers' claim regardless of political considerations. The Estates of the Empire originally offered 1,600,000 talers against the Swedish demand for 20 million. Salvius (and Queen Christina) eventually lowered this sum to 5 million. This figure was accepted by the Estates; the Emperor's consent was bought by Swedish abandonment of the Austrian and Bohemian Protestants. Their confiscated estates were not returned to them and the denial of religious toleration in their home lands made them perpetual exiles— but they were now assured at least of a financial compensation as most of them were serving in the armies of the Swedes and their allies.

The signing of the peace treaty took place on 24 October 1648 in the lodgings of the imperial ambassador in Münster. It was ratified on 8 February 1649, when the peace was solemnly placed under the common guarantee of Sweden and France. Details of its execution were settled at a congress which sat in Nürnberg from April 1649 to June 1651. Here [Italian field marshal Octavio] Piccolomini, representing the Emperor, showed himself a skilful diplomatist; he carried a number of interpretative amendments favourable to the house of Austria, for which Ferdinand raised him to the dignity of a prince of the Empire.

The peace of Westphalia remained in force until the end of the Holy Roman Empire in 1806. In its German as well as European aspects, it marked the end of the middle ages and heralded the era of the secular concert of Europe.

The Reign of Louis XIV

Maurice Ashley

In the following excerpt, historian Maurice Ashley evaluates the reign of Louis XIV. When first minister Cardinal Mazarin died in 1661, Louis, at age twenty-three, became the absolute monarch of France. His main objective at this time was to establish his supremacy by becoming personally involved in affairs of state and limiting the power of French noblemen. Louis also aspired to be the greatest Catholic king, patterning himself after the kings of the Holy Roman Empire. He offered aid to defeat the Turks and protect Catholics in Protestant nations and tried to convert the Huguenots, French Protestants. Like much of Europe, seventeenth-century France was primarily agricultural, and the French economy depended upon the overly taxed peasants. The king's goals as conqueror were also funded at the expense of the peasants; however, the people revered Louis as the conquering hero. Louis also supported developments in science and the arts, and it was his glittering court that gave him the name the Sun King. Although the seventeenth-century French were the most cultured people in the Western world, Louis XIV failed to unify the nobles or eliminate feudalism and religious intolerance, which paved the way for revolution.

The second half of the seventeenth century is generally described as "the age of Louis XIV." But modern French historians tend to concentrate on the conditions of the peasantry in relation to the social structure of the kingdom and to be unemphatic about the role of

Excerpted from Maurice Ashley, *The Age of Absolutism, 1648–1775* (Springfield, MA: G & C Merriam Company, Publishers, 1974).

the King himself, for he was a man and not a class. On the other hand, the numerous biographers of Louis XIV are mainly concerned with the King and his glittering Court while more or less ignoring the peasantry, who did not inhabit the palace of Versailles. No doubt the role of the King can be exaggerated, but it should not be ignored.

Establishing Absolute Rule

It would be difficult to show that any important changes of policy resulted when Cardinal Mazarin died in 1661 and Louis XIV, at the age of twenty-three, announced that henceforward he was going to be his own first minister. What was significant was that by then Louis had sown his wild oats and was prepared to become an industrious ruler. Mazarin had taught him most of the arts of government, while his Spanish mother had stressed the value of strict Court etiquette. He learned that it was necessary to think things out, to study the relevant information placed at his disposal before reaching a conclusion; thus when he was asked for even a small favour his custom was to reply "I will see." As to the Court, its elaborate ceremonial was intended to impress upon the world the King's supremacy. As Professor [Pierre] Goubert has written, "since the greater part of the Court, the pulpit and the town of Paris proclaimed that he was the lieutenant of God upon earth, it prepared to cry out with [French prelate Jacques Bénigne] Bossuet: 'Oh kings, you are as gods' nothing of all this could surprise him." Indeed it was to draw attention to his isolation far above ordinary mortals that the main changes after Mazarin's death were directed. Louis excluded not only the princes of the blood [royal family] from his councils of state but also his mother, who had been Regent of the kingdom during the eighteen years since his father had died. His only brother was allowed no place in the government nor any political post and in later years his only son was also kept in his place. Nothing was allowed to detract from the glory of the sun king. He employed the same three ministers who had served Mazarin, [Michel] Le Tellier, who was responsible for the army, [Hughes de] Lionne who was concerned with foreign policy, and [Nicolas] Fouquet, the superintendant of finance. But the King expected to be consulted about everything. On Monday, Wednesday and Saturday he presided over the ministerial council, the *conseil d'en haut;* on Tuesdays and Thursdays he generally attended the council which dealt with financial matters; and Fridays were devoted to religious questions in collaboration with the Archbishop of Paris and other leaders of the Church. It is sometimes argued that all this was a façade, that the real work was done by others. The King himself would never have admitted as much. He did not like anything to be kept from him and believed that most problems could be solved by the application of commonsense. But it is probably true that his principal interest lay in foreign affairs. "You will always," he wrote in instructing his son about his duties, "see me dealing directly with foreign ambassadors, receiving dispatches from abroad and writing a large part of the replies to them, while giving to my secretaries the substance of the way in which others are to be answered."

Solving Internal Problems

The period of peace which followed Louis XIV's accession to power enabled him to put his house in order. One should not underestimate the effect of the two Frondes [political parties who opposed the government and encouraged rebellion against the King's court while Louis was a child] upon his mind. During the second Fronde a Paris mob actually penetrated into his bedroom in the Palais Royale. It was because of the behaviour of the Prince de Condé and other princes during the second Fronde that the King excluded them from his councils, although he was later reconciled to Condé and employed him as a military commander. Because he had seen Frenchmen fighting one another it has been suggested that unity and consensus "became a near-obsession with him in later years." The decision that he ultimately took to remove himself and his Court from Paris to Versailles, where a royal château had been sufficiently enlarged to enable him to keep an eye upon most of the higher nobility, must have been partly motivated by memories of the Fronde.

Before he died Mazarin had recommended to the King the abilities of [Jean-Baptiste] Colbert, who came from merchant stock and had looked after the personal financial affairs of the Cardinal. Colbert was a master of the skills of administration. On Louis XIV's initiative he ferreted out the peculations or at any rate the irregularities of the able and cultivated Nicolas Fouquet. Once the King was satisfied that Fouquet had benefited himself overmuch from the exercise of his office while neglecting the true needs of the country, he had him arrested and insisted that he should be imprisoned for life. Here again Louis was moved by memories of the Frondes, for he feared that a man as rich and successful as Fouquet might become a disruptive influence. He came to trust the less glamorous Colbert, who was in due course appointed Controller-General of Finance, Minister for the Navy, Minister for the Arts and director of the royal building programme, which, after war and sex, was the monarch's chief passion. . . .

What was the foreign policy for which Louis XIV needed an army, a navy and plenty of money? This has been the subject of violent debates and various explanations of his purposes have been offered. It has been suggested that he wanted to attain the "natural frontiers of France," that is to say the Pyrenees, the Alps and the Rhine. But there is no evidence for this and in fact the Pyrenees had already been reached, after twenty-four years of war, before Mazarin died. Secondly, it is argued that the King subjected all other aims to that of winning the succession to the Spanish empire after Philip IV died and left a child and a weakling as his only direct heir. Another explanation is that he sought by dominating Germany to gain the imperial crown which had long been the monopoly of the Habsburg family. Again, it has been urged that he was guided by a desire for *gloire* which did not mean merely self-glorification but the glorification of his country as symbolically embodied in himself by God. Lastly, he has been pictured simply as a pragmatist who exploited his opportunities as they came his way. In fact, it does not seem that he had any steady purpose, but that he merely followed the same lines as the great Cardinals, Richelieu and Mazarin, who both wanted to drive back the Habsburgs and give France an independent role in Europe. Louis regarded the Habsburgs of Spain and of Austria as his natural and hereditary enemies who had been able in the past to fasten a stranglehold on France. Once the Pyrenean frontier had been established, Louis laboured to push forward the French frontiers to the north-east and to the east as far as he could in Spanish Flanders, Alsace-Lorraine and northern Italy. Thus rational considerations were fed by his ambition. As [historian] Louis André wrote,

> After 1663 Louis XIV ceased to be satisfied with the domains that he possessed and aimed to increase them at the expense of the Habsburgs. His pride and his desire for glory involved a wish to achieve success by arms, to make conquests beyond everything. Here again the King was in accord with the wishes of his subjects who also sought glory, above all since the treaty of the Pyrenees. Everyone thought that "to be a conqueror is the most noble and most elevated of aims."

The Role of a Catholic King

Another ambition of Louis XIV was to justify his title of the most Christian king. He wished to emulate the most Catholic king of Spain and the Holy Roman Emperor. To begin with, Louis thought of becoming a crusader. . . . He furnished six thousand men to fight against the Turks in 1664 and offered the Holy Roman Emperor twenty thousand men to help drive the Turks out of Europe. Later in his reign when the Turks attacked Vienna, he hoped that if the Austrian capital fell, he would be able to pose as the saviour of the West. During his reign he used his influence to protect Roman Catholic minorities, for example in England and the United Netherlands. He encouraged the Duke of Savoy to repress the Protestants. Logically therefore he had also to suppress the heretics and unbelievers in his own kingdom. Essentially, however, the driving force of his religious policy at home was his desire to ensure political unity. So while maintaining as far as he could liberty of action in relation to the Papacy, which at times he attempted to humiliate, he wanted to discipline the Jansenists, who were Roman Catholic ascetics advocating an austere life and upholding the doctrine of salvation through grace alone. Furthermore he embarked on the wholesale conversion of the French Protestants or Huguenots who had enjoyed privileges conferred upon them by the Edict of Nantes in the reign of Louis's grandfather. It has recently been argued with considerable plausibility that the King of France was not really aware of the drastic methods used to compel conversions by [François-Michel Le Tellier, Marquis de] Louvois, who succeeded his father as Secretary of State for War in 1666. Louis thought that the conversions, achieved by force or bribery, were genuine and that the Edict of Nantes could be revoked because it had become superfluous. But in his early years he himself was not a *dévot*. He flaunted his mistresses, acknowledged their children, and laughed at clerical hypocrisy along with the great [playwright] Molière (Jean-Baptiste Poquelin). His own conversion did not come until late in life. As Goubert writes, "the Most Christian King thought only of glory, not yet of salvation.". . .

The Importance of the Peasantry

The achievements of the monarchy were founded upon the unceasing labour of the peasantry who were allowed, if they put on their best clothes, to wander in the gardens of Versailles and to supply cannon fodder for the royal armies. The rise of the bourgeoisie had not yet diminished the agricultural basis of the economy which was inherited from the Middle Ages. At the beginning of the seventeenth century fewer than a million out of fifteen million inhabitants of France lived in towns. The peasants owned less than half of the land. They had to pay taxes to the government, feudal dues to the bigger landowners and tithes to the Church. It has been estimated that the share extracted by the nobility and the Church from the peasants' output was of the order of thirty to forty per cent. Many different kinds of service had to be provided by them. They might be able to maintain a satisfactory standard of living when the weather was fine and the harvests were good, but in bad times they were ill-fed and not infrequently starved. It is one of the ironies of French agriculture that the peasants often grew insufficient grain to feed their own families and were forced to buy bread out of their earnings. Naturally the position varied from province to province and where the peasant was able to diversify his crops or supplement his farmwork by doing casual work of one kind or another or by fishing and poaching he was better off. But little progress in agricultural technology is recorded; traditional and old-fashioned methods were used. Books dealt with the art of gardening, the pursuit of hunting or how to make jam, not with the rotation of crops. Ploughing was tedious and wasteful, often producing poor yields. In one year out of two the grapes failed to ripen; in one year out of eight or ten the harvest was insufficient. Moreover industry and commerce contributed in only a small degree to the national income. The trading companies created by Colbert were unsuccessful: practising merchants refused to join these companies which were so strictly regimented by the government. France relied essentially upon its rich soil and its hardworking people.

Modern French historians in describing the difficulties under which the peasants laboured have perhaps given a somewhat exaggerated impression. When compared with the serfs of parts of Germany, or of Poland, Hungary and Russia the French were fairly comfortable and were at least free to express their grievances without being whipped by their masters. There were undoubtedly many wealthy peasants who concealed their well-stocked barns from the view of the tax gatherers. Even compared with the Dutch and English tenantry (though feudalism came to an end earlier in England than in France) they cannot have been too badly off. After all, everywhere agriculture was dependent on the weather; nowhere except in the United Netherlands and in parts of eastern England was technological progress noticeable at this time. Nowhere were peasants more hard working or less adaptable than in France. If they had not been so, Louis XIV would never have been able to continue his wars as long as he did. . . .

A Culture of Contrasts

Certainly there are always two sides to every question and historians must not permit themselves to be influenced in any way by propaganda to make the French of the seventeenth century into ogres or criminals. They were, after all, the most cultured people in the Western world of their time; their drama, literature and painting were outstanding. It can be maintained that after 1678 all Louis XIV's wars were defensive, even the war that he began in 1688 in an effort to intimidate the [Holy Roman] Emperor. War does not necessarily ruin an economy if it is not fought on a nation's own soil. English historians have argued that in many respects war (which was the characteristic occupation of most governments in the seventeenth century) was a stimulant; for example, the output of the peasants fetched good prices from large armies that needed to be fed, provided that these armies did not forcibly plunder but rather bought what they needed. With the rise of national "standing" armies after the Thirty Years' War, soldiers could no longer live off the countryside with impunity. War also stimulated industrial development. Ship-building, iron foundries and the cloth industry were given plenty of work. In fact France did not suffer economic ruin as the result of Louis XIV's wars.

In many ways then the France of Louis XIV was a land of contrasts: contrasts between the peasants who starved to death in years of bad harvests and the wealthy farmers who were able to provide for their posterity; contrasts between the economical procedures of Colbert and the lavish expenditure of his master on wars and building and gilding his palaces; contrasts between the gardens of Versailles with their fountains and lakes and the workmen who died of marsh fever in digging the canals that brought the water from the river to the palace. One may also contrast the teaching of Jacques Bénigne Bossuet, Bishop of Meaux, who preached on the divine right of kings with the writings of highly intelligent members of the same generation who enjoyed a freedom of mind not usually associated with countries where totalitarianism or tyranny prevail. François Fénelon, Archbishop of Cambrai, and Marshal Vauban had telling criticisms to make of the way France was governed and an "opposition" to the King has even been discerned especially from the 1690s onwards. The French monarch craved, above all else, harmony and unity; yet as soon as he ceased to be a victorious conqueror and became a loser and a persecutor he no longer commanded adulation and died unmourned. The glories of Versailles had their seamy side. As Professor Albert Guérard wrote, "The palaces of the time lacked elementary sanitation; the aristocrats bathed less frequently than in the Middle Ages; stench was fought with perfume." "Classical France," as it was called, was a way of life but had no philosophy. The Bourbons' failure to create political unity, to destroy the galling remains of feudalism or to accept religious toleration paved the way ultimately for revolution.

Lessons in Kingship for the Dauphin

Louis XIV

The following is an excerpt from *Mémoires de Louis XIV pour l'instruction du Dauphin,* a collection of thoughts prepared by Louis XIV (1638–1715) to be used as instruction for his eldest son and heir, the dauphin. According to Herbert H. Rowen, translator of the *Mémoires* and editor of the collection of historic writings from which this selection is taken, Louis XIV began to record these ideas and his evaluation of events in 1661, when he became a father. Louis comments on the importance of absolute rule by pointing out the dangers of giving even the smallest claim to the people, yet he also explains out that the king should rule not for the good of himself but for the good of the state. As the king must represent himself above all others, Louis explains that he must be virtuous, intelligent, and stand firm on his decisions.

It is beyond dispute that that subjugation which compels a sovereign to let his people lay down the law to him is the worst calamity into which a man of our rank can fall. Perhaps if we judged things rightly, we would say that a private man who can take orders is happier than the prince who cannot command, for the former is confident that the modesty of his status can be attributed only to the orders of his fate, while the latter is always in danger of having the re-

Excerpted from Louis XIV in *From Absolutism to Revolution, 1648–1848,* edited by Herbert H. Rowen. Copyright © 1969 Herbert H. Rowen. Reprinted with permission from Prentice-Hall, Inc., Upper Saddle River, NJ.

spect in which his virtue is held diminished by a stain upon the brilliance of his character. The grandeur and majesty of kings come not so much from the scepter which they hold as from the way in which they hold it. To assign the right of decision to subjects and the duty of deference to sovereigns is to pervert the order of things. The head alone has the right to deliberate and decide, and the functions of all the other members consist only in carrying out the commands given to them.

The Dangers of Giving Power to the People

If I showed you before the wretchedness of princes who entrust their peoples and their dignity to the guidance of a prime minister, I have all the more reason to demonstrate to you here how wretched are princes who have been surrendered to the heedlessness of an assembled populace; for the prime minister, after all, is a man whom you choose according to your own lights, whom you bring into government only so far as you please, and who has the principal influence in affairs only because he has first place in your heart. In appropriating your wealth and your authority for himself, at least he retains gratitude and respect for your person; and, no matter how great we make him, he cannot escape ruin whenever we have the strength simply to want to maintain him no longer. He is at most a single companion beside you upon the throne; if he despoils you of a part of your glory, at the same time he spares you from the thorniest of your problems; his interest in his own glory urges him to maintain yours; it is his pleasure to conserve your rights as property which he enjoys in your name; and if he shares your diadem [crown] with you, at least he works to leave it intact for your descendants.

But it is otherwise with the power which an assembled people takes for itself. The more you grant it, the more it claims; the more favors you bestow upon it, the more contempt it feels for you; and what it once has in its possession is held by so many arms that it cannot be wrested away without the greatest violence.

Among the multitude who comprise these great assemblages, those who act with the greatest licence are always the least intelligent, if you defer to them once, they claim forever after the right to determine your plans as the fancy strikes them; and the constant necessity to defend yourself against their assaults furnishes you with more troubles than all the other interests of your crown. Thus it is that a prince who wishes to leave an enduring peace to his people and an intact dignity to his successors, cannot be too careful in repressing such turbulent audacity.

But I have dwelled too long upon thoughts which appear useless or can serve only to help you recognize the wretchedness of our neighbors, since it is certain that in the state where you will reign after me you will find no authority which is not proud to derive its origins and its powers from you, no corporation which dares to voice its decisions in any but terms of respect, no company which does not feel the duty to seek its greatness principally in the good of your service and its sole security in humble submission. . . .

There is not the slightest doubt that we have nothing of which we should be more zealous than that pre-eminence which constitutes the principal beauty of the place we hold. Whatever marks it off or preserves it should be infinitely precious to us; what is at stake is not only our own interest, for it is a possession for which we are accountable to the public and to our successors. We cannot dispose of it as the fancy strikes us, and we should not question that it is one of the rights of the crown which cannot validly be given away.

Those who believe that such claims as these involve nothing but ceremony are gravely mistaken, for in this matter everything must be considered and everything has its importance. The people over whom we reign are unable to see into the heart of things, and hence base their judgments upon what they can see on the surface; most of the time they proportion their respect and their obedience to the spectacle and the rank which they observe. As it is important for the public that it should be governed by only one man, it is also important to it that the man who performs this function should be so far above other men that no one could be mistaken for him or compared to him, and one cannot deprive the head of the state of the least mark of superiority which distinguishes him from the other members, without doing harm to the entire body of the state.

The Qualities of a King

But keep still in mind, my son, that the pre-eminence which you should most seek and which will distinguish you to greatest advantage will be that which comes from your own personal qualities.

High rank is never more solid or assured than when it is supported by singular merit; and this is what has doubtless persuaded some that it might be advantageous to the reigning prince to see those who are closest to him by birth greatly distinguished from him by their conduct. This wide interval which his virtue puts between him and them makes him appear more brightly and brilliantly before the eyes of the entire world. His lofty and solid qualities of mind obtain wholly new luster from the lack of distinction of those who come near him. The grandeur and firmness of soul which are visible in him are enhanced by the contrast with the weakness of soul observed in them; and the love of work and true glory which he displays is infinitely brighter when one discovers elsewhere nothing but ponderous sloth or love of trivialities.

Thanks to this difference, all eyes are fixed upon him alone; all requests are addressed to him alone, all respects are paid to him alone, everything is hoped for from him alone; nothing is undertaken, nothing is expected, nothing is done, except through him alone. His favor is regarded as the only source of all good things; men believe that they are rising in the world to the extent that they come near him or earn his esteem; all else is cringing, all else is powerless, all else is sterile, and it may even be said that the brilliancy he possesses in his own state passes by transference into foreign lands. The shining image of the greatness to which he has raised himself is borne everywhere on the wings of his fame. Just as his subjects admire him, so neighboring nations are soon awed by him. If only he is able to make good use of these advantages, there is nothing either under his sway or beyond it which in the course of time he cannot succeed in doing.

But although these reasons may seem quite plausible to you, and my explanations may perhaps give you cause to believe that they are not wholly unfamiliar to my feelings, do not think that if you should have brothers one day, my passion for you would be so blind that I myself would seek to give you all the advantages which I have just discussed with you; on the contrary, I would truly endeavor to give you all the same instruction and the same examples, but it would be your task to distinguish yourself from them by your particular skill in profiting by these lessons. . . .

Avoiding Weakness and Personal Interests

Kings are often obliged to do things which go against their inclinations and offend their natural goodness. They should love to give pleasure and yet they must often punish and destroy persons on whom by nature they wish to confer benefits. The interest of the state must come first. One must constrain one's inclinations and not put oneself in the position of berating oneself because one could have done better in some important affair but did not because of some private interest, because one was distracted from the attention one should have for the greatness, the good and the power of the state. Often there are troublesome places where it is difficult to make out what one should do. One's ideas are confused. As long as this lasts, one can refrain from making a decision. But as soon as one has fixed one's mind upon something which seems best to do, it must be acted upon. This is what enabled me to succeed so often in what I have done. The mistakes which I made, and which gave me infinite trouble, were the result of the desire to please or of allowing myself to accept too carelessly the opinions of others. Nothing is more dangerous than weakness of any kind whatsoever. In order to command others, one must raise oneself above them and once one has heard the reports from every side one must come to a decision upon the basis of one's own judgment, without anxiety but always with the concern not to command anything which is of itself unworthy either of one's place in the world or of the greatness of the state. Princes with good intentions and some knowledge of their affairs, either from experience or from study and great diligence in making themselves capable, find numerous cases which instruct them that they must give special care and total application to everything. One must be on guard against oneself, resist one's own tendencies, and always be on guard against one's own natural bent. The craft of a king is great, noble and delightful when one feels worthy of doing well whatever one promises to do. But it is not exempt from troubles, weariness and worries. Sometimes uncertainty causes despair, and when one has spent a reasonable time in examining an affair, one must make a decision and take the step which one believes to be best. When one has the state in view, one works for one's self. The good of the one constitutes the glory of the other. When the former is fortunate, eminent and powerful, he who is the cause thereof becomes glorious and consequently should find more enjoyment than his subjects in all the pleasant things of life for himself and for them. When one has made a mistake, it must be corrected as soon as possible, and no other consideration must stand in the way, not even kindness.

The Golden Age of Dutch Commerce

Charles Wilson

In the following excerpt, historian Charles Wilson, formerly of Jesus College at Oxford, provides an overview of the colonial trading empire developed by the Dutch during the seventeenth century. Wilson contrasts the East and West India Companies, the two primary trading companies of the Dutch Republic. The older East India Company continued to flourish in Asia, but it faced difficulties with colonists who sought autonomy in South Africa. According to Wilson, the West India Company unsuccessfully pursued South American markets while colonists in North America sought a measure of independence that challenged the economic success of trade in the American colonies. However, Dutch exploration continued: The western coast of Australia was discovered by a Dutch ship traveling to Java, and the expeditions of Abel Tasman led to the discovery of Tasmania and New Zealand.

B etween the truce with Spain of 1609 and the Treaty of Breda with England in 1667, the Dutch created a new colonial trading empire. They did it in competition with two other powers—a declining Portugal, upon whose colonial heels they trod nearly everywhere except in North America, and the English, who were also preparing themselves for colonial adventure. Few spectacles in modern history are more remarkable than the explosive expansion of Holland and Zeeland, these two small waterlogged provinces that formed the heart of the Republic. For more than a century the

Excerpted from Charles Wilson, *The Dutch Republic and the Civilisation of the Seventeenth Century.* Copyright © 1968 Charles Wilson. Reprinted with permission from The Orion Publishing Group Ltd.

Netherlands economy had been developing on the principle of a division of labour. The Netherlanders concentrated on those trades and industries that yielded high rates of return. The less profitable they left to others. They therefore naturally extended their enterprise to these remote areas of the world that were confidently expected to yield, if not gold and silver, at any rate spices, fine textiles, tobacco, sugar and similar products of high scarcity value. They were already equipped by experience to navigate in far waters. There was probably no better school of navigation and seamanship than the seas between the Bay of Biscay and the Baltic.

The Trading Companies

The chosen instruments of colonial expansion were the East India Company and—much later and less successful—the West India Company. Like the government of the Republic itself, like the navy too, these companies were organised on a more or less federal basis. The East India Company, granted its charter in 1602, was the result of a belated realisation that the original pioneer companies were all getting in each other's way and that as a result profits were lower and costs higher than they could have been. But the new corporation, ruled by its seventeen directors (the *Heeren XVII*), retained six regional "chambers" based on the old companies at Amsterdam, Middelburg, Delft, Rotterdam, Hoorn and Enkhuizen. The corporation disposed of the talents of Dutch navigators who had formerly served with the Portuguese. Nor had the earlier voyages, ill-organised though they were, been entirely wasted. Cornelis Houtman's first voyage of 1595 had been literally a "pilot plant" for later expeditions. The Amsterdam merchants who organised it had acquired all the information they could about the journeys of [English explorers Sir Francis] Drake and [Thomas] Cavendish. Where possible they had employed pilots and sailors who had served in earlier English expeditions. (Among those on board were John Davis and James Lancaster, who were later to be in charge of the English East India Company's expedition to the same waters.)

The same pattern of control as had manifested itself in the politics of the Republic was now repeated in the East India Company. Gradually the small "chambers" fell under the dominance of Amsterdam. By the end of the century a group of a hundred or so Amsterdammers held nearly half the capital of the Zeeland chamber. More than half the total capital of the entire company was held in Amsterdam. In the second half of the seventeenth century, the nature of this Amsterdam control itself altered. Active merchants played a diminishing part. Regents—rentiers, professional administrators—came to dominate its affairs.

The West India Company presented a strong contrast to the older company. It was the brain child of the Calvinist, Orangist party, strongly influenced by southern immigrants whose driving ambition was to strike a last fatal blow at Spain and Portugal. [Dutch statesman Johan van] Oldenbarneveldt had delayed its foundations in the interests of his policy of conciliation with Spain. Once he was out of the way, the West India Company went forward. Amsterdam was less enthusiastic about this enterprise than it had been twenty years earlier about the old. Even so it subscribed on a very large scale. By 1670 half the capital of the West India Company was likewise owned by Amsterdam shareholders.

Trading in the East

Yet there the resemblance between the companies ended. In the East the Dutch company forged ahead. By the mid-century, it had established itself by conquest in the Moluccas, at Batavia; Malaya, at Pulicat in India; and Zeelandia in Formosa. It had made monopoly contracts with native rulers like the Sultan of Ternate. Elsewhere it traded alongside the English or Portuguese in competition for the favours of the local chieftains. This last was to be, in spite of additional conquests after 1650, the most important area of trade. In everything except the spices of the Moluccas and Ceylon, that is to say, the Company's business was highly competitive. Hence the presence of those who, from the formidable founder of Batavia, Jan Pieterszoon Coen, onwards, believed in a policy of conquest to eliminate European competition and bring local rulers under control.

Coen had laid down his formula to the directors in 1614 and it was in very clear terms:

> Your Honours should know by experience that trade in Asia must be driven and maintained under the protection and favour of Your Honours' own weapons, and that the weapons must be paid for by the profits from the trade; so that we cannot carry on trade without war nor war without trade.

This was strong medicine for the cautious *Heeren* at Amsterdam. Fortunately perhaps for them, there was never much they could do about it. As a much later official at Batavia remarked, "The Directors in the fatherland decide matters as it seems best to them there; but we do here what seems best and most advisable to us."

Territorial conquest nevertheless remained limited—in Asia to Java, the Moluccas and Ceylon, in South Africa to the Cape settlement. Originally founded to trade in pepper and spices, the Company changed tack later in the seventeenth century. As European demand for oriental textiles grew, the importance of spices declined. In the next century textiles were joined by tea, coffee and porcelain as homeward cargoes. Within its area of conquest, the Dutch Company, like its English rival, became a territorial colonial power in the eighteenth century. Yet even here it remained, as Professor [C.R.]

Boxer has said, "an alien body on the fringe of Asian society." The trading activities of the Dutch did little to alter the fundamental forces of economic, social or religious custom which decided the shape and structure of society in Java or Ceylon. *A fortiori* the same was true of areas like the Indian mainland, China and Japan where the Europeans came as traders not as conquerors.

The Dutch in South Africa

The Cape of Good Hope [in South Africa] was incidental to the Company's plans. Soon after their foundation they had tried to seize Mozambique as a port of call for their ships to be re-victualled. They failed. In 1620 the English East India Company had taken formal possession of the Cape, but then failed to occupy it. It therefore remained until Jan van Riebeeck took it in the name of the Dutch Company in 1652.

The Cape was not a safe roadstead for shipping (in fact it was very dangerous) but it provided a healthy stopping place, and reduced the appalling mortality at sea that marked these long voyages to and from the East. But as a settlement it was, in the eyes of the directors, an incubus [a nightmarish burden]. Its main function was to supply victuals for the Company's ships. The main duty of the governor was to keep the costs of food and maintenance as low as possible. The second half of the century therefore saw a conflict between the Company and the "free-burgher" colonists who had been allowed to farm the land and provide provisions. They wanted, not unnaturally, to get the best prices they could for their produce. As long as the Company rule lasted, the conflict went on. "Trekking," a phenomenon often thought of as a nineteenth-century peculiarity, began in the late seventeenth century. It was the instinctive reaction of men trying to escape from the rigid autocracy of Company rule. Visitors already noticed the difference between the urbane bureaucrats, professional men and merchants who formed the Cape community itself, and the rougher, tougher *boeren* who had moved out further and further into the hinterland. It was a distinction which was to last. . . .

Trading in the West

The West India Company was from the start a belligerent mixture of trade and religion. Most of its directors were strong Calvinists from the south whose dominating idea was to combine business with a religious crusade against popery [Catholicism]. They were almost uniformly unsuccessful. After a promising beginning, the campaign against Brazil became hopelessly bogged down, its costs an endless drain on the finances of the Company. Sugar, the commodity in which the Company in Brazil principally dealt, was a highly fluctuating and speculative business. Markets were impossible to predict, profits precarious. The brilliant capture of the silver fleet by the Dutch Admiral Piet Heyn in 1628 enabled the Company to declare a bumper dividend but it was almost the last for thirty-five years. The West African trade yielded some profit too, but this was absorbed in the enormous costs of the fiasco in Brazil. The Company ended by going into the slave trade, especially the profitable but illegal export of slaves to the Spanish American colonies. Yet as a whole the history of the West India Company was a dreary tale of muddle and near-bankruptcy. It showed how wise was the normal Dutch policy of keeping politics and religion out of business.

Like the East India Company, the West India Company never penetrated the tropical countries to which it traded. Like the older Company it established one colony of white settlement—New Netherland on the banks of the Hudson and the shores of Manhattan Island. In 1609, two years after Christopher Newport had brought his battered ships into Chesapeake Bay and initiated the English settlement of America, Henry Hudson sailed west in search of a north-west passage to India. Hudson, though English, was in the employment of the Dutch East India Company. He failed to find what he was looking for, but found instead the river which bears his name. This he believed to be the opening of a channel which would lead him through into the Pacific. When this optimistic assumption proved wrong, his backers lost interest. But that was not the end of the story. Other merchants had spotted the possibilities of the fur trade. A company was founded. Blockhouses flying the Dutch flag sprang up, one on the island of Manhattan, another—"Orange"—where Albany now is. The trickle of immigrants began to realise that New Netherland had other commercial possibilities too. Surrounded by the more populous and growing settlements of New England and Virginia, the Dutch colony was strategically placed to act as an entrepôt [intermediary center of trade] for the entire east coast.

The Dutch in America

Unfortunately, the directors of the West India Company at home, under whose aegis the colony stood, failed to see eye to eye with the colonists. A dispute arose not unlike that which was to arise between the Cape colonists and the directors of the East India Company. The directors hedged and vacillated over schemes of further colonisation. The governor was at loggerheads with the colonists over their demands for more say in local affairs. By 1649 three delegates of the citizens of the colony embarked for home to submit petitions against the entire system of control by the West India Company. The leading spirit was Adriaan van der Donck, a man of remarkable and articulate vision. His petition on behalf of the languishing colony ended with a plea for more immigration, more civic freedom. Only this, he said prophetically, could save the existence of the colony:

> The most terrible ruin will follow and this province will become the defenceless prey of its neighbours. The Dutch free burghers already living there will be forced to seek refuge elsewhere or to subject themselves to a foreign nation. The very name of New Netherlands will be lost and no Dutchman will any longer have any say in affairs here.

The mission was not altogether without effect. The reins were loosened a little. A modest measure of self-government was allowed. Immigrants flowed in (many of them foreigners) but the colony remained small. Meanwhile, from 1660 onwards, the English government was set upon enforcing a re-invigorated navigation system designed to prevent the Dutch from buying from or selling to English colonies except in carefully selected areas of trade. The Dutch colony in North America cut clean across these ambitions. Its most profitable business was in smuggling goods through to New England and buying (so it was said) wool from the New Englanders to supply to the Dutch cloth industry in defiance of all the regulations which were trying to restrict that supply. An economic challenge of this kind from a militarily weak and isolated foreign community was too much to be tolerated. After a suitably pious prelude of protest and claims based on heavily doctored history, an expedition set out to capture the colony. In 1664 New Amsterdam became New York. There was no bloodshed. (A common Protestantism counted for something, even in the seventeenth century.) But another chapter of Dutch colonisation and settlement was at an end, though Dutch continued to be spoken amongst the descendants of the settlers for another century. But Dutch craftsmanship continued identifiably in such manufactures as silverwork. Personal ties remained strong. Late in the eighteenth century a gigantic land speculation in Pennsylvania and New York was floated by a Dutch company, the *Hollandsche Land Compagnie*. It was an American of Dutch descent who cut the Erie Canal and poured the first kegful of lake water into the Atlantic. It was the first of the famous members of the Roosevelt family, Nicolas, who organised the first steamboat service from Pittsburgh to New Orleans. The Dutch did not quickly forget their traditional skills.

The South-West Pacific

In the meantime, other Dutch discoveries had taken place which were to have consequences equally great to the British Empire. These were the opening up of the south-west Pacific. There was a tradition that south of New Guinea lay a great continent—a tradition which possibly originated in half-remembered tales of earlier voyagers, possibly in the old theory that the southern hemisphere must contain as much land as the northern in order to maintain the stability of the earth—a nice instance of how the Middle Ages occasionally came to the right conclusion for the wrong reason. 1606 saw the first authenticated discovery of Australia by the Dutchman Willem Janszoon who, coming from Bantam in the *Duifken*, crossed the dangerous region of shoals and islands separating New Guinea from Australia and penetrated into the Gulf of Carpentaria, reaching the west coast of Queensland. The Dutch explorers were not impressed by what they found in these lands of promise; they wrote:

> This extensive country, for the greatest part desert, but in some places inhabited by wild, cruel, black savages, by whom some of the crew were murdered; for which reason they could not learn anything of the land or waters, as had been desired of them, and, by want of provisions and other necessaries, they were obliged to leave the discovery unfinished; the furthest point of the land was called in their Map, Cape Keer-Weer (Cape Turn-Again).

Ten years later, the Dutch accidentally discovered western Australia. A Dutch ship taking the route south of the tropics from the Cape of Good Hope to Java overran the passage westwards before turning north to Java and sighted the west coast of Australia. During the following decade, the whole of the west coast was charted, and in 1627 another Dutch ship explored about half the southern coast. The new continent was christened *New Holland,* but thereafter Dutch interest flagged; Janszoon's successors conceived no more affection for it than he. It promised no spices, food or even fresh water. Meanwhile other Dutch seamen were exploring in the north and in 1623, one had crossed the Gulf of Carpentaria and discovered Arnhem Land.

Discovering Tasmania and New Zealand

Dutch enterprise in the south-west Pacific culminated in the voyages of the great commander and navigator Abel Tasman and his chief pilot and planner, Frans Visscher, sailing under the patronage of the governor-general of the East Indies, Antony van Diemen. The immediate motive of the expedition was strategic; in South America the Dutch were at grips with the Spaniards; their problem was to find access to the Spanish colonies in South America without having to go all the way round the north Pacific and down the Californian coast, risking the twin hazards of calms and adverse winds. Tasman's aim was to steer a passage south of Australia; his voyage brought him to an island (Tasmania) which he named Van Diemen land; then, turning east into the open ocean, he came to an unknown land which he called New Zealand. He followed the coastline to its most northerly point which he called after his patron's wife, Maria van Diemen, then, convinced that the west wind track to South America was navigable, he sailed back to Batavia by the northern coast of New Guinea.

Tasman's discoveries made him the greatest explorer since Magellan; they were not to be surpassed in importance until the time of [English explorer James] Cook. As a result of his voyages and those of his predecessors, the Dutch had come to know a great deal about western and northern Australia, though they still mistakenly believed New Guinea to be contiguous with north-east Australia. They also knew the southern coast as far east as Tasmania. But these were not the most attractive or fertile stretches of the south coast and the east coast—the regions which make up the greater part of the populated continent today remained outside the scope of their knowledge and interest. Obsessed by the narrow conception of colonial trade as a quest for spices, the Dutch explorers were blind to the vast potentialities of these continents which they discovered, charted and left sprinkled with Dutch names. . . .

To summarise: within half a century of their earliest voyages, Dutch traders and adventurers had sketched the future course of European colonial development. They had laid the foundation of an eastern and a western Empire; they had established a settlement in the pleasant lands of south Africa and another on the Atlantic seaboard of America: they had discovered and charted considerable stretches of territory in Australia and New Zealand. Yet the Hollanders' enterprise failed to live up to its early promise. Except for the East Indies and some islands and territories in the West Indies and South America, the Dutch settlements either stagnated, or fell supinely before the aggressive enterprise of newcomers, or simply failed to take root.

The Fall of the Ottoman Empire

William Stearns Davis

The Ottoman Empire made one last effort to resume its glory as a conqueror by capturing Vienna in 1683. As a result of corruption within the government, demoralization of the people, and mismanagement of the military, the Turks were doomed to fail, writes the late William Stearns Davis, a former professor of history at the University of Minnesota. According to Davis, the sultans abused their power, making it difficult for the last great viziers, Mohammed and Ahmed Kiuprili, to overcome a century of corruption and stagnation. Led by the ambitious vizier Kara Mustafa Pasa, the Turks advanced on Vienna, and a surprised Austria nearly lost the city. The king of Poland, however, arrived on roads unprotected by the Turkish army, and after days of fighting, liberated Vienna from the Turkish troops that surrounded it. Kara Mustafa Pasa escaped but was killed on December 25, 1683.

For over two hundred years after the crossing of the Hellespont the Ottoman sultans, despite occasional repulses, seemed steadily advancing from glory to glory. But after the conquest of Cyprus in 1571 they won few additional territories. For a little more than a century the boundaries in the Near East remained fairly static, then in 1683 the Turks made a new and vigorous effort to resume their conquering path by capturing Vienna. They failed absolutely, and very soon were struggling as desperately on the defensive as had been the West when Solyman I [1520–1566] was girt with the sword of Osman.

Excerpted from William Stearns Davis, *A Short History of the Near East* (New York: The Macmillan Company, 1922).

The Causes of Ottoman Decline

What were the causes of this century of stagnation (always equivalent to degeneration in an Oriental despotism), and of this decisive reverse? Some of the more general factors were undoubtedly these:

I. The Ottomans had now driven through the relatively weak South Slavs and Magyars, and were directly opposed to the more military Germans and Poles.

II. In their rear they always had Persia, a rival Moslem Empire, quite strong enough to press hard on their eastern Sanjaks whenever the Sultans became too involved in the West.

III. The Ottomans had now been in Europe over two hundred years, an extremely long time for an Oriental race and dynasty to retain its virility and aggressiveness.

IV. The development of the art of war into a real science under the impulse of such great captains as Alexander Farnese [regent for Philip II of Spain], Maurice of Nassau [stadtholder of the Dutch Republic] and Gustavus Adolphus [king of Sweden] was something which the Turks were unable to imitate. The tactics that had quite sufficed against Louis of Hungary at Mohacz had become hopelessly antiquated by the middle of the seventeenth century when the Turks had to confront soldiers trained in the horrible but effective school of the Thirty Years' War.

The Ottomans in fact would doubtless have experienced a great military disaster long before 1683 had not this period of their stagnation coincided with the century of the Wars of the Counter Reformation, the Thirty Years' War, and of the first decades of Louis XIV; when the Christian powers were rending one another, and when Austria (the Turks' most formidable Christian neighbor) very often had the Swedes or French upon her back. The feuds of Christendom were thus once again the salvation of Islam.

Nevertheless in addition to these various factors over which, circumstances considered, the Ottomans might possibly have pleaded that they had no control, there were other evils more specific which were not really beyond the powers of a vigorous government to rectify. The first two Kiuprili viziers (1656–1676) did indeed accomplish something in preventing the ruin of the state, but they were after all only ministers and not sovrans, and they were in a position to treat merely the symptoms, not the fundamentals of the disease. During the seventeenth century the following concrete abuses were helping to pull down the still vast and imposing Ottoman Empire.

The Abuse of Power

The Padishahs [Turkish sultans] had "become invisible." Many of them had been reared in the harem in strict seclusion until totally bereft of any political education. They were incessantly trembling for their lives, until some revolution called them not to the bowstring but to supreme power. The Sultans had now ceased to preside at the council of viziers, to hear litigants, or to enjoy any opportunity to get unbiased reports about the bad deeds of their officials.

Along with this evil there went the inordinate influence of harem women and of eunuchs. Even if these persons were not iniquitous, they had never the least ideas of what might benefit the state. Frequently their intrigues could induce the Sultan to depose or even to bowstring [strangle with a bowstring] a highly competent vizier. "The Sultan governs no longer; the grand vizier is hindered in governing; the power is actually in the hands of negro eunuchs and purchased slave-girls." This of course was hardly true of the two great Kiuprili viziers, but it never ceased to be a constant danger.

The outrageous taxation of the subjects, especially of the Christian rayahs, [a person who is not Mohammedan], wrought general demoralization. The imperial officials increased taxes at pleasure, and often levied new and unauthorized imposts. "The tears of the oppressed will drown the Empire in the waves of perdition." All this in other words meant economic decline and fiscal demoralization.

The feudal spahis—holders of the military fiefs—by the seventeenth century were allowed to evade systematically their martial duties. Many fiefs were awarded as perquisites to harem women, to court eunuchs, to the sultan's dwarfs and mutes—persons utterly incapable of the slightest military service. The result was that this feudal cavalry, once a great factor in the armies, dwindled down to some 7,000 or 8,000 riders, and these often inefficient and ill-disciplined.

Most serious for the government was the change in the recruitment of the Janissaries [elite troops]. In the seventeenth century the blood-tax of Christian boys was dropped, and Moslems (to the general satisfaction of the Faithful) were now allowed to enroll in this privileged corps. Under Solyman I there had been some 12,000 Janissaries; a century later there were over 46,000. But their devotion and discipline were now utterly relaxed. They lost much of their value in battle; yet in Constantinople they often terrorized populace and sultan by their outrageous mutinies and constant demands for more bounties and perquisites. "The formidable corps of 'slave-soldiers' had given place to an impudent and seditious city guard."

Along with this recruitment of the guard-corps from the regular Turkish population went a corresponding decline of the promotion of "slaves" and other ex-Christians to high office in the army and civil service. The administrative incapacity of the native Moslems wrought endless confusion in "The Ruling Institution." The ablest of the Kiuprili viziers failed in the end to reinvigorate the state, thanks largely to sheer inability to find competent officials to execute good laws. . . .

The Great Viziers

It was not until 1656 that the Ottoman magnates persuaded the Sultan-mother . . . to offer the grand vizierate to the man whom circumstances were already designating as the preserver of the Empire. In that year, says the exultant Turkish historian, "the demons of cruelty, debauchery, and sedition, who had reached their meridian in [the preceding decades] . . . were obliged to yield up their crown of dominion, when the voice was heard which proclaimed Kiuprili Grand Vizier of the Empire."

Mohammed Kiuprili was the grandson of Moslem Albanians who had emigrated to Asia Minor. He began his career as a kitchen boy. By sheer ability he rose to such eminence that all patriotic factions united to put him on the very steps of the throne. He only accepted office on condition that the Sultan-mother and the Sultan should let him act as practically the unchecked dictator of the realm. The Sultan-mother in behalf of her son actually swore to his arrogant terms,—that all his measures should be ratified without discussion; that he should have complete and unquestioned power to appoint, to reward, and to punish; that no great man or favorite should be allowed any influence against him; and that all accusations or insinuations against him should be instantly rejected. Under these conditions he undertook to save the afflicted Empire.

Kiuprili was grand vizier from 1656 until his death in 1661. During that time he walked in the steps of Murad IV, and restored order to the realm by the pitiless execution of all evil-doers, however high their station. His spies soon were everywhere, reporting past delinquency or present sedition. He hanged the Greek patriarch for writing a letter expressing the hope that the Ottoman power soon would crumble. He was equally severe with lawless and fanatical dervishes [a Moslem order] and ulemas [religious teachers]. Kiuprili never wasted his time with threats and warnings. "His blows outsped his words." Thirty-six thousand persons are said to have been executed by his orders within five years. The chief executioner of Constantinople later declared that within that time he had himself strangled 4,000, and thrown the corpses in the Bosphorus. Kiuprili seems to have followed out this policy in good faith, believing it to be the only method for purging the Empire of evil elements. Possibly in this he was not, considering existing conditions, very greatly mistaken.

The Vizierate of Ahmed Kiuprili

On his deathbed Kiuprili was asked, by his sorrowing master, who could best continue his work of reformation. "I know of none better than my son, Ahmed," was his candid response; then he gave the Sultan four maxims: "Listen not to the counsels of women; let not a subject become too rich; by every means fill the treasury; keep continually on horseback and give constant employment to the army." Mohammed IV was too sluggish to obey these directions personally, but he promptly made Ahmed Kiuprili his grand vizier. The latter became the real ruler of Turkey from 1661 to his death in 1676; and he is justly eulogized both by Ottoman and Christian historians as "the greatest statesman of his country." Unlike his father (perhaps merely because his father had finished a necessary if ungrateful work) he was usually humane, and he made a really earnest effort to lessen the burdens of taxation, and to protect the masses from the exactions and violence of the feudal Spahis, the begs, and others among the mighty. Despite evidences of decadence in the Empire matters had not gone so far that this wise and just minister could not accomplish a perceptible if only temporary improvement of the state.

Ahmed Kiuprili was defeated indeed in the great battle of St. Gotthard by the Austrians, but in other wars (with the Poles and Venetians) he was usually successful. Unfortunately a large part of his worthy civil reforms perished with him, when in 1676 there died this true "light and splendor of the nation; the conservator of good laws; the vicar of the shadow of God." It was not in the power of Mohammed IV to find a third prime minister like unto him. The next grand vizier, Kara Mustafa ("Black Mustafa"), who held power from 1676 through 1683, was rather a showy, ambitious personage, exceedingly covetous, who never subordinated his personal schemes to the weal of the Empire. The result was that the forces of decay—partially arrested by the two great Kiuprilis, resumed their potency, and were presently blazoned to the world by a great military disaster.

The Battle of St. Gotthard

Without power to affect fundamental reforms it is not surprising that even the great Kiuprili viziers could not give back to the Empire successful aggressiveness. The Ottoman military pride, however, died very hard. The monarchy was still indeed imposing in its size. It could still muster armies extremely formidable to the weaker European powers or to those beset by desperate feuds with their Christian neighbors. During a twenty-five-year war (1644–1669), during which Venice vainly sought effective help from the West, the Turks wrested from her Crete ("Candia") and practically banished her from Greek waters, save only from her possession of Corfu (old Corcyra) and other Ionian Isles. In 1672 the Sultan became also involved in a war with Poland, in which the Turks captured and for years retained possession of the strong fortress of Kemenets and wrung from the ill-governed Slavic "Commonwealth" the cession of most of Podolia. This last result, however, was far more due to the generally distracted state of Poland rather than to any inferiority of her armies.

When in 1673 the struggle was renewed, and Kiuprili laid siege to the other great fortress of Chotin, it was only to see his army sorely defeated in a great pitched battle.

This was by no means the first indication that Ottoman leaders would have done well to hesitate ere they attempted offensive warfare with the scientifically organized and commanded armies of the greater Christian powers. As a rule during this period Turkey had at least nominally kept up the old relations with France, and considered her an "ally"; but this friendship often became very cold. Louis XIV, much as he hated Austria, was entirely willing to teach the Sultan that he could only hope to prevail over the "Holy Roman Emperor" when he made Ottoman ambitions subserve French policy. In 1664 Ahmed Kiuprili ventured to invade the Austrian lands in a year when the Emperor and Louis were actually at peace. The French king promptly offered so large an army to assist the Austrians that the latter became alarmed lest they be put under too heavy obligations. They only accepted 6,000 troops, but these were the very pick of Louis's forces under the Count de Coligny. Kiuprili, with a host of 120,000 Orientals, meanwhile advanced, ravaging the Christian territories, until by the monastery of St. Gotthard on the Raab he met the Imperialists . . . with the new French auxiliaries. There were barely 20,000 Christians in their entire army, but they were led by great captains. When the Vizier saw the white perukes of the French as they charged to battle he demanded in amazement, "Who are these girls?" But, raising their dreaded cry, "*Allons! Allons! Tue! Tue!*" Coligny's men speedily scattered the Janissaries with a terrific onslaught. The Turks were driven discomfited from the field. The Emperor (fearing too much French assistance) soon, it is true, made peace on terms extremely favorable to the Ottomans, but the latter indeed should have had their warning. St. Gotthard had taught the world that the small Western armies, properly led, could now rout the Sultan's huge hosts in open battles.

The Second Siege of Vienna

Matters thus drifted till 1683, when the grand vizier, Kara Mustafa,—Ahmed Kiuprili's son-in-law, to be sure, but no heir to his probity and intelligence,—opened his ears to the projects of certain Hungarian rebels against the Hapsburgs. He mobilized the whole available strength of the Ottoman Empire and undertook to do that which Solyman I had failed to accomplish. With over 200,000 men he pushed up the Danube against Vienna.

The moment seemed not ill-chosen. Louis XIV was probably about to resume his old wars with Austria. The French king even exerted his diplomacy to prevent the Hapsburgs from getting allies, his own apparent desire being that Vienna should fall, and that then he (as the all-powerful champion of Christian civilization) could intervene to expel the Turk to his own great benefit. Kara Mustafa in his turn appears to have been dreaming a disloyal dream of carving out a separate kingdom for himself in the Danube valley. In any case, when he made his attack, Leopold of Austria was taken almost unawares. He could barely throw 13,000 men into Vienna and flee himself to Passau, calling loudly for help to the lesser German princes, and especially to the valorous John Sobieski, the elective king of Poland, the victor of Chotin. The latter responded fairly promptly, not because he loved Austria greatly, but because the safety of Poland would have been in sore jeopardy if the Turks were once fairly ensconced at Vienna.

Sweeping up the Danube valley with his enormous host, swollen now by Wallachian [of what is now Romania] vassal contingents and by Hungarian malcontents, Kara Mustafa encamped before Vienna on July 14, 1683. The failure of the Austrian ministers to realize their danger betimes and bring up prompt assistance almost ruined the situation for their master. The imperial general, Charles of Lorraine, with a very weak field army, did his best to ease the pressure on the garrison by cutting off the Turkish supplies, as well as by a valorous and successful defense of Pressburg. If, however, the grand vizier had known his business, or Count Stahremberg (the governor of the besieged capital) had flinched in the slightest, Vienna, at least for the moment, would have gone the way of Constantinople. Kara Mustafa, however, wasted several precious days getting comfortably encamped in the suburbs, and in that short interval the garrison got the defenses in some kind of order. Then at length began the incessant assaults and the inflexible resistance. . . .

The Deliverance of Vienna

The Polish army had mobilized slowly, and slowly it had been joined by a force of Saxons, Bavarians, and various other German volunteers. Added to Charles of Lorraine's forces, the whole relieving host numbered barely 70,000, but they were soldiers hard and fit, the match for any in the world, save possibly their French rivals. While Stahremberg looked forth from St. Stephen, John Sobieski from the Kahlenberg was viewing the besieged capital. Even across the years may be realized his tension when he beheld "the immense plain covered with pavilions, and innumerable multitude of horses, camels and buffaloes. Two hundred thousand men, all in motion, . . . while [around the city] the fire of the besiegers was incessant and terrible, and that of the besieged such only as they could contrive to make," with the tall steeples of Vienna barely appearing above the haze of fire and smoke.

Sobieski instantly saw, however, that the Vizier had delivered himself into his hands. Kara Mustafa had dwelt in a fool's paradise. Confident that the Poles could not arrive ere the city surrendered, he had neglected to block the roads by which the relieving army must approach. The experienced Ibrahim, Pasha of Buda, now besought him to draw off his best troops from before the walls, and dispute the difficult ravines west of the city, by which alone the rescuers could advance. The Vizier would have none of this advice. He virtually allowed the Christians to advance with his own army spread in a long, thin circumference around Vienna, and with no sufficient concentration at the point where Sobieski was sure to strike. The King exultantly took in the situation at a glance. "This man knows nothing of war," he declared. "We shall certainly defeat him!"

On the morning of the 12th, the Poles and the Imperialists rushed down from the Kahlenberg. There was hard fighting at some of the villages, but on the whole the Christian victory was surprisingly easy. The battering charges of the Polish and German cavalry swept away the Ottomans. The Janissaries were caught in their trenches between the relieving army and the rejoicing garrison and were almost cut to pieces. By night the whole great Infidel host was flying in headlong rout, in one of those enormous panics that now and again will seize upon Oriental armies. At next dawn the victors looked about for foes to contend against. They were nowhere. At ten o'clock that morning the rabble of Turks was racing across the Raab, covering in one night a journey they had consumed eight days in making on the advance.

The besiegers lost 10,000 men slain outright (their headlong flight prevented greater slaughter), 300 heavy cannon, 5,000 tents. Treasure of 15,000,000 crowns was taken, whereof 400,000 were in the Vizier's private coffers. All the Turkish standards were captured, save only the "Sacred Standard of the Prophet," which the fugitives saved by desperate exertions. Kara Mustafa fled precipitately to Belgrade, leaving the Christian allies to sweep in the Hungarian fortresses. At Belgrade, frantic with wrath and terror, he proceeded to execute those sagacious officers whose military advice he had wantonly disregarded. But before he could slay them all, the news of his calamity had reached Stamboul. In anguish and fury the Sultan ordered the ministers of death to Belgrade. On December 25, the bowstring in its turn tightened around Kara Mustafa, and all his ill-gotten wealth was confiscated for his master's treasury.

The Second Siege of Vienna marks the "high tide" for the attack of the Turanian Turks upon Europe. Doubtless they could not have made Vienna a second Constantinople set on the edge of Germany, but if even for a while they had possessed themselves of the city the blow inflicted in one way or another upon Western civilization would have been great. Such a calamity John Sobieski averted. "This time" the Turks had been repelled from Central Europe "never again to return thither."

Seventeenth-Century Art and Culture

PREFACE

While the art and culture of the Renaissance reflect the pursuit of the ideal, the art and culture of the baroque period provide a more realistic picture of seventeenth-century life. Access to art in the 1600s was no longer limited to the elite; an emerging middle class shared an interest in art, music, and fashion. Many artists were actually hostile to life in the royal courts. Whereas some mocked and parodied the court, others simply rejected the court as a subject, preferring to examine the life of artisans and farmers. Eastern art and culture had its own evolution apart from the Renaissance. Although Eastern artists of the seventeenth century came from the elite classes, they found meaning in all aspects of their unique culture. The art and culture of both worlds reveal the sense of individual power that was emerging during the seventeenth century.

Although some historians of Western civilization reserve the term *baroque* for artistic style, others use the term to describe a way of life, arguing that the baroque period exemplified people's interest in exploring the limits of human potential. Whether used to describe the art or the culture of the seventeenth century, the baroque reveals the tension of the age. People of the Renaissance strove toward the ideal, but during the baroque period people began to explore their individuality, and from this conflict between singularity and the ideal emerged a unique style.

The most obvious expression of the baroque is found in its architecture and music. Baroque architects designed ornate castles and churches. Baroque musicians composed elaborate and expressive operas, accompanied by grand pipe organs or huge choruses and orchestras. In painting, artists employed light and shadow to reveal the individuality of landscapes and human faces. Tragic stories of great heroes and extravagant comedies about human frailty dominated the theater and literature. Some scholars claim that at the height of the baroque, architects, sculptors, painters, poets, and musicians strove to accomplish the impossible in all directions.

Although some seventeenth-century artists came from the emerging middle class, which made it possible for them to reject the influence of the court, other artists did not have the means to support their own work and depended on patronage. As a result, the courts of Europe continued to influence the art of the seventeenth century. Moreover, the court itself began to express the baroque temperament. Members of the court and the emerging middle class created dramatic personas with magnificent costumes, elaborate coiffures, masks, and makeup. During the seventeenth century, people began to develop elaborate courtly manners, with dramatic displays of obeisance to duty and honor. People expressed themselves in extremes, pursuing both religious piety and carnal passion.

The grandiose and extravagant baroque, however, was a product of Western civilization. In the East, artists often sought the greatest meaning in the simplest form. As these artists found meaning in all objects, even the most mundane subject could have significant spiritual and artistic significance. However, Eastern art and culture during the seventeenth century were no less extreme. Whereas poets and painters sought simplicity, architects built elaborate temples and palaces for Eastern rulers and spiritual leaders.

Whether in the East or the West, people of the seventeenth century began to perceive themselves and their world in a new way. No longer focused on the ideal, they revealed in their art and culture the limits of human potential from the indulgence of royalty to the struggles of the peasant.

Music During the Baroque Period

Don C. Walter

The baroque period was characterized by a positive, vigorous, passionate style, and the music of the period was no exception. In the following excerpt, historian Don C. Walter explores not only the instruments and the music of the baroque but also its influence on those who
lived during the period. Unlike the music of the Renaissance, Walter
writes, baroque music was grandiose and thus required instruments that
could fill great halls and accompany large choruses. The baroque period, therefore, is characterized by the development of the pipe organ
and orchestral instruments. Baroque was more than an artistic style; it
was a part of courtly life. For example, Walter explains, music was an
important part of the court of Louis XIV, and musicians wrote music to
accompany the king and his court throughout their daily activities, from
getting dressed to going on the hunt. Musicians who came under the
king's protection, such as Jean-Baptiste Lully, became very successful
in their time.

The Baroque period was ushered in by a wave of intellectual, spiritual and physical activity. In that age we find the activities that are
the practical basis of our systematic civilization of today. The Renaissance had failed to fulfill the hopes and ideals that had produced it.
From the final decades of the Renaissance, characterized by doubt and
contradiction, arose the positive style of Baroque art, which was full of
vigor, strong emotion, symbolism, and subtlety. Renaissance music was

not made for the concert stage; its charm and delicate nuances are lost in a big auditorium, and the few forms in which it was composed were insufficient to meet the needs of a changing society.

The Role of the Pipe Organ

One of the most striking features of the Baroque was its fondness for the grandiose. This was evidenced by the prominent role assigned to the pipe organ and to music which required large choruses and massive effects.

In 1619 the pipe organ was on the threshold of its greatest era. Michael Praetorius described it in this way:

> The organ possesses and encompasses all other instruments of music—large and small, however named—in itself alone. If you want to hear a drum, a trumpet, a trombone, cornetts, a recorder, flutes, pommers, a shawm, a dulcian, racketts, sorduns, krummhorns, violins, lyres, etc., you can have all these and still many more unusual and charming things in this artful creation; so that when you have and hear this instrument, you think nought but that you have all the other instruments one amongst another. . . .

Organs of some sort have been used by man since well before the time of Christ. The Greeks and Romans employed their water-driven organ, known as a *hydraulis,* at circuses and festal gatherings. The Hebrews refer to a form of organ in the early synagogue services. In the Middle Ages, the Byzantines had similar large instruments that were admired by visiting Westerners. By the end of the ninth century, the organ made its way into most of the European churches, which have remained its principal home since that time. The organs of the medieval churches must have been cumbersome and overpowering monsters. The keyboard had not yet been developed; to select a tone, one pulled out a long slat which covered the end of one or more pipes. Compressed air was then free to rush in and produce a sound. The separate or combined use of various ranks of pipes, which we call registration, did not appear until the fourteenth century. Keys also began to replace slats at about this same time, but the keys were much wider than those used today and separated from one another by some distance. Around 1400 organ builders began to eliminate spaces between the keys, but it took almost another century to bring the keys down to the comfortable size of today. When this was accomplished, there was a rapid development, which led to the great organ described by Praetorius.

When we speak of a Baroque organ as such, we usually refer to a small instrument of great clarity and mellowness of tone, but lacking in ability to execute dynamics. All contrasts in dynamics followed the Baroque idea of contrasting sonorities and tone qualities which could be achieved on the organ by changes in registration. Although the small Baroque organs were widely used, the great organ experienced the most remarkable development and popularity.

Closely paralleling the development of the organ in France and northern Germany was the cultivation of its music. Probably the greatest center of organ music development was Lübeck, in northern Germany, which was known as the "Organ City." Three of Lübeck's five Gothic cathedrals had two organs each and the largest of these cathedrals, the Marienkirche, had three. The outstanding organists of the time were those who played at the Marienkirche: Franz Tunder (1614–1667), who is often credited with being the founder of the North German School of organ music, and his son-in-law, Dietrich Buxtehude (1637–1707). These men, along with Johann Sebastian Bach (1685–1750), are ranked with the greatest organists of all time.

Most of our modern orchestral instruments were in use or were developed during the Baroque period. Brass and woodwind instruments were effectively used, although modern types of valve mechanisms were not patented until the early nineteenth century. It was customary for instrumental music of the sixteenth and early seventeenth centuries to be composed for organ, harpsichord, or lute, but since there was no traditional instrumentation for brass and woodwind ensembles, composers experimented with all sorts of instruments in a wide variety of groupings. Some of the best ensemble and multiple choir music of the early Baroque was produced by the Gabrielis, Andrea and Giovanni, in Venice. A generation later, however, Girolamo Frescobaldi (1583–1643) and Heinrich Schütz (1585–1672) were also composing effectively in this new medium.

The Court of Louis XIV

To better understand how Baroque society used the music of its day, a reference to the music of the French court of Louis XIV is enlightening. The music of the court was literally a part of its magnificent décor. It was as necessary to the proper succession of events as were the elaborate costumes of those in attendance; music served the ear much as the presence of the musicians served the eye and added color, dignity, and beauty to the most routine functions. The entire day was carried out with carefully wrought background music, and this background was the most magnificent the world had ever seen.

Musicians in Louis XIV's court were artisans in the same manner as the architect, the jeweler, the hairdresser, and the sword maker; but all of these artisans shared an exalted equality, and each maintained a goal of excellence which would admit nothing but the best. Life itself was a cheaper commodity and more readily expendable than was superior craftsmanship. Within the court, there was music to rise by, to eat breakfast by, to set the mood for making one's toilet, music for dalliance, music for worship, and music for dancing. The King had his twenty-four violins in constant attendance. Lesser dignitaries in the court had their own music at hand in proportion to their position. The King had outdoor music for his stable, for the hunt, for processions, and for spectacles of every sort. All of this vast quantity of musical production served first a decorative and pleasing purpose, but it also carried on the important function of creating an air of magnificence.

Much of this decorative music was preserved and put into print for further usefulness in successive events, but little thought was given to preserving it for posterity; it was simply filed away. In 1680 André Philidor was appointed "Keeper of the Library of the King's Music." He began the gigantic task of bringing together all of the music ever produced in France, but never accomplished it. A century later the French Revolution disrupted the still uncompleted project. However, much of the military music of the day, and that composed by Philidor and by Jean-Baptiste Lully, was preserved.

Jean-Baptiste Lully (lew-lee') (1633–1687) was the most successful composer of his time. His success was due not only to his high degree of musical talent but also to his political talent, his opportunism, and his driving ambition. Born in Florence, Italy, Lully came to France as a boy. In 1652 he entered the service of the young King, Louis XIV who was the same age as Lully. Under the protection of Louis, he engaged in a series of shrewd maneuvers that made him successively composer of the royal chamber music, superintendent of the King's music, and finally holder of the royal patent. The latter position gave him a virtual monopoly on French operatic composition and production, and, at his death, he had accumulated a large fortune from his operatic ventures as well as from his real estate speculations.

The Influence of Lully

Lully's operas differ basically from those by Italian composers. His works emphasize choruses, huge ballets, and spectacular stage scenes. The Lully type of overture, usually called the French overture, has imposing dotted rhythms in the slow first part and fugal passages in the fast second section. The French overture form was widely used by Baroque composers for half a century after Lully's death, and it is still occasionally heard today. The opening *sinfonia* or overture of Handel's *Messiah* is an excellent example of the French overture. In composing his operas, Lully used varied and interesting orchestral accompaniment and completely disregarded expense in the cost of staging and costuming his work. These factors, combined with the musical genius of his composition, made his productions suitable for the exacting taste of Louis XIV, who was

Lully's principal auditor.

Lully had achieved such status by 1655 that he petitioned King Louis XIV for an orchestra of his own and was granted an organization of seventeen players. This was later expanded to twenty-one and, without doubt, this orchestra and the twenty-four violins of the King were the two finest string orchestras in all of Europe.

After the death of Lully in 1687, French music began to turn away from the expressive grandeur generally associated with the Baroque age to seek a more delicate, highly ornamented, and entertaining style which was known as the *Rococo*. This name, derived from the French word *rocaille* (ro-kie') (a kind of artificial rock work), denotes in the visual arts, a style rich in curving forms of rocks, shells, and plants, and in other graceful motifs imitating natural forms. Rococo was also called a "gallant" style, this word reflecting its origins in the aristocratic manner of the times. Rococo music appeared in the late years of court life under Louis XIV and reached its height under Louis XV, who reigned from 1715 to 1774. The style was almost entirely French but its influence was felt in Germany and Italy, where it can be detected in some of the works of Georg Philipp Telemann (1681–1767) and Domenico Scarlatti (1685–1757). . . .

Musical culture during the last part of the seventeenth century was dominated by French, Italian, and English musicians. The French exported orchestra players; the Italians exported composers, conductors, and singers to most of the courts of Europe; and the English followed the lead of the Italians with Henry Purcell, composer to the Royal court, as their greatest master. This period in history produced a bewildering array of musical forms. Those of choral music were only slightly less complex than those of the instrumental. Further confusion arose when only a few of these forms were standardized or accepted on an international scale.

The Vitality of Baroque Painting

Carl J. Friedrich

From the glittering beauty of the sensuous female nudes of Peter Paul Rubens to the unexpected inner life of the human being captured by Rembrandt, most of the great nations of Europe produced magnificent baroque painters, according to historian Carl J. Friedrich in the following excerpt. Friedrich provides a brief history of several baroque painters and examines the origins and elements of their style, listing many of their great works. The late Carl J. Friedrich was a prolific writer on history, government, and politics, and a professor at Harvard University.

T he baroque developed certain formal elements peculiar to painting. Among the outstanding traits of the new and vital style were
chiaroscuro (contrast of light and shade); the extensive use of tonal
gradation rather than clear colors, combined with the gradual elimination of distinct outlines and the merging of objects into the surrounding background; and finally the employment of large quanti-
ties of pigment and the consequent visibility of brush strokes. Continuing the trends of the renaissance, the baroque painter decorated
the interior of palaces and chapels, created great altarpieces, but also
developed further the landscape and the portrait as movable decora-
tions for the rooms of princes and wealthy burghers alike. A truly adequate appreciation of the art of baroque painting would necessitate,
just as in the other arts, a discussion of the early baroque and of the
so-called mannerism of the late sixteenth century. The towering ge-

nius of Michelangelo would once again have to be considered together with such masters as Carracci and Caravaggio. Titian, Tintoretto and Veronese would likewise have to be analyzed.

The Opening of the High Baroque

Assuming these antecedents of early baroque, we may say that all the great nations of Europe, except England and Germany, produced magnificent painters in the period of the high baroque. At the opening, around 1600, we find the Italians in the lead with Guido Reni (1575–1642) whose mature period began with his famous Aurora, and more specifically with Pietro da Cortona (1596–1669) whose frescoes in the Palazzo Barberini were among the most jubilant creations of the high baroque. At the other end of Europe, the first phase of high baroque was unquestionably dominated by the brilliant work and outstanding personality of P.P. Rubens (1577–1640). Ill-reputed among moderns on account of his lusty and sensuous female nudes, Rubens actually painted with a verve and a sense for the glittering beauty of colored surface that makes him unique in the history of painting. Trained in Antwerp and Italy (1600–1608) he was profoundly stirred by the magic color effects of Titian and his school, especially Tintoretto, as well as by the two incomparables: Raphael and Michelangelo. With the inception of our period, Rubens began to dissolve the fixed and isolated figure of renaissance painting. Figures were placed into more animated relations with each other, and an increasingly unified movement pulsed through his great canvases. At the same time, the colors gained in richness, variety and interrelationship. Pathos and sensuality combined to fill Rubens' canvases with a life that shows cosmic unity in all its parts; after 1620, some magnificent landscapes showed the same profound change. His success became overwhelming, and he developed a large workshop at Antwerp in which many assistants executed the great dynamic designs which he sketched. But after his great diplomatic mission to Spain and England, 1628–30, during which he tried to re-establish peace, Rubens withdrew and a late, more spiritual style appeared which was less vital but more subtle. Among his greatest, most celebrated works were the altarpieces now in the cathedral of Antwerp, Venus Facing a Mirror (1618), The Fall of the Damned (1620) and the Drunken Silenus (1618) at Munich, the Medici cycle painted for Marie de' Medici's Luxembourg Palace (1621–25) and now in the Louvre, the Altar of St. Ildefonso and The Festival of Venus (1630–32) at Vienna; and from his final period The Garden of Love (1635) and the great landscapes showing his country estate at Steen. From Rubens influences radiated into Italy, France and Spain; but perhaps his greatest follower was Anthony van Dyck (1599–1640).

Van Dyck was a member of Rubens's workshop from 1616 to 1620, then went, via England, to Italy, returning to Antwerp in 1627. In 1632 he became the court painter of Charles I and remained in that position until his early death. Van Dyck was most renowned for his portraits. In his later period he imposed a marked restraint upon baroque forms. In this respect his artistic development resembled trends in France. Van Dyck was more reserved and subtle than Rubens, and displayed a delicate taste in his use of color. No one has ever portrayed the noble grandeur of British aristocracy more convincingly than he, and his influence is clearly recognizable in the work of Gainsborough and Reynolds. Among the most celebrated of van Dyck's canvases I should mention The Betrayal of Christ (1620) at Madrid, Susanna and the Elder (before 1622) now at Munich, Madonna with Ste Rosalia (1629) at Vienna, Lamentation (1630) at Berlin, Maria Louise de Tassis (about 1628) in the Liechtenstein Gallery, Queen Henrietta (1634), Charles I on Horseback (about 1635) at London, and The Children of Charles I (1637) at Windsor. No greater contrast can be imagined than that between van Dyck's affinity for all that is noble and reserved, and J. Jordaens's (1593–1678) and Adriaen Brouwer's (1605/6–38) earthy, lowbrow scenes of peasant life. Yet these scenes, apart from their subject matter, were extraordinary in their masterly handling of complex design and highly dynamic motion.

The Artists of Sevilla

The true kinship of van Dyck was with Diego de Silva y Velasquez (1599–1660), who served Philip IV and [his prime minister, Gaspar de Guzmán de Pimental, conde de] Olivárez throughout his life. Velasquez was a student of F. Pacheco (1564–1654), whose daughter he married. Pacheco in turn was the center of a remarkable group of artists and writers in Sevilla which included Cervantes, Góngora, Quevedo. Like Zurbarán (1598–1664) he deserves an independent evaluation, but Velasquez towers above them both as one of the very greatest painters Europe produced. In some ways, the baroque had no more striking representative then Velasquez. His portraits like those of King Philip IV are unrivaled as embodiments of the divine right of kings to rule and to be honored as representatives of God on earth. His Góngora (1622), now at Boston, caught the haughty and self-centered personality of this quintessentially baroque poet. Velasquez evolved from a relatively rigid style of painting which clearly separated figures and shapes toward a much looser and dashing treatment which exerted a profound influence upon the French Impressionists. In his most brilliant period he painted such extraordinary canvases as The Surrender of Breda (1635) now at Madrid, and the numerous portraits of Philip IV and of Olivárez, especially the famous ones on horseback. His portrait of Pope Innocent X (1650) now at Rome is among the most striking psychological studies of the period; only Rembrandt probed as deeply into the personality of the human beings he painted. His numerous studies of court dwarfs, like those of Sebastiano de Morra (1643) revealed the same penetration. Among his late paintings, The Tapestry Weavers (1657) and the Venus (1657–58) now at London were especially impressive in their subdued vitality. Velasquez was twice in Italy, in 1629–31 and in 1649–51, and the result of these visits was a loosening of his style. Deeply affected by the art of Tintoretto and Titian, Velasquez always retained an unbaroque quality of clear and distinct coloring; sharp contrasts were not lacking, and a certain static element, while rooted in his temperament, gave his painting a "classic" aspect which links him to French tendencies. The art of the renaissance was similarly alive in B.E. Murillo (1618–82), called "the Raphael of Sevilla." Characteristically Spanish in his merging of naturalism and mysticism, Murillo was probably the most universally admired Spanish painter. Many of his most celebrated canvases belong to our period, like The Flight to Egypt (1648) and the somewhat saccharine scene of a small Jesus offering refreshment to a small St. John, as well as the great representations of the legend of St. Francis (1645–46). But Murillo was above all the painter of the Madonna, tenderly portrayed as the virginal mother of Christ. His compositions were devoid of tightness; he used the chiaroscuro with exceptional warmth, fitting soft pastel colors like cirrus clouds into the sunset of a summer evening. The contrast between Murillo's gentleness and Zurbarán's monumental and heroic figures conveys something of the rich range of Spanish life and art, comparable to the contrast between Lope, Calderón, and Góngora.

The French Flavor of Baroque

No clear lines ran from the great Spanish painters to France's outstanding men, Poussin, Claude Lorrain, Champaigne, the brothers Le Nain, Vouet, who all conveyed a specific French flavor, modified by Italian and Flemish influences. Indeed, these painters present a problem comparable to that of French literature, which is highlighted by the term *classicism*. This classicism has been treated as an absolute antithesis to the baroque; but . . . it was a specifically French form of baroque, modified when compared with Italian, Flemish or Spanish baroque, but differing from it no more than the persistent folkways of these peoples.

Simon Vouet (1590–1649) spent many years in Italy, and while he brought to France the baroque ideal of bodily beauty, he nonetheless modified Italian ideas sufficiently to become the teacher of an entire generation, more especially of Eustace Le Sueur (1616–55) and Charles Le Brun (1619–90). Le Sueur, who is spoken of as "the French Raphael," was deeply religious and infinitely refined. This very French artist achieved his greatest triumphs in twenty-two canvases which he painted for the Hôtel Lambert, between 1645 and 1648. Le Brun was, in a way, the first of a long line of French artists who, superb craftsmen, have nevertheless exerted an unfortunate influence by their tendency to be academic intellectuals who permitted their clear thoughts to dominate their cool hearts. Greatly admiring Poussin, whose formal perfection he urged as the ideal against Rubens's powerful colors, Le Brun was in no way comparable to Poussin's willful and stubborn genius. Indeed, the two greatest French painters, Nicolas Poussin (1593–1665) and Claude Gellée, called Lorrain (1600–1682), spent most of their lives in Italy, and more especially in Rome, where Poussin played a vital part in the passionate rivalries which divided the artists of the Eternal City.

The Landscapes

In many ways Poussin was the counterpart of [French playwright Pierre] Corneille. His striking landscapes, with classical themes, could easily be visualized as stage settings for Corneille's stately dramas. The constructed, stagy effect was as baroque as was Corneille's characterization, and the handling of colors and scenery similarly resembled the ornamented diction of the great dramatist. . . . Poussin painted wide, open, heroic landscapes which breathed order. Yet there always seemed to be an undercurrent of passion, of mysterious subdued tension—a strange expectancy enlivens these great scenes for the beholder, if he takes the time to contemplate them as idealized reality. Besides, Poussin painted some magnificent scenes of earthy and sensuous pleasure, of mighty clash of arms. Among his greatest (and they are difficult to reproduce in small compass) are the Bacchanal with the Lute Player (after 1630) at the Louvre, the Parnassus (1630) at the Prado, The Rape of the Sabine Women (1637–39) at the Metropolitan, the Triumph of Pan (one of four painted for [Cardinal] Richelieu) at the Louvre. The great landscape canvases of his late period, especially the Winter of the Four Seasons cycle (1660 and later), also at the Louvre, was as baroque in conception and execution as any painting of the period; but Landscape with Diogenes (1648) at the Louvre and Apollo and Daphne (1665) at the Louvre were likewise baroque in conception and execution. Only the brief period 1640–47, the first two years of which he spent in Paris, showed an academic effort to paint like Raphael, but I must confess that a picture like The Discovery of Moses (about 1645) at the Louvre strikes me as intensely baroque in its very setting.

The Court and the Countryside

If Nicolas Poussin may be called an epic painter who depicts the heroic in all its ramifications, Claude Lorrain was the lyric painter par excellence. [German poet Johann von] Goethe . . . remarked that there was "not a trace of reality in his pictures, but the highest truth. Claude Lorrain knew the real world by heart down to its smallest detail, but he used it as a means for expressing the cosmos of his beautiful soul. This is true idealization; it knows how to use real means in such a way that the truth which appears produces the illusion of being real." It was one of the most curious features of Lorrain's remarkable achievement that he remained free from all dominant Italian influences though living in Italy most of his life. Claude Lorrain was the incomparable master of sunsets and their golden sheen upon the waters of quiet harbors, of the indirect light through mist that makes a pastoral landscape glow, of the balanced elaboration of a welter of palace fronts, ships with their masts and sails and the manifold appointments of a waterfront. It is almost impossible to gather from any black and white reproduction the limitless peace and the cosmic sense which emanates from these canvases. The baroque sense of unity was superbly expressed. A bachelor all his life, Lorrain lived in virtual retirement from the world, painting the quiet scenes which were much in demand for the great baroque palaces of Rome and elsewhere. Among the greatest were the following: Harbor in Mist (1646), Landscape with Flight to Egypt (1647), Adoration of the Golden Calf (1653), and the wonderful cycle of Morning, Noon, Evening and Night (1661–72). Lorrain kept a diary of his development, the *Liber veritatis,* containing many sketches which show the vivid animation underlying his great paintings.

Compared to the genius of Poussin and Lorrain, the splendid craftsmen who remained in France seem academic and weak, with the single exception of the brothers Le Nain. Their extraordinary work, much of it concerned with life on farms and in inns, showed the baroque spirit of naturalism at work in true polarity to the stately, even pompous, paintings of Philippe de Champaigne (1602–74). The latter's Richelieu as well as his Louis XIII were singularly vivid examples of the courtly side of baroque art. All the splendor, the theatrical gravity, found perfect form in these portraits of the two men who by their singular combination of talents did more than any others to consummate the task which the baroque sense of power and unity called for in the political field, and which the emergence of the modern, national, bureaucratic state institutionalized— to repeat once again our major theme. That Champaigne should at the same time have painted with depth of appreciation representative figures of Port Royal is testimony to his artistic sensitivity, which intuitively grasped the basic polarity of the age.

The Dutch Baroque

This basic polarity is perhaps nowhere as clearly seen as in the contrast between a great court painter, such as Champaigne or Le Brun, and the work of the greatest Dutch baroque, rooted in the life and feeling of the common folk, the burgher and peasant of the Dutch lowlands, especially as exemplified in Frans Hals (1584–1666) and Rembrandt Harmenez van Ryn (1606–69). Among the incredible welter of brilliant talent that strode upon the scene of western paintings, these two were perhaps the most striking baroque figures, although van Ostade, van Goyen, Hobbema, Ruysdael, Vermeer, Jan Steen and Wouwerman certainly have great claims upon our recognition and attention. Especially Vermeer has had a renaissance; his extraordinary capacity to elicit in the beholder the poetic qualities of a simple scene has found many admirers; his clearly demarcated treatment of color and line made him, however, a somewhat typical figure without the more striking characteristics of the baroque age.

Frans Hals was perhaps the most extreme representative of that lust for life and nature, of that abandon and physical impulse which the age offered. Who does not know his famous Malle Bobbe, his lute players and fisher lads, his startling self-portrait, so-called. But Frans Hals must have had a unique psychological insight into the recesses of "abstract" thought and what produces it: his portrait of René Descartes is probably the most remarkable picture of a great philosophic genius. This aspect of Frans Hals's nature and art has only recently found adequate interpretation. It has now been shown that underlying his dash and naturalistic vivacity, there was a hard, geometric core of structure and design which gave his compositions a Cartesian quality of rationalist rigidity.

Although Hals's portraits are most widely known and provided him with the greatest immediate fame, his Banquets of Officers (five in all, dated 1616, 1624, 1627, 1633 and 1639, all at Haarlem) were the most striking products of his art. His manner of painting was revolutionary in its impressionistic liveliness and vivacity. The colors were brilliant, but fused; only in his later period did Hals employ black extensively. The individual figure in his group portraits lives a distinct life of its own, yet there is always a unity achieved through interrelated movement. Hals has been called the most sober, the most guarded of Dutch painters. This is true only in the sense that he possessed a veritable passion for reality. If one goes over the several great feast scenes, from the Officers in Georgedoelen (1616) to the same topic in 1639, one finds an increasing unity of design. But the most extraordinary symphonic accord was achieved in his late group of Regents of the Old Men's Hospital (1664), where he himself spent the last years of his life, evidently quite impoverished. Other key paintings: Jonkheer Ramp and his Sweetheart (1623) at New York; The Merry Drinker (about 1627) at Amsterdam; Malle Bobbe (about 1640) at Berlin; and The Gypsy Girl (about 1635) at Paris.

The Masterpieces of Rembrandt

In the work of Rembrandt baroque painting rose to universal significance and appeal. Like Raphael, Leonardo and Michelangelo, Rembrandt is in his most personal works "for all times and nations." At the same time, we have to recognize that Rembrandt was clearly and strongly linked to the baroque in such masterpieces as The Night Watch (1641), which has been called the greatest baroque painting. In a very personal manner Rembrandt from the outset struck against the idealizing tendencies coming from Italy. With startling realism, he depicted the human body with all its shortcomings of age. Witness Rembrandt's Ganymede, where an idealized youth was transformed into a terrified child, wetting in its distress at being carried off. . . . Rembrandt appears to have reveled in the ugly, the lowbrow, the coarse. Among paintings he owned, Adriaen Brouwer occupied a high place. It was a result of the determined search for man and nature as they appear to common folks in street and field. This insistence upon realistic representation had even a political significance: the protest of the Netherlander who had won his freedom from the mighty king of Spain, surrounded by his courtiers and elegant ladies as portrayed by Rubens and Velasquez. Similarly, Dutch painters preferred the simple charms of farm life to the heroic landscapes of a Poussin. But we must not forget the corresponding scenes in the work of the brothers Le Nain, and the occasional canvases of Velasquez.

Starting with the cult of "realism," Rembrandt eventually achieved a new spirituality by somehow investing all that is human with an unsuspected inner life. His expressive handling of light and dark and his baroque efforts at unity and universality through the complete dissolving of outline were unique. His pictures were the quintessence of what painting can accomplish when it sets itself the task of portraying the a "soul that lives in all things," of which Spinoza was to formulate the definitive philosophic statement. Color and light, surface and space were made to serve the purpose of rendering visible the inner life of all beings and more especially of man. The complete freedom and independence upon which Rembrandt insisted all his life, even when it meant suffering and poverty, was an essential condition of his achievement. "The external tragedy of his life—economic ruin after great success and social ostracism after brilliant rise which made him ever greater and more sovereign—is closely connected with this willfulness of the genius who abandons all social bonds."[1] In Rembrandt's work, nature became animated and spiritualized.

Capturing Humanity

Among his greatest paintings must be counted, besides The Night Watch already mentioned, The Anatomy of Dr. Tulp (1632). Here we have the first group picture which seems to live a life of its own in the situation it portrays: the passionate interest in a problem of natural science. Therefore light is concentrated on the arm of the corpse. Samson's Wedding (1638) showed a marked development of Rembrandt's style in the direction of atmospheric chiaroscuro. The bride, flooded by light, was surrounded by a waving, flowing commotion of human activity. The Night Watch (1641) carried this tendency further; each individual was made an integral part of the drama of the whole. Working as if a spectator of the great scene, Rembrandt recreated a moment of intense activity, when the parade was gathering, moving toward order, but as yet free, in entirely unpremeditated activity.

> Rembrandt's bold innovation in transforming a group portrait into a dramatically animated crowd stemmed from truly Baroque impulses. He created a tremendous burst of movement of utmost complexity, brushing aside all rem-

nants of the more static order which the Renaissance tradition had continued
to impose upon his forerunners. The Baroque favored both complexity and
unification of movement, and Rembrandt succeeded in expressing both, sub-
tly subordinating the diversity of action to a concentric trend within the
whole.[2]

A similar extraordinary scenic effect was achieved in some of his great
etchings, more especially the one where Christ is shown in the midst of
a multitude (Hundred Guilder print) (before 1650). But Rembrandt had
still a long way to go before he arrived at his greatest heights, the superb
art with which he captured the quintessence of a human being. After
about 1650 he became primarily occupied with this almost superhuman
task; for who "would know what is in another's heart"? In this last period, the surrounding space and all decorative detail tended to disappear.
For example the famous Portrait of an Old Lady (1654), now at
Leningrad, concentrated upon the face of the old woman, lost in medita-
tion. Her eyes are turned inward, her hands quiet and absorbed. "Design
and outline are those of a monument and the painting is great and significant, but the picture is not monumental in the usual sense of rigid im-
mortalization. All forms are softened and instead of eternity, the elusive,
fleeting quality is caught of a life which is here concentrated in one
changeable moment."[3] In this, as in other paintings of this period, such
as The Man with Golden Helmet (after 1650), we find the peculiar treatment of light, luminous and illuminating, yet devoid of a clear source, often like a fluid emanating from a misty atmosphere of darkness. A new
clarity, a combination of outer brilliance and inner life (excelling Velasquez and van Dyck), was reached by Rembrandt in such portraits as
that of Jan Six (1654), and in this same spirit he painted the grandiose
scene of The Syndics (1661–62). A final and perhaps ultimate combination of all of Rembrandt's originality was revealed in The Return of the
Prodigal Son (1668–69). The intense religiosity of Rembrandt, which his
sketches of the Life of Christ so beautifully embodied, was here given final form: the inner light of Protestant faith animates not only the painter,
but the face of the father, forgiving and sorrowful, the abject figure of the
son, and the reverent attitude of the onlookers wrapped in darkness. Here
what is penultimate in the spirit of baroque feeling was achieved.

Notes

1. Hamann, *Kunstgeschichte* (1933), 592.
2. Jacob Rosenberg's *Rembrandt* (2 vols., 1948), 177–78.
3. Hamann, op. cit., 606.

The Golden Age of the Theater

Richard S. Dunn

William Shakespeare and Ben Jonson in England, Lope de Vega and Pedro Calderón de la Barca in Spain, Molière and Jean Racine in France—these and other dramatists marked the late sixteenth and seventeenth century as the golden age of the theater. In the following excerpt, Richard S. Dunn examines some of the leading dramatists and the social and political climate of the theater during the seventeenth century. Dunn is professor of history at the University of Pennsylvania.

Late sixteenth and seventeenth-century literature [was] the most enduring achievement of the age. In poetry the spectrum ran from such monumental epics as [Torquato] Tasso's *Jerusalem Delivered,* [Edmund] Spenser's *Faerie Queene,* and [John] Milton's *Paradise Lost* to daringly experimental lyric verse by [John] Donne and the other English metaphysical poets, [Louis de] Góngora in Spain, and [Joost van den] Vondel in Holland. Miguel de Cervantes wrote the first great novel, *Don Quixote.* John Bunyan wrote one of the most enduring Christian allegories, *Pilgrim's Progress.* Bunyan, [Francis] Bacon, Milton, Sir Thomas Browne, and many others contributed to the amazing development of English prose style. In 1559 the English language was a clumsy instrument for the conveyance of ideas or the creation of moods, but by 1689 English prose writers could generate the utmost power or shade the most delicate nuance. Correspondingly, in France, such prose stylists as [Michel de] Montaigne, [Blaise] Pascal, [François de] La Rochefoucald, and [Nico-las] Boileau were purifying and polishing their tongue so as to ex-ploit its elegance, precision, and wit.

Above all, this was the golden age of the theater—the age of [Christopher] Marlowe, [William] Shakespeare, and [Ben] Jonson in England; of Lope de Vega and [Pedro] Calderón in Spain; of [Pierre] Corneille, Molière, and [Jean Baptiste] Racine in France. For both the English and the Spanish stage, the peak years can be specified rather precisely—from 1580 to 1640. The heyday of the French theater came a little later, between 1630 and 1680. Seven-teenth-century drama, like its twentieth-century counterpart, was as much show business as art. The circumstances of theatrical produc-tion reveal a great deal about contemporary social and economic conditions. And the plays themselves, written to please a capricious public, illustrate most of the generalizations . . . about the religious and intellectual climate and the political structure of European so-ciety in the late sixteenth and seventeenth centuries. . . .

The Drama of Shakespeare

William Shakespeare (1564–1616) was of course the greatest Eliz-abethan dramatist and also probably the most popular playwright of his day, though the audiences at the Globe and Blackfriars certainly did not appreciate how far he towered over all other English poets. Contemporaries saw Shakespeare as a complete man of the theater, author of three dozen successful plays, and actor and shareholder in the chief theatrical troupe of the period, the Lord Chamberlain's Company, later called the King's Company. Regrettably little can be discovered about Shakespeare's career. His life is better documented, however, than that of any other Elizabethan playwright except Ben Jonson. A great many people have refused to believe that a Stratford glove maker's son, with only a grammar-school education, could possibly write *Hamlet*. It makes them happier to suppose that the plays were secretly written by some aristocrat with a university ed-ucation, such as Francis Bacon or the earl of Oxford. There is no way of reasoning with people who equate genius with book learn-ing or blue blood. But it should be emphasized that the Elizabethan stage provided a suitable career for an ambitious country boy of mid-dling birth like young Shakespeare. Players and playwrights could make a good living, even though they ranked socially just above beggars and whores. The theatrical life could be brutal. Christopher Marlowe died in a tavern brawl, stabbed through the eye, and Ben Jonson narrowly escaped execution for killing an actor in a duel. Shakespeare was much more even tempered than Marlowe or Jon-son. He worked hard in London for about twenty years, and once he had earned enough money, retired in comfort to the Warwickshire

This print depicts a scene from William Shakespeare's Hamlet.

country town he loved much more. Obviously he composed his plays quickly, even if not as fast as some of the hack writers who teamed up in threes or fours to cobble together a play in a few days.

Shakespeare always carefully designed his plays for the two dozen actors in the Lord Chamberlain's Company. The protagonist in the late plays is generally older than in the early plays, because Richard Burbage, the company's leading actor, had grown older. There are never many female roles in Shakespeare's plays, since women were represented on the Elizabethan stage by boy actors, less experienced and effective than the men in the acting troupe. Shakespeare published some of his poetry, but he published none of his plays, regarding them as company property without independent literary value. Fortunately, since his plays were popular, eighteen of them were printed in pirated versions during Shakespeare's lifetime. And even more fortunately, his friends (spurred on by Ben Jonson's careful edition of *his* plays in 1616) collected the plays in a folio volume in 1623, printed "according to the True Originall Copies." Actually, some of these folio texts are quite imperfect. *Macbeth,* for instance, has survived only in a shortened, doctored acting version, perhaps used for touring in the provinces.

Pleasing the Court

Even before Shakespeare's retirement from the stage in 1613, London theatrical conditions were beginning to change. His younger colleague Ben Jonson (*c.* 1573–1637) was writing biting comedies set in contemporary London and bookish tragedies set in ancient Rome, which pleased the courtiers in the box seats much more than the groundlings in the pit. Francis Beaumont and John Fletcher were collaborating on a series of tragicomedies, a fancy new kind of escapist entertainment, far more frivolous than Shakespeare's tragedies and more exotic and farfetched than his most romantic comedies. Such plays did better in small enclosed theaters like Blackfriars than in big open arenas like the Globe. Playwrights were getting more daringly controversial. A sensational hit of 1624, Thomas Middleton's *A Game at Chess,* lampooned Prince Charles's expedition to Spain to woo the Infanta [daughter of the king]. This play ran at the Globe for nine consecutive days while the royal court was out of town, and grossed £1,000, with customers lined up for hours to get in, before James I heard about it and banned further performances.

As Puritan criticism of the London theater grew louder, the acting companies allied themselves with the Stuart court. James I and Charles I spent much more money on theatricals than had Elizabeth. James I employed Ben Jonson to write court masques, in which the songs, dances, scenery, and costumes greatly outweighed the libretto. Jonson dedicated his splendid anti-Puritan play *Bartholomew Fair* to James, who must have enjoyed Jonson's portrayal of the unctuous hypocrite Zeal-of-the-land Busy. In 1632 the real-live Puritan William Prynne produced a thousand-page diatribe against the stage called *Histriomastix,* written in a style very reminiscent of Zeal-of-the-land Busy. Prynne had seen only four plays, but he damned the theatrical profession wholesale, implied that Charles I's queen, Henrietta Maria, was a whore because she acted in court masques, and demanded that her royal husband close the theaters. "Do not Play-Poets and common Actors (the Devil's chiefest Factors) rake hell and earth itself," he asked, "so they may pollute the Theater with all hideous obscenities, with all the detestable matchless iniquities, which hitherto men or Devils have either actually perpetrated or fabulously divulged?" Prynne had his ears cropped for publishing this polemic, and the play-poets continued their pollution undisturbed for another decade. By the 1630's the London stage was certainly somewhat decadent. Dramatists provided their jaded audience with hectic spectacles of lust and debauchery. There is a corrosive brilliance to this Caroline drama quite different from the adolescent rampaging of Kyd and Marlowe in the 1580's and from the witty naughtiness of the Restoration stage after 1660. The Puritans quickly took their revenge. In 1642, as soon as they gained control of London, they closed the theaters, and they kept them closed for the eighteen years they remained in power.

When the London playhouses reopened after the return of Charles II in 1660, the theater was a strictly upper-class form of entertainment. Restoration drama was more sophisticated, more libertine, and more limited than Elizabethan drama had ever been. Actresses now assumed the female roles, and the plays were staged within a proscenium arch [over the stage area], with elaborate scenery, stage machinery, and artificial lighting. But the public theater was no longer a roaring business. An average of ten new plays a year appeared on the London stage between 1660 and 1700, as against a hundred a year between 1580 and 1640. Although the Restoration playhouses were small, the audience was not large enough to support two theaters simultaneously. Charles II was an ardent playgoer, and he honored Nell Gwyn, the most popular actress of the day, by taking her as his mistress. Great aristocrats such as the second duke of Buckingham amused themselves by writing plays. The best Restoration playwrights— [Sir George] Etherege, [William] Wycherley, [William] Congreve, [Sir John] Vanbrugh, and [George] Farquhar—wrote their plays when they were very young men and quickly retired from the stage. John Dryden (1631–1700) produced a series of stately heroic dramas, but the Restoration stage is best remembered for its witty, indecent comedies of manners, which perfectly mirrored the cynical, farcical temper of the late seventeenth-century English aristocracy.

The Drama of Spain

The Spanish theater enjoyed its *siglo de oro,* or golden age, during exactly *those years*—1580 to 1640—when the Elizabethan public stage was flourishing. . . .

Lope de Vega (1562–1635) was the Spaniards' answer to William Shakespeare. He had the same middle-class background, a better formal education, and a far more explosive temperament. He conducted a long series of passionate love affairs, generally with married women, and took up the last of these mistresses after he had become a priest. Lope de Vega was a fantastically prolific writer. In less than fifty years he turned out 1,500 *comedias,* of which nearly five hundred still survive! In his sixties he was writing two plays a week. Lope enjoyed immense celebrity and earned a fortune from his plays, but he valued them much less highly than his now-forgotten epics. "If anyone should cavil about my *comedias,*" he once wrote, "and think that I wrote them for fame, undeceive him and tell him that I wrote them for money." Unlike Shakespeare, however, Lope de Vega did publish a large number of his plays. The fact that most of them follow a single pattern helps explain how he was able to turn them out so quickly. The first act introduces the action, the second act scrambles it, and the third act builds up to the denouement, delayed as long as possible, for once the audience guessed it, they walked out! Lope de Vega's *Discovery of the New World by Christopher Columbus* exemplifies his dramatic technique. In the first act of this play, Columbus secures the backing of Ferdinand and Isabella for his voyage—according to Lope, in 1492 he was looking for the New World, not a new route to Cathay. Since it was impossible to keep the audience guessing as to whether Columbus would find the New World, Lope brought his Spaniards to the West Indies early in the second act, and concentrated thereafter on their patronizing treatment of the childlike Indians. In the third-act climax, a demon inspires the Indians to kill some of the gold-crazy Spaniards and pull down their cross. Instantly a new cross miraculously rises and the stupefied savages are converted to Christ. Every scene and every speech in this drama had the authentic, trivial ring of true life. Other dramatists might feel impelled to explore the obvious moral issues raised by this story; Lope de Vega was content to amuse his audience with a sparkling, colorful romance.

The Critics of Theater

By the 1630's the Spanish stage was declining, for several reasons. No playwright after Lope de Vega had his range and universal appeal. The collapsing Spanish economy shrank box-office receipts. The clergy, like the Puritans in England, criticized the immorality of actors and actresses with mounting indignation and pressed the government to close the theaters. During the reign of Philip IV (1621–1665), such clerical agitation had small effect, for this dissolute monarch—the patron of [painter Diego Rodríguez de Silva] Velázquez—was an ardent lover of plays and of actresses. Philip IV turned the Spanish drama from a popular art form into a royal hobby. He built a palace theater and spent so lavishly on court productions that the leading acting companies came to depend on his patronage. The king would disrupt public performances in the Madrid theaters by commanding certain actors and actresses to come immediately to the palace to rehearse for royal performances!

The changing character of the theater is reflected in the plays of Pedro Calderón (1600–1681), the chief Spanish dramatist after Lope de Vega. Whereas Lope wrote for the people, Calderón wrote for the court. In his youth, up to 1640, Calderón wrote comedies about lovesick grandees in pursuit of their mistresses and tragedies about jealous grandees in pursuit of their wives' lovers. His plays are more subtle and complex than Lope's, but less variegated. Everything hinges on the aristocratic code of honor, which the proud Spaniards cultivated as a substitute for their lost political power and prestige. Calderón clearly approves of the way his gentlemen fight duels at the twitch of an eyebrow and murder their adoring wives on the rumor of infidelity. During the crisis of the 1640's, with Catalonia and Portugal both in revolt, all theatrical activity ceased temporarily. Calderón himself took holy orders, and for the last thirty years of his life wrote only *autos sacramentales* and operatic court masques. He left no successors. By the close of the century, the professional theater in Spain was dying; it was in worse plight than in England, where the court circle kept the London stage alive.

The Role of Patronage in France

In France, the great theatrical age began about 1630, just as it was drawing to a close in England and Spain. The first French professional acting companies had begun operating in the late sixteenth century, but they put on crude shows for uncultivated audiences and did better in the provinces than in Paris. In these early years, no Frenchman remotely comparable to Marlowe, Shakespeare, or Lope de Vega wrote for the stage. The political turmoil during the sixteenth-century wars of religion and again during Marie de Medici's regency certainly delayed the development of the French public theater. Finally, [Cardinal] Richelieu's administration gave France the self-confident stability which England and Spain had achieved fifty years earlier. In 1629 two auspicious events occurred: an accomplished troupe of actors established fixed residence in a Paris theater, and an immensely talented dramatist, Pierre Corneille, produced his first play. When the French theater began to flourish in the 1630's under Richelieu's patronage, it provided entertainment for the elite, like the English theater of the same period, patronized by Charles I, and the Spanish theater patronized by Philip IV. The French drama remained closely tied to the royal court throughout its period of greatness, 1630–1680. Corneille, Racine, and Molière never wrote for the kind of huge and diversified audience which had thronged to the Elizabethan and Spanish playhouses at the turn of the century. Their audience was sophisticated but limited. In seventeenth-century Paris there were never more than three theaters, playing three evenings a week. Playwrights and actors could not make ends meet without royal patronage. Richelieu opened the finest theater in Paris, pensioned dramatists, and subsidized actors. [His successor, Cardinal] Mazarin was less generous, but Louis XIV in his youth was extremely fond of the theater, and his support kept afloat five acting companies: three French, one Italian, and one Spanish. Molière's company, for example, was not only subsidized by Louis XIV, but given the use of a royal theater. In addition, Molière held a court appointment as the king's bedmaker. Many of his plays were commissioned by the king for production at Versailles. Louis also pensioned Racine, without quite appreciating what he was paying for. The royal pension list for 1664 includes the following entries:

To the Sieur Racine, a French poet	40 louis d'or
To the Sieur Chapelain, the greatest French poet who ever lived	150 louis d'or

In the drama, as in art and literature, the Bourbon monarchy wished to cultivate a pure and dignified classical style. Court patronage helped to steer seventeenth-century French playwrights away from the exuberant romanticism of the Elizabethan and Spanish stage. In the time of Richelieu, French critics adopted the Aristotelian rules for dramatic composition. Seventeenth-century French playwrights generally observed the three unities of time, place, and action, and avoided Shakespeare's rambling plots and his mixture of high tragedy and low comedy. The spectator is spared the sight of murders, duels, and similar violent acts which are instead decorously reported by messengers. This classical influence is particularly evident in seventeenth-century French tragic drama, whose themes and plots are largely derived from Greek and Roman sources. French tragedies tend to be more literary and less stageworthy than the romantic tragedies of Elizabethan England and Habsburg Spain. But the French neoclassical tragedians were not blind copyists. They always reworked ancient history and myth to suit seventeenth-century taste, expanding the love interest and expunging the pagan religious element. Racine's Greek heroines and Corneille's Roman heroes are always recognizably ladies and gentlemen of the Bourbon court.

The French Tragedians

Pierre Corneille (1606–1684), the first great French dramatist, wrote a number of effective comedies but is best remembered as a neoclassical tragedian. In 1636 his *Cid* caused a sensation. Corneille's mastery of dramatic verse, his fiery lyricism, his characterization and plot structure, thrilled and shocked his audience as Marlowe's *Tamburlaine* had hit the Elizabethans, only more so, for *Le Cid* is a much finer play. It tells a tale of star-crossed lovers, kept from each other by a feud between their families. When the boy kills the girl's father, her love conquers her sense of filial honor, and she agrees to marry him. This ending scandalized the moralists, and the resulting furor had a somewhat unhappy effect on Corneille. In his subsequent plays he tried to please the critics with safer themes, extolling family honor, patriotism, monarchy, and Christianity. His favorite setting was imperial Rome, which gave him abundant opportunity to moralize on the virtues of benevolent despotism. Corneille never recaptured the verve, passion, and warmth of *Le Cid*. By the 1660's he had woefully lost his touch, and in a pitiful effort to outdo his young rival, Racine, he produced in his late years a series of grotesquely contrived melodramas.

Jean Baptiste Racine (1639–1699) was a poet of surer taste and control than Corneille, and he perfected the French neoclassical tragic style. At the age of four Racine was sent to school at the Jansenist stronghold of Port-Royal, and he emerged with an austere piety akin to Pascal's, and a deep love of the classics. He quickly established his reputation at court with a play about Alexander the Great, tactfully dedicated to Louis XIV. His next play, *Andromaque*

(1667), was a great success. It told the story of Hector's widow after the fall of Troy, forced to choose between marrying her Greek captor and seeing him kill her child; in other words, here once again was Corneille's theme of love versus honor—in a presentation graced by an exquisitely euphonious and precise verse style. In later plays, Racine reworked the tragic themes of his favorite Greek poets. *Phèdre,* perhaps his best play, follows Euripides' *Hippolytus* so closely that some scenes read like translations from the Greek. Suddenly, at age thirty-seven, Racine retired from the secular stage. His last two plays are biblical dramas designed for private performance by schoolgirls, in reversion to the early sixteenth-century amateur theatrical tradition.

The Comedy of Molière

The great comic master of the seventeenth-century French stage was of course Molière (1622–1673), whose real name was Jean Baptiste Poquelin. His father, a prosperous Paris furniture maker, sent the boy to a Jesuit school for the sort of classical education which Descartes, Calderón, Corneille, and thousands of other Jesuit pupils had received. Young Poquelin was determined to be an actor, and he endured a strenuous apprenticeship to prove himself. In 1643, taking the stage name of Molière, he helped to organize a Paris troupe, which rapidly went bankrupt. Molière and his companions toured the provinces for twelve years before they felt ready to attempt another assault on the capital. While touring, Molière wrote his first plays. In 1658 his troupe reappeared in Paris, performed successfully before the young king, and received the use of a theater in the Louvre palace. During the remaining fifteen years of his life, Molière wrote and produced a brilliant constellation of farces, parodies, and satires for his company. He generally took the lead role of valet or comic marquis himself, for Molière was a wonderfully accomplished comic actor. He made the Paris bourgeoisie and the Versailles aristocracy laugh at themselves. He mocked bourgeois greed in *The Miser,* and social climbing in *The Bourgeois Gentleman.* He mocked the rottenness of court society in *The Misanthrope,* and the hypocrisy of canting clerical bigots in *Tartuffe.* He mocked medical quackery in *The Imaginary Invalid,* and overly educated women in *The Female Savants.* Unlike Corneille and Racine, Molière was a total man of the theater. His plays read well, but they act better, and they remain more vibrantly alive than any other seventeenth-century plays except Shakespeare's. Molière's humor is realistic and hard-hitting, like Ben Jonson's but more universal and humane. His style is witty and urbane, like that of English Restoration comedy, but less smutty and trivial. Naturally he stepped on many toes. The clergy were so incensed by *Tartuffe* that the play was banned for five years, and only the king's patronage shielded Molière from heavier punishment. No doubt Molière was lucky that he wrote *Tartuffe* before Louis XIV had become pious and persecuting. No doubt he would have been silenced fast enough had he ventured to mock Bourbon absolutism or ask his royal patron to laugh at himself. Nevertheless, it remains ironic that the best social satire of the century was sponsored by the most complacent and authoritarian monarch in Europe.

With Molière's death, Racine's retirement, and Louis XIV's growing preoccupation with international war, the great age of the French theater drew to a close. To compare the art of Molière and Racine with that of Lope de Vega and Shakespeare is to see once again the bewildering diversity of European culture in the early modern period. Artists and intellectuals lived in closer proximity than ever before, yet the international cultural community established during the Middle Ages and the Renaissance had been shattered. Scientists, to be sure, cooperated with unprecedented fruitfulness, sharing discoveries and building on one another's experiments and theories. Painters, sculptors, and architects congregated in Italy and in a few of the large northern cities for their training and roved over Europe in search of commissions. This helps explain the spread of the Baroque style from Italy to Spain, Belgium, and Austria. But the Baroque was not all-conquering. In philosophy, as in theology, there was no consensus, scarcely even a dialogue. The art and thought of the seventeenth century has a deeply fragmented quality which reflects the loss of traditional religious unity and the rise of autonomous sovereign states. Catholics and Protestants evolved distinctly different responses to art. Literature, always the most chauvinistic art form, acquired a self-consciously national style in each vernacular language. At the close of the century, sophisticated persons everywhere wanted to copy French taste, but this attitude was symptomatic of the coming era, the Enlightenment. The seventeenth century was intellectually disorderly, contentious, intolerant. Audiences were easily unsettled by shocking ideas. Iconoclasts like Galileo and [philosopher Baruch] Spinoza were muzzled. Even poets like Milton and Molière risked persecution for their polemical art. Yet no censor or inquisitor could suppress the general intellectual revolt against authority, the richest legacy of the age.

Literature of the Seventeenth Century

George Clark

In the following excerpt, the late historian George Clark examines the influence of politics, economics, and culture on the writers of the seventeenth century. The salons of France provided more opportunity for creativity and individuality to flourish, and as the literary class grew and took direction from the aristocracy, the upper classes began to look toward literature to guide them in their social behavior. The late seventeenth century also saw the development of argumentative articles that began the age of the political pamphlet. Furthermore, improvements in communication and the spread of education spurred the development of journalism.

If the question were asked what the seventeenth century did for the permanent enrichment of human life, it would be answered differently according to the scales of values which were applied, but, whatever disagreement there might be about some of its other legacies, all would concur in setting a very high price on its great works of poetry and imaginative prose. . . . A few great masterpieces of seventeenth-century literature, though they have meant different things to different generations, have been continuously prized. Others have been forgotten and revived, some of them to be forgotten again. Still

Excerpted from Sir George Clark, *The Seventeenth Century* (London: Oxford University Press, 1929).

others are attractive to students who want them as expressions of the civilization which made them. The whole mass is only a selection, and a selection made for changing needs, but it is sufficient to set the seventeenth century among the great creative periods.

The National Literatures

This is true especially of three among the national literatures which have ranked highest in their influence on the world, and of two among those of the next lower level. In England the Elizabethan glory was at its brightest when the century opened. The whole life of [John] Milton fell within it. When it ended the "Restoration" drama had almost run its course; the prose and verse of the Augustan age were nearing their best. In France, with much else, it produced in both comedy and tragedy all the greatest works of that classical drama which is still the highest and typical embodiment of the French genius. In Spain, as in England, its earlier years fell within a time, already begun, of many-sided splendour. It gave to the Spaniards the most famous of their dramatists, and to all the world Don Quixote. The language of Spain's neighbour, Portugal, is now little read by foreigners, but the Portuguese account some of their seventeenth-century writers among their greatest. In the same way the Dutch, although they are deprived by accident of the confirmation of foreign opinion, regard [Joost van den] Vondel as their greatest poet and his time as the best in their literary annals.

When we pass to the other countries of Europe, we do not find any of which the same can be said. In Sweden it was a good period, but, on the whole, a period of promise rather than of maturity. In Germany there was decline: foreign influences and false standards overcame all but a few writers of powerful individuality. Poland and Hungary look back on this as a time of decadence. Even in Italy, but lately the source of inspiration for the whole of Europe, although there was much literary activity about the princely courts, its results were feeble. There was no prose of any importance except in treatises or sermons. In poetry nothing remained alive except intellectual ingenuity and a prettified sensualism. The lyrics of the period are, for the most part, slight in content, strained and artificial in form.

The Influence of Politics

The good health of literature was in fact dependent on political vigour. Where the life of the state was robust even when, as in England, it was turbulent, men found better things to write than in the misery of Germany or the stagnant passivity of the Italians. There is never a complete divorce between letters and politics. The literary languages of Europe, as they have been formed from the multitude of dialects, have crystallized round political centres, separating when these have divided, coalescing as they unite. A language cannot be defined except as the speech of an organized people, and a literature cannot arise except in the medium of a common life. Battles and the enforcement of justice, civil strife and the fortunes of kings, make a large part of the common stock of imaginative experience: they colour even the most personal affections and ideals. In the seventeenth century this was true to an exceptional degree. It was the age of the political ode and the political satire. The drama, free from the tutelage of the church, had entered the service of the other great institution of ceremonial and pageantry, the royal court. The minds of the spectators were reflected in its choice of subjects. Even where political discussion was prohibited the dramatists had their minds full of state affairs. It was by making them monarchs or state conspirators that [William] Shakespeare and [Jean] Racine alike raised their heroes to the tragic scale of grandeur. Among the human types which the dramatists, the writers of "characters," or the novelists portrayed, none were more shrewdly observed than the counsellors, the place-hunters, the sycophants and adventurers who clustered round the kings. Constitutional history and political theory fall into a wrong perspective if they take the point of view merely of obligation and utility, forgetting that the state, as the focus of the most unquestioning loyalties and the arena of the keenest of all contests for power, is, like love and war, one of the themes of the literary artists.

The Age of Patronage

In bringing about this result the force of political passions was seconded by the social conditions of authorship. The royal protection accorded to the drama was not so much a part of the diversions of kings as of their work as rulers. The more enlightened European rulers well understood how much they could do by judiciously distributing favours among the literary men, and teaching them, as they taught the nobles, to look to royal bounty for the fulfilment of their ambitions. It was the age of patronage in every walk of life, but in none more than in literature. Noblemen and other writers who needed no protectors were less prominent among the writers than they had been in the sixteenth century. Authorship was less often an incident in a life of action and adventure, more often a means of livelihood. It was coming to be normally a professional pursuit. The amateur was less to the fore than he had been in the days of [Sir Philip] Sidney and [Michel de] Montaigne.[Miguel de] Cervantes, early in the period, belonged to the old heroic line, but most of the great writers were comparatively sedentary men. They could earn something from the sale of their books or from the box-offices of the theatres, but these were seldom sufficient rewards, and even these could scarcely be earned without the good offices of some noble-man who would accept a dedication or gave his livery to a company of players. A patron might provide a minor office at court, a tutor-ship, a pension in cash, an ecclesiastical benefice, at the very least hospitality and a passport to fashionable society. His requirements might vary as much as his benefactions. He might be content with a flattering dedicatory epistle and with the friendship and gratitude of his client, or he might demand some more direct literary service such as a defence of his policy or a panegyric on his family. But whatever he demanded and whatever he gave in return, he was almost indis-pensable to the author. Authors sought after the most powerful pa-trons they could get. In London, where the aristocracy was never overshadowed by the crown, the Stuart kings merely played their part as the first among equals; but in the absolutist countries the kings were as much the masters in literary patronage as they were in politics or society.

The Academies

The dependence of letters on worldly power moulded not only the relation of the individual writer to his own patron or patrons, but also the relations of authors among themselves. The men of words, es-pecially perhaps those of less than the highest merit, are gregarious. Vanity and jealousy are among their besetting faults, but even these lamentable qualities, so far from discouraging intercourse, find their most nourishing pasture in a social circle. From the dawn of the Ital-ian renaissance, and indeed from even earlier times, there had been academies, some more freely formed and others under princely aus-pices. In the course of time they had become specialized, and we have noticed the considerable services of those devoted to science and learning. For pure literature this form of association is less cer-tainly beneficial than where the object is co-operation in acquiring knowledge. Its influence is almost sure to be in the direction of set-ting up and enforcing rigid standards, and, although this may be a useful service to the correction and improvement of language, it is dangerous to apply it to the substance of literature, to sentiments and even to matters of style and to the forms of expression in verse and prose. Thus the French academy has undeniably done much good by its dictionary, which was begun in 1639 and first published in 1694; but by its distribution of praise and blame in higher matters, al-though it has been one of the formative influences of French litera-ture, it has probably at times exalted mediocrity and depressed true genius. If that is in some measure true of the greatest of all modern academies, it is far more so with the numerous fantastically named societies which in Italy, Germany, and elsewhere carried on the tra-dition of those of the Renaissance. The mutual admiration of poetasters who met to exchange verses in the characters of shepherds could only result in a deterioration of taste. The exceptions are those where the academies were strengthened from without. In France the connexion with the monarchy, in Holland the solidity of the national culture, outweighed the tendency to frivolous ingenuity.

The Salons

In many ways like the academics, but much more favourable to real individuality, were those other characteristic resorts of the authors of the time, the *salons*. In the history of French literature a great place must be assigned to the Hôtel de Rambouillet, which has been called, with pardonable exaggeration, the first society on this side of the Alps which united the aristocracies of rank and of genius in one circle. There, under the eyes of a gifted hostess, [Cardinal] Richelieu used to meet the great dramatist [Pierre] Corneille. A *salon* is less formal than an academy, more purely a social gathering, less pleased with erudition and more given to wit. Its conversation revolves round the women, and the literature of the second half of the seventeenth century bears many signs that its writers met ladies of fashion on terms of social equality. "The town" became one of the favourite settings for verse, and when the country was described, it was the country as it is seen by the guests in a château or mansion. The literary class was growing more numerous and more compact. Like the learned class it was taking its tone and manners from the aristocracy. It helped in the formation of the standards and social consciousness of the upper classes. At the time when the old feudal aristocracy was silently assimilating recruits from the *bourgeoisie* of every country from Ireland to Naples, men and women were specially self-conscious in matters of deportment. When Molière satirized the *Bourgeois Gentilhomme* and the rich peasant who married above his station, his audiences were crowded with newcomers to high life who laughed the more because they were separated from Monsieur Jourdain and George Dandin, [the play's main characters], only by the thin partition of conformity to accepted usage. Even Molière, who saw through pretentious shams as well as any man who ever lived, could flatter the complacency of the "best people," and from about his time it became the general rule that the pen was a modest auxiliary of the purse.

The Development of Journalism

For the causes of another great change in the purposes of writing we must look also to the improvement in the methods of communication. Together with the spread of education, the rise of postal systems and the other changes connected with it were making a deep impression on the habits of the general population. Letter-writing was ceasing to be a luxury confined to the rich and learned. More and more as time went on it was becoming an everyday incident for commonplace people. That meant not only a widening of the common man's horizon; it also meant that it became less and less easy for governments to control the exchanging of news. They had, of course, their very skilful experts for opening and reading letters; but now they could open only a small proportion of those that were sent, and their chances of damming up a broad stream of information or opinion were diminishing. An increasing number of people had regular confidential correspondents who sent them political or commercial reports from a capital to the provinces, or even from one country to another. The trade in news was facilitated and grew. Professional writers of newsletters had existed in all countries for a long time and were still to go on for some time to come. In Queen Anne's reign, for instance, Abel Boyer, the historian, used to send a newsletter to the ambassador, Lord Strafford, at The Hague by every post for a guinea a week. But it was not by this old-fashioned system that Boyer made his living. He published an excellent monthly magazine. In much the same way Henry Oldenburg, the first secretary of the Royal Society, gave up his plan of sending monthly reports of scientific progress to individuals, and started, as a private venture, the society's *Philosophical Transactions*. It had become safe to sell the news broadcast, and it paid better to make it common property than to dole it out furtively to a limited clientele.

Journalism was born and grew to maturity in the seventeenth century. A string of dates will show that plainly. In 1609 comes the first printed periodical, the *Strassburger Zeitung*. In 1621 come the first English newspapers (printed in Holland for British soldiers there). In 1631 Richelieu started the first official newspaper, the *Gazette de France*. Its English counterpart was started in 1665 and became the *London Gazette* in 1666. In 1665 was the first review, the *Journal des Scavans*. In 1702 began the first daily newspaper, the *Daily Courant*. Each of these was imitated rapidly in many parts of the world: "the press" was beginning to be one of the main institutions of Europe. In several ways, it is true, its later developments were as yet only dimly foreshadowed. The purveyance of news was at first in other hands than those which wrote to influence opinion. The earliest newspapers were like their forerunners the newsletters, collections of information from correspondents, facts about war and politics or signs and wonders. They did not meddle with literature, and the literary or scientific journals also kept to their own bounds. One-sided news was common enough: the Protestant correspondent in the Thirty Years' War has his way of telling the story, and the Catholic his own. But the leader-writer came late: it was not for some time that argumentative articles began to be combined with the news in the same sheet, and not until much later that the newspaper leader became the principal vehicle for forming political opinion. The seventeenth and eighteenth centuries, or more exactly the period from the Reformation to the French Revolution, constituted the golden age of the political pamphlet. Special circumstances made this phase begin and end at rather different times in different countries. For England [Thomas Bobington] Macaulay [1800–1859], in his essay on [essayist Joseph] Addison [1672–1719], defined its height as the time from the end of the licensing of the press to the beginning of the regular reporting of parliamentary debates. In France the great days of the pamphleteers began somewhat earlier; but everywhere, though their character and influence varied with the social and political conditions, the later seventeenth century saw them in full cry.

Matsuo Bashō: Master of Haiku and *Renga*

Harold G. Henderson

In the following selection, the late Harold G. Henderson, a noted authority on Japanese art, explores the life of seventeenth-century Japanese poet Matsuo Bashō. By examining the poet's haiku, Henderson reveals Bashō's development as an artist. For example, Henderson reveals Bashō's attitude toward poetry by describing his experience as a haiku master, or teacher. The author tells the story of Bashō's guidance of his pupil Kikaku in the proper use of metaphor by providing Kikaku's verse and Bashō's illustrative revision. Henderson examines the haiku that reveals Bashō's spiritual and secular life, taking the reader on Bashō's journeys through Japan. According to Henderson, Bashō is best known for a haiku technique that evolved during the seventeenth century, known as *renga,* or linked verses. In his *renga,* Bashō develops his use of internal comparison. Henderson, who had lived in Japan, was assistant curator of Far Eastern art at the Metropolitan Museum of Art and taught Japanese and the history of Japanese art at Columbia University.

S hortly after 1600 the chaos of civil war that had prevailed for centuries was brought to an end, and Tokugawa Ieyasu established the Shogunate, a military government that allowed no rivals and was only nominally subordinate to the Emperor. In 1638, under the third shogun, a completely pacified Japan was officially isolated from the world, and in 1644 Matsuo Bashō was born.

Bashō would probably have been a poet in any age, but that in which he found himself was peculiarly favorable for the development and appreciation of his genius. Life for all was once more stable and secure; a rich and leisured *bourgeoisie* was being born; and samurai—men of the warrior class—who could no longer turn their energies to the arts of war, tended to turn them to the arts of peace. And of these arts poetry was one of the most popular.

The Education of Bashō

At the age of eight—possibly later, accounts differ—Bashō, who was of samurai blood, was taken into the service of a nobleman, the lord of a castle in Iga, in the south of Japan. There he became the page of the lord's son, Sengin, a lad just a few years older than Bashō himself. The two lived in close companionship, with Sengin not so much Bashō's master as his close friend and guide. From Sengin, and from Sengin's master, Kigin, Bashō learned the art of poetry as it was then known.

Apparently Bashō started composing at the age of nine, but his first recorded verse—it is hardly a poem by any standards—dates from the time he was about thirteen. It was written for the year of the bird (1657), and is a sort of *jeu d'esprit* rejoicing that that year falls between the years of the dog and the monkey, which it does in the Japanese table of calendar signs.

> Oh! It's the friend
>   of the dog and the monkey!
>   The year of the bird!

In its way this effort is almost a caricature of contemporary verse, as it depends for its effect on a "literary" allusion. Only in this case the allusion is to a story any Japanese child would know—the tale of Momotarō, a boy who slew many demons with the help of his three retainers, a dog, a pheasant, and a monkey.

Renouncing the World

In 1666 Lord Sengin suddenly died, and within two months Bashō had gone to the monastery at Kōyasan and had "renounced the world." There can be no doubt that he was utterly broken up at the death of his much-loved master, and that the impression it made influenced his entire life. More than twenty years later he went back to Iga in the spring, and stood again under the cherry trees where he and Sengin had worked and played so long, and with a heart too full to make a normal poem, all he could say was:

Many, many things
  they bring to mind—
    cherry blossoms!

However, though Bashō had given up "the world," this did not mean that he confined himself to a monastery, and we next hear of him at Kyoto, studying haiku under Kigin and beginning to make a name for himself. When Kigin went to Edo (the present Tokyo), Bashō followed him; and two years later, when he was thirty, Bashō started a school of his own, taking as his first pupil the son of a rich merchant, a young boy who afterward became famous in his own right under the name of Kikaku.

Bashō had not at this time reached the height of his powers, but there is a famous tale of the period that well illustrates his attitude toward poetry. One day when he and Kikaku were going through the fields, looking at the darting dragonflies, the boy made a seventeen-syllable verse:

Red dragonflies!
  Take off their wings,
    and they are pepper pods!

"No!" said Bashō, "that is not haiku. If you wish to make a haiku on the subject, you must say":

Red pepper pods!
  Add wings to them,
    and they are dragonflies!

The *Renga* Model

Gradually Bashō's school increased in numbers and repute, and in the next few years in addition to his haiku he contributed to several books of *renga* or "linked verses." In 1679 he wrote his first verse in the "new style," which came to be associated with his name and was taken as a model by many later haiku poets. This verse, even more important for its technique than its contents, was:

On a withered branch
  a crow has settled—
    autumn nightfall.

There are at least two points of technique which made it a model. First, the over-all mood or emotion is produced by a simple description, a plain statement of fact which makes a picture. Second, the two parts that make up the whole are compared to each other, not in simile or metaphor, but as two phenomena, each of which exists in its own right. This may be called "the principle of internal comparison" in which the differences are just as important as the likenesses. Here it is not simply that "over the withered landscape the autumn nightfall settles like a crow." It is also the contrast of the small black body of the crow with the vast amorphous darkness of the nightfall—and whatever else the reader may find in it. It is easy to see how the use of this technique helps to give depth to haiku, and to make them starting points for thought and imagination.

Bashō himself did not always follow this model, but in most of his subsequent haiku—even those that are lot so wholly objective—"internal comparison" is at least implied. Unless this is realized, much of the effect of his poems is lost. A good illustration is the haiku where the cherry blossoms (emblems of transient beauty) are used both as background and for comparison with what they "bring to mind."

At the time the "crow" verse was written Bashō was consciously looking for the poetic beauty to be found in things not themselves particularly beautiful. He was still developing both his technique and his poetic insight Two years later, in 1681, something happened to him. He announced that his life, simple as it was, was "too worldly," and he began the serious study of Zen—the Buddhist sect which gives most attention to contemplation. It was after this, in the last ten years of his life, that nearly all of his finest poetry was written.

A Turning Point

Early in 1686 Bashō wrote what is probably the best-known haiku in the Japanese language—one which he himself considered as marking the most important turning point in his poetic life. The poem itself is deceptively simple. Literally translated, it is:

> Old pond:
>> frog jump-in
>>> water-sound

Many competent critics have found in this a deep and esoteric meaning; others have considered it too darkly mysterious to understand at all. Perhaps some light may be thrown by the fact that the last two lines were the first to be composed. The circumstances seem well attested. Bashō was sitting in the garden of his little house in Edo with some of his friends and pupils, when suddenly a sound was heard, necessarily during a period of silence. Bashō, without premeditation, looked up and said: *"Kawazu tobikomu mizu no oto"* (frog-jump-in water-sound). This was immediately recognized as a possible ending for a haiku, and after the others had made various suggestions, Bashō completed it with "old pond" for the first line. If this story is correct, the closest possible English for the poem would seem to be:

> Old pond—
>> and a frog-jump-in
>>> water-sound.

In form this is quite similar to the "'crow" poem, but the "internal comparison" between the old pond and the sudden sound is certainly deeper and much more subtle than that between the crow and the autumn nightfall. And the over-all mood induced by it certainly reflects a very different attitude toward life.

The Spirit of Zen

If this were the only poem that Bashō had ever written, one might wonder whether the poet really put into it all the deep meaning that one finds. But the proof is overwhelming that, consciously or unconsciously, Bashō did put into most if not all of his later haiku all the meaning that anyone can find, and probably much more. It has been my own experience that the more one reads them, the more one finds depth in each single one, even in those that appear most trivial. One gets a feeling that they are somehow all parts of one whole. Japanese who have had the same experience have explained it by saying that Bashō was so imbued with the spirit of Zen that it could not help showing in everything he wrote. This is quite possibly true, but as an explanation it suffers from the fact that nobody has yet been able to define what the "spirit of Zen" actually is. Zen "illumination" (*satori*) is apparently a strong emotional experience for which there are no words. It has been called a "realizing of reality," and some Christian theologians have praised it as being "the highest form of natural mysticism." About all that non-Zen people can do is to observe its effects on Bashō and on his poems. Among the qualities which are often considered as indicative of his Zen are a great zest for life; a desire to use every instant to the uttermost; an appreciation of this even in natural objects; a feeling that nothing is alone, nothing unimportant; a wide sympathy; and an acute awareness of relationships of all kinds, including that of one sense to another. Whether or not these qualities are due to Zen, they do exist in Bashō's haiku, at least in the originals.

Only comparatively few of Bashō's poems are obviously religious, though several seem to be records of semi-mystic experiences. For example, in his *Sarashina Journey* Bashō records that while he and his pupil Etsujin were journeying through the mountains of Kiso, they found themselves climbing a steep and dangerous path. On their left was a deep gorge, and at its bottom, thousands of feet below, a rushing river. They took each step in terror, until they came to the fragile ivy-covered rope bridge which spanned the gorge and which they had to cross. Bashō gives no details of his feelings, but appends the haiku:

Around existence twine
  (Oh, bridge that hangs across the gorge!)
    ropes of twisted vine.

There are also other poems, which would be obviously religious to a Japanese Buddhist of any sect.

Octopus traps: how soon
  they are to have an end—these dreams
    beneath the summer moon.

Octopus traps are earthenware pots, set horizontally in shallow water, into which during the nighttime the animal backs as if it were a crevice in the rocks. In the morning it is unable to get out. In the original, which is prefaced with the words: "On board a boat," the effect of *wo* is to make the moon the subject, and suggest that it looks down on the whole sea- and landscape, and all its "ephemeral dreams." Here the religious implications are obvious, even if we do not go into the Buddhist symbolism of the boat and the moon. It is, however, worthy of note that whenever Bashō uses the word "dream" he seems also to be thinking of human life; and perhaps it is even more noteworthy that to him the "illusion" of the world does not seem to mean that it is in any sense unreal, but rather, as with St. Thomas Aquinas, that it is far more real than it seems.

The vast majority of Bashō's haiku are not obviously religious, whatever the Zen content may be. They are for the most part simple descriptions of actual scenes and events, with just enough detail given to allow the reader to put himself in Bashō's place and so share his emotions. . . .

In addition to the *Sarashina Kikō,* Bashō wrote several other prose works. The most famous of these is *Oku-no-Hosomichi, Narrow Roads in Oku,* a collection of notes of a six months' journey which started from Edo in the spring of 1689, went through parts of northern Japan, and ended at the sacred shrine of the Sun Goddess at Ise. It is quite short and contains only about fifty of his haiku. Yet it is undoubtedly one of the great works of Japanese literature, and it has probably been annotated and commented on more than any other work of its size in the world. Comment is unfortunately often necessary as Bashō's prose is, like his poetry, extremely condensed, and he is constantly making allusions that were clear in his own day, but which are not clear now.

Even the title has been the subject of controversy, partly because *michi* (road) may be either singular or plural, and partly because the word *oku,* which is an epithet applied to the northern provinces, has a basic meaning something like that of "the interior." The same point comes up in one of the poems, where a song of *"oku"* is contrasted to the sophisticated art of the cities *(fūrū).* Bashō is reporting a conversation held shortly after his entering the *"oku"* country:

"My host asked first: 'At the crossing of the Shirakawa Barrier, what poem did you compose?'

"The troubles of the long journey had tired me in body and mind, and moreover, I was carried away by the scenery and the old-time feeling that it evoked, so that I was not in any condition to compose a poem at the moment. But thinking it a pity to pass in silence, I made this one:

The beginning of all art:
a song when planting a rice field
in the country's inmost part.

"I gave him this for an answer, and we added a second and a third verse to it, and so made it into a *renga* [a linked verse]."

Many pages of comment have been written about this poem, and many explanations of it have been given. One is that Bashō, coming as he did straight from the ultra-refinement of Edo, was struck with the fact that only rice culture made its luxury financially possible. Another, that he was pointing out the necessary connection between true refinement and natural simplicity. A third is that Bashō was simply paying a compliment to his host. The poem means different things to different people, and the reader may take his choice. . . .

[Another] haiku from *Oku-no-Hosomichi* . . . needs discussion here, because it requires a type of reader co-operation to which most foreigners are unaccustomed:

Into the sea
it drives the red-hot sun—
the river Mogami.

In the prose text Bashō has previously told us that the time is summer, and that he has boarded a boat to go down the river, which is large and swift. But this information is not really needed to give a feeling of the welcome coolness after a hot day, and the rush of waters. And even a slight attempt to put ourselves into Bashō's position is enough to make us realize that he must be looking down the river, and westward across its mouth, to where the red ball of the sun is sinking into the waters. It is only after we have done this that we can begin to share in the emotions that prompted him to make the poem.

In 1694 Bashō died, and died as he would have wished, on one of his beloved wanderings, and surrounded by many of his friends and pupils. During his last illness he was constantly discussing religion and philosophy and poetry (three things that were almost one to Bashō), and when it became evident that he was dying his friends asked him to give them a "death poem"—the sum of his philosophy. Bashō refused, on the ground that every poem in his last ten years, starting with the "old pond" haiku, had been composed as if it were a death poem. But on the next morning he called them to his bedside, saying that during the night he had dreamed, and that on waking a poem had come to him. And he gave them:

On a journey, ill,
and over fields all withered, dreams
go wandering still.

Surely as lovely a farewell as any poet ever gave to the world.

A Walk Through the Taj Mahal

François Bernier

Built in Agra in northern India between 1632 and 1638, the Taj Mahal, designed by Muslim architect Ustad Ahmad Lahori, is considered one of the most beautiful buildings in the world and the finest example of the late style of Indian Islamic architecture. The Mogul emperor Shāh Jahān ordered the building of the mausoleum after the death (1629) of his favorite wife, Mumtāz Mahal. The tomb is adorned with fountains and marble pavements, and the garden contains four water channels to echo the four rivers of Islamic paradise. The white marble exterior is inlaid with semiprecious stones arranged in Arabic inscriptions, and the dome forms a bulb that tapers to a spire topped by a crescent. The building remains perfectly preserved. The following is an excerpt from a letter written in July 1663 by François Bernier during his travels in India. Bernier describes in detail what he sees as he walks through the Taj Mahal, providing references to European structures, dimensions, and taste not only to provide his readers with perspective but also to confirm his belief that the Taj Mahal should be counted among the wonders of the world.

I shall finish this letter [of 1 July 1663] with a description of the two wonderful mausoleums which constitute the chief superiority of Agra over Delhi. One was erected by Jehan-Guyre [Jahangir] in honor of his father Ekbar [Akbar]; and Chah-Jehan [Shah Jahan] raised the other to the memory of his wife Tage Mehale [Mumtaz Mahal], that extraordinary and celebrated beauty, of whom her husband was so en-

Excerpted from François Bernier in *Taj Mahal: The Illumined Tomb* (Seattle: The University of Washington Press, 1989), edited and translated by W.E. Begley and Z.A. Desai.

amored that it is said he was constant to her during life, and at her death was so affected as nearly to follow her to the grave.

I shall pass Ekbar's monument without further observation, because all its beauties are found in still greater perfection in that of Tage Mehale, which I shall now endeavor to describe.

On leaving Agra, toward the east, you enter a long, wide, or paved street, on a gentle ascent, having on one side a high and long wall, which forms the side of a square garden, of much greater extent than our Place Royale, and on the other side a row of new houses with arcades, resembling those of the principal streets in Delhi. After walking half the length of the wall, you find on the right, that is, on the side of the houses, a large gate, tolerably well made, which is the entrance of a Karvan-Serrah [caravansarai] and on the opposite side from that of the wall is seen the magnificent gate of a spacious and square pavilion, forming the entrance into the garden, between two reservoirs, faced with hewn stone.

This pavilion is an oblong square, and built of a stone resembling red marble, but not so hard. The front seems to me longer, and much more grand in its construction, than that of S. Louis, in the rue S. Antoine, and it is equally lofty. The columns, the architraves and the cornices are, indeed, not formed according to the proportion of the five orders of architecture so strictly observed in French edifices. The building I am speaking of is of a different and peculiar kind; but not without something pleasing in its whimsical structure; and in my opinion it well deserves a place in our books of architecture. It consists almost wholly of arches upon arches, and galleries upon galleries, disposed and contrived in a hundred different ways. Nevertheless the edifice has a magnificent appearance, and is conceived and executed effectually. Nothing offends the eye; on the contrary, it is delighted with every part, and never tired with looking.

The last time I visited Tage Mehale's mausoleum I was in the company of a French merchant, who, as well as myself, thought that this extraordinary fabric could not be sufficiently admired. I did not venture to express my opinion, fearing that my taste might have become corrupted by my long residence in the Indies; and as my companion was come recently from France, it was quite a relief to my mind to hear him say that he had seen nothing in Europe so bold and majestic.

When you have entered a little way into the pavilion approaching toward the garden, you find yourself under a lofty cupola, surrounded above with galleries, and having two divans or platforms below, one on the right, the other on the left, both of them raised eight or ten French feet from the ground. Opposite to the entrance from the street is a large open arch, by which you enter a walk which divides nearly the whole of the garden into two equal parts.

This walk or terrace is wide enough to admit six coaches abreast;
it is paved with large and hard square stones, raised about eight
French feet above the garden; and divided the whole length by a
canal faced with hewn stone and ornamented with fountains placed
at certain intervals.

After advancing twenty-five or thirty paces on this terrace, it is
worthwhile to turn around and view the back elevation of the pavilion, which, though not comparable to the front, is still very splendid,
being lofty and of a similar style of architecture. On both sides of the
pavilion, along the garden wall, is a long and wide gallery, raised like
a terrace, and supported by a number of low columns placed near
each other. Into this gallery the poor are admitted three times a week
during the rainy season to receive the alms founded in perpetuity by
Chah-Jehan.

Resuming the walk along the main terrace, you see before you at
a distance a large dome, in which is the sepulchre, and to the right
and left of that dome on a lower surface you observe several garden
walks covered with trees and many parterres [ornamental gardens]
full of flowers.

When at the end of the principal walk or terrace, besides the dome
that faces you, are discovered two large pavilions, one to the right,
another to the left, both built with the same kind of stone, consequently of the same red color as the first pavilion. These are spacious
square edifices, the parts of which are raised over each other in the
form of balconies and terraces; these arches leave openings which

*Carved from pristine marble and considered an architectural wonder,
the Taj Mahal was built by order of the emperor Shāh Jahān as a
mausoleum for his wife, Mumtāz Mahal.*

have the garden wall for a boundary, and you walk under these pavilions as if they were lofty and wide galleries. I shall not stop to speak of the interior ornaments of the two pavilions, because they scarcely differ in regard to the walls, ceiling, or pavement from the dome which I am going to describe. Between the end of the principal walk and the dome is an open and pretty large space, which I call a water-parterre, because the stones on which you walk, cut and figured in various forms, represent the borders of box in our parterres. From the middle of this space you have a good view of the building which contains the tomb, and which we are now to examine.

This building is a vast dome of white marble nearly of the same height as the Val de Grace of Paris, and encircled by a number of turrets, also of white marble, descending the one below the other in regular succession. The whole fabric is supported by four great arches, three of which are quite open and the other closed up by the wall of an apartment with a gallery attached to it. There the Koran is continually read with apparent devotion in respectful memory of Tage Mehale by certain Mullahs [Muslims trained in traditional religious law and doctrine] kept in the mausoleum for that purpose. The center of every arch is adorned with white marble slabs whereon are inscribed large Arabian characters in black marble, which produce a fine effect. The interior or concave part of the dome and generally the whole of the wall from top to bottom are faced with white marble: no part can be found that is not skilfully wrought, or that has not its peculiar beauty. Everywhere are seen the jasper, and jachen, or jade, as well as other stones similar to those that enrich the walls of the Grand Duke's chapel at Florence, and several more of great value and rarity, set in an endless variety of modes, moxed and enchased in the slabs of marble which face the body of the wall. Even the squares of white and black marble which compose the pavement are inlaid with these precious stones in the most beautiful and delicate manner imaginable.

Under the dome is a small chamber, wherein is enclosed the tomb of Tage Mehale. It is opened with much ceremony once in a year, and once only; and as no Christian is admitted within, lest its sanctity should be profaned, I have not seen the interior, but I understand that nothing can be conceived more rich and magnificent.

It only remains to draw your attention to a walk or terrace, nearly five-and-twenty paces in breadth and rather more in height, which runs from the dome to the extremity of the garden. From this terrace are seen the Gemna [Jumna] flowing below, a large expanse of luxuriant gardens, a part of the city of Agra, the fortress, and all the fine residences of the Omrahs [umaras] erected on the banks of the river. When I add that this terrace extends almost the whole length of one side of the garden, I leave you to judge whether I had not sufficient ground for asserting that the mausoleum of Tage Mehale is an astonishing work. It is possible I may have imbibed an Indian taste; but I decidedly think that this monument deserves much more to be numbered among the wonders of the world than the pyramids of Egypt, those unshapen masses which when I had seen them twice yielded me no satisfaction, and which are nothing on the outside but heaps of large stones piled in the form of steps one upon another, while within there is very little that is creditable either to human skill or to human intervention.

The Middle Class in Seventeenth-Century France

John Laurence Carr

Although the hereditary nobles of France experienced a reduction in power and freedom in the seventeenth century, the bourgeoisie, or middle class, experienced an improvement in status and wealth, writes John Laurence Carr in the following excerpt. Comprised of merchants, lawyers, doctors, bankers, clerks, and shopkeepers, the middle class had greater wealth with which to purchase goods, educate their children, and enjoy and participate in the arts. Carr explores aspects of the bourgeois way of life, including, an interest in fashion, etiquette, and life in Paris, from the filthy crime-ridden streets to the cafés and parks where the middle class socialized. Carr is a senior lecturer in French at the University of Glasgow.

The most obvious and outstanding characteristic of the Age of Louis XIV was the fact of absolute monarchy—an achievement that was the culmination of the efforts of [Cardinal] Richelieu, whose toughness coupled with intelligence brought admirably useful qualities to the task; of [Cardinal] Mazarin, whose insinuating diplomacy assisted the secular realization of absolutism; and of Louis XIV, whose concept of glory and national grandeur crowned the splendid edifice. . . .

Excerpted from John Laurence Carr, *Life in France Under Louis XIV.* Copyright © 1966 John Laurence Carr. Reprinted with permission from Chrysalis Books.

As far as the common people were concerned, this change in the balance of power between the social orders in France brought little respite from their eternal miseries, and in some ways added to them. But . . . other classes of society were infinitely better off under the Roi Soleil ["Sun King"] than under faction and disorder, for, whereas the nobility had clearly to accept reduced freedom of action under a strong and powerful monarchy, two kinds of Frenchman were to benefit from the change: first, the middle classes, from whom Louis chose his principal ministers and advisers and, secondly, that sector of middle-class society which we call the World of Letters. It is a curious paradox that, though the centre of political and social gravity shifted under Louis XIV from Paris to Versailles, the noble became a mere palace servant, whilst the Third Estate in the towns preened itself in a way unknown since the Renaissance.

The Members of the Middle Class

This Third Estate divided itself up into categories. The most important was called the bourgeoisie, which consisted of all those who, without being of noble birth, did not earn their living by manual occupations. Thus lawyers and others who had purchased offices from the Crown and thus had acquired privileges and exemptions . . . were high upon the list, and might one day become *noblesse de robe*. Then we must count the professional men, doctors and some men of the law, municipal officers like mayors and *échevins* [alderman], wealthy merchants and industrialists. Financiers too came into the third class of society. So did bankers and tax-collectors. So did a so-called petite bourgeoisie, consisting of lawyer's clerks and shopkeepers.

Paradoxically again, the Century of Absolutism was also the Century of the Middle Classes. Since taking over the reins of power, Louis XIV had resolutely confined the nobility to that place in society which he desired them to occupy. This royal policy permitted more sunshine to fall upon the hard-working *honnête-homme,* the middle-class merchant or technocrat grateful to offer his services. For there was now an elegance abroad—a nobility of the heart, possessed superlatively by the man in the middle of the social scale, the honest bourgeois.

As we have said, the king chose some of his most trusted servants amongst the middle classes. The fortification genius, [Sébastien Le Prestre de] Vauban, was one of these and [controller general of finance Jean-Baptiste] Colbert was another. Son of a cloth merchant, Colbert was bred in retail trade and commerce which, largely because of the ancient law about *dérogeance,* [which prohibited nobles from working], was territory forbidden to the French nobility. It was Colbert who, by incessant publicity and effort, kept the French economy as busy as it could possibly be, and ultimately ensured that, looking back, [French writer] Voltaire could decide that the Age of Louis XIV had something in common with the Italian Renaissance in this respect. Intensely patriotic and mercantilist in his theories, Colbert offered French industry all the protection it needed to flourish. This protection took the form of customs-barriers, credits, financial assistance, the supply of labour, tax-relief, temporary monopolies and so forth.

Colbert himself was the hardest worker of all. At 5:30 in the morning he entered his study, and spent up to 16 hours a day at his desk. In 1673 he tried to make the guild system universal so that industry would work more smoothly and more efficiently. And he was a harsh taskmaster and a self-seeking overlord when he wished. To [architect Louis] Levau, who had not produced enough tin, he pointed out that His Majesty's needs had to be met with prompt and adequate supplies; and he hounded down the wealthy financier [Nicolas] Fouquet, whose trial dragged on for such a length of time. Furthermore he provided more than adequately for his own kith and kin during his years in power and favour; he married his daughters to wealthy and influential spouses, and managed to amass for himself a huge fortune during his career. Still that was typical of his social group, which became justifiably rich and influential as the king opened more and more doors to their ambitions. . . .

The Bourgeois Way of Life

The middle classes seem to have been happy enough under Louis XIV, who allowed them a raison d'être ["reason for being"]. This pleased them, for status contributes as much to happiness as wealth. Their accumulating riches meant that they could lead a life of comparative ease, surrounded by the rewards of industry and shrewd investment. Their furniture tended to be of the finest wood and looked as though it was meant to last for ever. Their houses became larger and larger; and it is not without significance that by 1705 [Abraham] Du Pradel was prompted to attack these rich burghers in his *Traité contre le luxe,* whilst in the following year [Conrart] De Valentin's poem *Le Franc Bourgeois* took them to task on the same issue.

But let us have an open mind, and imagine that, like the dwarf Asphodel in [Alain-René] Lesage's *Diable boiteux* (1707), we can remove roofs and peep into middle-class society. Surrounded by their army of retainers, the bourgeois spent their time in different ways. Some frequented the *Précieux,* [female writers and their writing style] in the salons; others learned how to play the guitar or the *clavecin,* the contemporary piano. Women took up such instruments in considerable numbers. They also turned to literary pursuits, so novels began to have a place in the reading list. The theatre too benefited by this leisured, cultivated public evolving from the hitherto fully-occupied middle classes.

Middle-class children received the education their parents could afford, which meant that in many cases boys had a private tutor, whereas girls still tended to go to the convent school, where the emphasis was naturally on religious instruction. After private tuition, boys were usually sent to college, which taught religion, but (thanks partly to the paganism of the classical authors they studied) managed to turn out a number of freethinkers.

Marriage was still arranged by parents, and [playwright] Molière found it necessary to draw attention to the abuses of such a system. Nevertheless, the thinker and reformer were in the minority, and *mariages de convenance* were the rule rather than the exception, which makes it understandable, if not pardonable, that so many extra-marital amours characterize the Ancien Régime in France.

Old-fashioned in some ways, the middle classes were nevertheless constantly preoccupied with the business of keeping up with current fashions, and this often led to conflict with superior authority. To a very real extent the king tried to regulate fashion. For example, a decree of 1660 renewed an earlier edict of 1656 forbidding the middle classes to wear cloth of gold or silver and certain adornments. Despite the fact that it was the king's wish, this edict had to be reissued no less than 11 times, which shows how wealthy the middle classes really were. And inventories of wardrobes of the period testify to open defiance of the veto. After all, a fine hardly deterred the original of the *Bourgeois gentilhomme* ["middle-class gentlemen"], determined to "cut a dash.". . .

In view of this external show of elegance and civilized living, it is surprising that more attention was not paid to the body beneath. Houses did not possess baths, but, if the bather were disinclined to travel to the bath-house, he could hire a portable *baignoire* [bathtub] for the day. Water was still considered somewhat dangerous. The *Civilité nouvelle* warned its readers: "To wash in water is bad for the sight, produces toothache and catarrh, makes the complexion pale, exposing the face to cold in winter and to sunburn in summer." However, despite general distaste for water and washing, it was considered fashionable at Versailles to attend the king's bathing parties. The custom naturally spread to Paris, and resorts by the Seine began to attract clientèle. Ladies in particular were expected to bathe in the comparative seclusion of bath-houses anchored in the river. In 1675 we learn that men aspiring to cleanliness were being urged to wash their feet regularly, that Turkish baths were flourishing in some quarters, and that portable apparatus was being conveyed to private houses for the use of rheumatic sufferers too. A current manual of gallantry invites the would-be socialite to take the following precautions: "One may go to the bath-house sometimes in order to have a clean body, and every day should take the trouble to wash one's hands with milk of almonds. The face must be washed almost as often." Not a very rigorous cleansing routine!

The Importance of Good Manners

But, if the current primers on gallantry lacked enthusiasm for hygiene, they showed no such restraint in dealing with etiquette. Indeed, as we have seen, so highly did seventeenth-century France rate good manners, that it is not surprising there were many books published on this subject. One of these, by a man called Courtin and entitled *Le Nouveau Traité de la civilité* (1675), speaks of the etiquette involved in paying and receiving calls. If the caller is a lady, the gentleman will don sword and mantle and meet her at the carriage. He will then provide a comfortable armchair, whilst he himself will make do with a stool (Versailles protocol had penetrated to society by now). At the end of the visit, the polite gentleman will escort her to her carriage and remain outside his house, without hat, until the conveyance has disappeared. . . .

Revolutions in table manners had occurred about 1648, when the plate replaced a slice of bread as a receptacle for food, and about 1655, when clean plates started to appear with each course. However, although in 1648 forks began to be used more and more generally, ten years later the king's sister was expressing distaste at guests helping themselves with fingers to meat from the royal platters. Alas, we may be surprised to know that her objection was connected more with the alleged crime of lese-majesty than with hygiene! Despite these curious anomalies and lapses, it is true to say that table etiquette was elaborate in the seventeenth century. For instance, once the large table-cloth which covered the knees of all the diners and therefore served as communal napkin had given place to the more modern tablecloth, in 1661 separate serviettes were introduced with intricate and sometimes emblematic folds, and the competent maître d'hôtel or footman was expected to know all these many variations, some 30 in all!

Courtin's book on etiquette explains how careful one should be not to offend public taste. The host was expected to sit not at the head of the table, but in the middle. After grace it was customary to pass around a bowl of scented water for the washing of hands; but it was an offence to use the same bowl as your host or a social superior. Spitting was to be done dexterously and unostentatiously, turning the head carefully to the side for the purpose. The knife was recommended to reduce the meat or bread to smaller portions: conversely, savage use of the teeth was discouraged. Elbows on the table were forbidden and the mouth was not to be over-stuffed with food. If knife and spoon were to be dipped into communal dishes, they had to be wiped first on a convenient piece of bread. Noises made whilst eating were frowned upon, as was blowing on the soup to cool it or licking the fingers to clean them. Picking the teeth with the knife or fork was inexcusable if enough tooth-picks were supplied. . . .

Despite these quaint ceremonials, table-manners tended to be cruder and less refined than today, even blowing the nose on the serviette being commoner than one might suppose. Indeed, amongst the inconsistencies of the Age of Louis XIV is the fact that, in spite of such crudities, it was considered bad manners to address a toast directly to a person. It was polite to exclaim "A la santé de Madame," [to Madame's health], but the height of bad manners to say "A votre santé, Madame," [to *your* health, Madame],—a distinction which must surely have eluded or mystified those unfortunates who were not conversant with that breeding-ground of eccentricities, the Palace of Versailles. For the middle classes were entrenched in the towns, and more readily understood customs that sprang from their own nursery of ideas, the City of Paris.

The Bourgeois Stronghold

Seventeenth-century Paris was small compared with the present city, being bounded virtually by the Place de la Bastille in the north-east, by the Boulevard Saint-Germain in the south, and possessing in 1684 only 23,272 houses and 500,000 inhabitants. The city was divided into 16 *quartiers,* a number to be increased to 20 in 1702.

Two kinds of residence could be seen in seventeenth-century Paris. The stone-built *hôtels* (townhouses) of the aristocracy and rich burghers, access to which was via the arched entrance to the courtyard; and the wood and plaster shacks of the humbler folk, some of which still survive in modern Paris. The lower floor of these hovels was often taken up by shops and stalls open to the four winds, and in many cases projecting into the street. Signs of quite inordinate dimensions jutted out from the houses and shops, until the police chief finally imposed upon an unwilling populace rules and regulations to limit their size.

Public squares were rare in this comparatively confined city. There were of course the Place Royale (nowadays the famous Place des Vosges) and the Place Dauphine, which has still preserved its seventeenth-century aspect. There were also the Place des Victoires, near the modern Banque de France, and the Place Vendôme which, like the Place des Victoires, contained an imposing statue of His Majesty. On the Pont-Neuf, the oldest bridge in modern Paris, stood an earlier version of the statue of Henri IV we see today. The Pont-Neuf and the Place Dauphine were the scene of the most fantastic trade. Itinerant vendors would sell you the latest illicit publication from the Netherlands, quack doctors and alchemists would try to persuade you to accept a quick remedy for all your ills, the marionette show would amuse you at a price, street singers or plain beggars would relieve you of any spare change the pickpockets had not been able to extract—and the policemen permanently located under the equestrian statue of Henri IV would be quite incapable of taking effective action to protect you against theft.

The Dangers of Paris

Paris by night was even more hazardous, and you would do well to travel the streets in considerable numbers, or, better still, stay at home. In many doorways there would probably lurk some likely malefactor to rob you, leave you naked or, if you resisted, slit your throat. . . .

Undermanned, the police had only 800 men taking it in turns to patrol the streets; so, by the time your cries had attracted their attention, your felon might well have escaped up the nearest dark alley. However, when he became Chief of Police in 1667, La Reynie cleaned up the city in more ways than one. In the first place, he revoked the right of asylum of certain enclaves in Paris, and forbade the carrying of weapons by ordinary citizens.

Secondly, the Lieutenant of Police turned to a problem affecting public health. The hygiene of the capital left much to be desired. Windows would suddenly open to discharge on the street below the contents of domestic utensils, and woe betide the man who failed to respond quickly enough to the cry "Gare l'eau," [watch out for the water]. Most houses were simply without toilet facilities of any sort, with the result that the street became a communal latrine, and the middle of the road ran with the foulest of streams. An order issued in 1662 forbade Parisians to pile excreta in front of their doors, in the highway, on the sides of the river and in public squares; but unfortunately the inhabitants of this great city did not obey the order. Nor were the royal residences much better looked after in this respect. The supplier of a new kind of toilet device tells us that in 1675 around the Louvre—especially in the courtyards, on the stairs, behind doors and in the upper corridors—all sorts of disgusting sights were to be encountered. Because of the dangers arising from lack of hygiene, in 1666 some attempt at street-sweeping was made and in 1667 La Reynie began to think about other possible measures. For instance, in 1668 he made primitive sanitary provision obligatory.

The Police Lieutenant also increased the number of street-lights in the capital between October and March each year. Lighting was by candles, but they must have been of a considerable size, since the lamps themselves, suspended over the street 20 feet in the air, had panels two feet square, and each candle lasted until midnight. . . .

The Café Society

The reign of Louis XIV witnessed the birth of society cafés, the first of them being the café Procope down the present Rue de l'Ancienne Comédie in the Saint-Germain-des-Pré district of Paris. Here tea was drunk by fashionable folk, but cocoa was much cheaper than tea, and was therefore consumed more freely by the humbler bourgeois. However, in 1671, the fashion changed and cocoa-drinking was held responsible for all kinds of maladies. Coffee had been known throughout the half-century; in 1669 Soliman Aga, an oriental envoy to the Court, popularized the infusion and three years later an Armenian trading at the Foire Saint-Germain opened a coffee-house. Mid-oriental proprietors joined in the rush, though doubts regarding the health-giving properties of the beverage were entertained. However, Procope and his colleagues soon overcame these difficulties, with the result that by 1716 there were no less than 300 cafés in Paris. Furthermore, middle-class homes adopted the drink and coffee became well-established in French life.

On a fine day, however, it was natural to prefer the parks to the coffee-houses. The choice was quite extensive. The elegant continued, of course, to find their pleasure in frequenting the Cours-la-Reine—so much in demand that it was extended into the evening, with torches and lanterns lighting up the fairy-like scene. Other places began to be used as the Cours became more crowded: the Mail, between the Arsenal and the river; the Palais-Royal near the Louvre; the Luxembourg Gardens in the Latin Quarter; the Place-Royale and the Jardin du Roi, which we now know as the Jardin des Plantes. But above all it was the turn of the Tuileries, especially for lovers. It had the advantage of being near the Cours-la-Reine, and when in 1664 . . . Colbert improved it, it was enhanced by fountains, trees and flowerbeds.

Other public parks attracted a crowd of sightseers. The Bois de Boulogne, which was at that time surrounded by walls, had been enlarged in 1670 by the addition of a large tract of woodland belonging to the nuns of Longchamp. This allowed the authorities to add a race-course, which is still the Mecca of Parisian society at certain times of the year. The Bois was also a place for illicit love-affairs—as indeed it is to this day. The coachman would say "Here I am paid to look after the cloaks, and keep silence!" Whilst the Bois de Boulogne attracted mainly the upper classes, living (as is usual) on the western fringes of the city where the prevailing wind carried the smoke away from their houses, the lower classes, residing on the less salubrious eastern side of town, enjoyed a stroll in the Bois de Vincennes. Here it was a short walk to the banks of the River Marne and the famous cabaret, La Pissotte. Stimulated by the open air, other thirsts would find satisfaction near the Gobelins (literally "The Goblins," but in fact called after a person) on a tiny stream called the Bièvre used by the dyers of Paris, or at Vanves on the south-west, whilst on the southern side proper it was not far to the park of Sceaux or to Bagneux. Saint-Cloud on the western extremity of the capital was also much favoured as a Sunday trip, or on Saint-Fiacre's day, when masked parties crossed the Seine by ferry. Truly then, as now, Paris catered for all tastes, without, however, ceasing to provide above all a setting worthy of the rich and increasingly powerful men of affairs, the bourgeoisie.

The Great Fire of London

Samuel Pepys

Samuel Pepys was an English diarist and naval administrator who became secretary to the admiralty in 1672. He lost his office, however,
and was imprisoned because of his alleged complicity in the Popish Plot
(1679). He was reappointed in 1684, and in that same year he became
president of the Royal Society. His celebrated diary provides vivid pictures of contemporary seventeenth-century life, and the highlights include the Great Plague and the Great Fire of London. The following excerpt from Pepys's diary describes his experiences during the four-day
fire that raged through London in 1666, destroying most of its public
buildings, numerous churches, and countless homes.

Some of our maids sitting up late last night to get things ready
against our feast today, Jane called us up, about 3 in the morning, to tell us of a great fire they saw in the City. So I rose, and
slipped on my nightgown and went to her window, and thought it to
be on the back side of Marke Lane at the furthest; but being unused
to such fires as fallowed, I thought it far enough off, and so went to
bed again and to sleep. About 7 rose again to dress myself, and there
looked out at the window and saw the fire not so much as it was, and
further off. So to my closet to set things to rights after yesterday's
cleaning. By and by Jane comes and tells me that she hears that
above 300 houses have been burned down tonight by the fire we saw,
and that it was now burning down all Fish Street by London Bridge.

Excerpted from Samuel Pepys, *A Pepys Anthology: Passages from the Diary of Samuel Pepys*,
edited by Robert and Linnett Latham. Copyright © 1987 The Master, Fellows, and Scholars of
Magdalene College, Cambridge, Robert Latham and the Executors of William Matthews. Reprinted
with permission from the University of California Press.

So I made myself ready presently, and walked to the Tower and there got up upon one of the high places, Sir J. Robinson's little son going up with me; and there I did see the houses at that end of the bridge all on fire, and an infinite great fire on this and the other side the end of the bridge—which, among other people, did trouble me for poor little Michell and our Sarah on the Bridge. So down, with my heart full of trouble, to the Lieutenant of the Tower, who tells me that it begun this morning in the King's bakers house in Pudding Lane, and that it hath burned down St Magnes Church and most part of Fish Street already. So I down to the waterside and there got a boat and through the bridge, and there saw a lamentable fire. Poor Michells house, as far as the Old Swan [theater], already burned that way and the fire running further, that in a very little time it got as far as the Stillyard while I was there. Everybody endeavouring to remove their goods, and flinging into the river or bringing them into lighters [barges used for transporting goods over short distances] that lay off. Poor people staying in their houses as long as till the very fire touched them, and then running into boats or clambering from one pair of stair by the waterside to another. And among other things, the poor pigeons I perceive were loath to leave their houses, but hovered about the windows and balconies till they were some of them burned, their wings, and fell down.

Having stayed, and in an hour's time seen the fire rage every way, and nobody to my sight endeavouring to quench it, but to remove their goods and leave all to the fire; and having seen it get as far as the Steeleyard, and the wind mighty high and driving it into the City, and everything, after so long a drought, proving combustible, even the very stones of churches, and among other things, the poor steeple by which pretty Mrs [Horsley] lives, and whereof my old schoolfellow Elborough is parson, taken fire in the very top and there burned till it fall down—I to Whitehall with a gentleman with me who desired to go off from the Tower to see the fire in my boat—to Whitehall, and there up to the King's closet in the chapel, where people came about me and I did give them an account dismayed them all; and word was carried in to the King, so I was called for and did tell the King and Duke of York what I saw, and that unless his Majesty did command houses to be pulled down, nothing could stop the fire. They seemed much troubled, and the King commanded me to go to my Lord Mayor from him and command him to spare no houses but to pull down before the fire every way. The Duke of York bid me tell him that if he would have any more soldiers, he shall; and so did my Lord Arlington afterward, as a great secret. Here meeting with Capt. Cocke, I in his coach, which he lent me, and Creed with me, to Pauls; and there walked along Watling Street as well as I could, every creature coming away loaden with goods to save—and here and there sick people carried away in beds. Extraordinary good goods carried in carts and on backs. At last met my Lord Mayor in Canning Street, like a man spent, with a handkercher about his neck. To the King's message, he cried like a fainting woman, "Lord, what can I do? I am spent! People will not obey me. I have been pull[ing] down houses. But the fire overtakes us faster then we can do it." That he needed no more soldiers; and that for himself, he must go and refresh himself, having been up all night. So he left me, and I him, and walked home—seeing people all almost distracted and no manner of means used to quench the fire. The houses too, so very thick thereabouts, and full of matter for burning, as pitch and tar, in Thames Street—and warehouses of oyle [oil] and wines and brandy and other things. Here I saw Mr Isaccke Houblon, that handsome man—prettily dressed and dirty at his door at Dowgate, receiving some of his brothers things whose houses were on fire; and as he says, have been removed twice already, and he doubts (as it soon proved) that they must be in a little time removed from his house also—which was a sad consideration. And to see the churches all filling with goods, by people who themselfs should have been quietly there at this time. By this time it was about 12 a-clock, and so home and there find my guests, which was Mr Wood and his wife, Barbary Shelden, and also Mr Moone. While at dinner, Mrs Batelier came to enquire after Mr Woolfe and Stanes (who it seems are related to them), whose houses in Fish Street are all burned, and they in a sad condition. She would not stay in the fright.

As soon as dined, I and Moone away and walked through the City, the streets full of nothing but people and horses and carts loaden with goods, ready to run over one another, and removing goods from one burned house to another—they now removing out of Canning Street (which received goods in the morning) into Lumbard Street and further; and among others, I now saw my little goldsmith Stokes receiving some friend's goods, whose house itself was burned the day after. We parted at Pauls, he home and I to Pauls Wharf, where I had appointed a boat to attend me; and took in Mr Carcasse and his brother, whom I met in the street, and carried them below and above bridge, to and again, to see the fire, which was now got further, both below and above, and no likelihood of stopping it. Met with the King and Duke of York in their barge, and with them to Queenhith and there called Sir Rd Browne to them. Their order was only to pull down houses apace, and so below bridge at the waterside; but little was or could be done, the fire coming upon them so fast. Good hopes there was of stopping it at the Three Cranes above, and at Buttolphs Wharf below bridge, if care be used; but the wind carries it into the City, so as we know not by the waterside what it doth there. River full of lighter[s] and boats taking in goods, and good goods swimming in the water; and only, I observed that hardly one lighter or boat in three that had goods of a house in, but there was a pair of virginalls [keyed instruments similar to a spinet, but without legs] in it. Having seen as much as I could now, I away to Whitehall by appointment, and there walked to St James's Park, and there met my wife and Creed and Wood and his wife and walked to my boat, and there upon the water again, and to the fire up and down, it still increasing and the wind great. So near the fire as we could for smoke; and all over the Thames, with one's face in the wind you were almost burned with a shower of firedrops—this is very true—so as houses were burned by these drops and flakes of fire, three or four, nay five or six houses, one from another. When we could endure no more upon the water, we to a little alehouse on the Bankside over against the Three Cranes, and there stayed till it was dark almost and saw the fire grow; and as it grow darker, appeared more and more, and in corners and upon steeples and between churches and houses, as far as we could see up the hill of the City, in a most horrid malicious bloody flame, not like the fine flame of an ordinary fire. We stayed till, it being darkish, we saw the fire as only one entire arch of fire from this to the other side of the bridge, and in a bow up the hill, for an arch of above a mile long. It made me weep to see it. The churches, houses, and all on fire and flaming at once, and a horrid noise the flames made, and the cracking of houses at their ruine.

So home with a sad heart, and there find everybody discoursing and lamenting the fire; and poor Tom Hater came with some few of his goods saved out of his house, which is burned upon Fish Street Hill. I invited him to lie at my house, and did receive his goods: but was deceived in his lying there, the noise coming every moment of the growth of the fire, so as we were forced to begin to pack up our own goods and prepare for their removal. And did by moonshine (it being brave, dry, and moonshine and warm weather) carry much of my goods into the garden, and Mr Hater and I did remove my money and iron chests into my cellar—as thinking that the safest place. And got my bags of gold into my office ready to carry away, and my chief papers of accounts also there, and my tallies into a box by themselfs. So great was our fear, as Sir W. Batten had carts come out of the country to fetch away his goods this night. We did put Mr Hater, poor man, to bed a little; but he got but very little rest, so much noise being in my house, taking down of goods. *(Lord's Day, 2 September 1666)*

1600

Nurhachi unites the Mongol tribes of Manchuria in northeast China to form the nation of Manchu; After a seven-year trial, the Inquisition burns Giordano Bruno at the stake in Rome. Bruno, an Italian philosopher and scientist, championed the theory of Copernicus, which brought him into conflict with the Inquisition; The British establish a commercial and political organization in India known as the East India Company; The players at the Globe perform Shakespeare's *Hamlet* for the first time.

1601

The Time of Troubles begins in Russia with the arrival of the false Dmitrys, a series of men who pretend to be the son of Ivan IV, who died during an epileptic seizure. The pretenders find support from competing domestic and foreign interests, and the power struggles continue until a new czar is elected from the Romanov family in 1613.

1602

The States-General of the Netherlands charters the Dutch East India Company to expand trade with its colonial enterprises in Asia, the Cape of Good Hope, the Strait of Magellan, Indonesia, Malaya, and Ceylon (Sri Lanka).

1603

Ieyasu establishes the Tokugawa shogunate in Japan and moves the capital to Edo (Tokyo); Stuart rule begins when King James VI of Scotland, the son of Mary, queen of Scots, is crowned James I of England after the death of Queen Elizabeth I.

1605

The Catholics who organized the Gunpowder Plot fail to blow up the British House of Parliament, beginning the persecution of Catholics in England that lasts throughout the century; Miguel de Cervantes publishes *Don Quixote de la Mancha*, the first modern novel; painter Peter Paul Rubens settles in Antwerp, establishing the Flemish baroque.

1607

James I grants the Puritans permission to found a colony in Virginia; the Puritans establish Jamestown, the first permanent English colony in America. The colony is the setting for the controversial story of the rescue of Captain John Smith by Pocahontas, daughter of Chief Powhatan.

1608

Samuel de Champlain establishes the French colony of Quebec; Francesco Maria Guazzo publishes the *Compendium Malefi-carum,* a manuscript on the practice of witchcraft and methods for discovering, interrogating, and executing witches.

1609

Philip II of Spain issues the Edict of Expulsion of Moriscos, or Spanish Muslims, and as many as 2 million Spanish citizens leave Spain; The *Relation* debuts in Germany as the first regularly published newspaper.

1610

Galileo sees the moons of Jupiter through his new invention, the telescope.

1611

James I passes an act of Parliament to have the Latin Bible translated into English; Rubens paints his *Descent from the Cross.*

1613

The British East India Company obtains permission from the Mogul Jahāngīr to set up a trading post in India; Mikhail Feodorovich Romanov is elected the new czar of Russia, establishing the Romanov dynasty, which ruled Russia for the next three hundred years.

1614

Shogun Ieyasu issues an order that suppresses Christianity throughout Japan; John Napier publishes the first logarithmic table and coins the word *logarithm.*

1616

The Dutch land at the Gulf of Carpentaria, beginning settlement of New Holland (Australia).

1618

Regents of the court of Emperor Ferdinand II are thrown out of the castle window in the Defenestration of Prague in Protestant Bohemia, which begins the Thirty Years' War; Johannes Kepler publishes *De cometis* and *Harmonice mundi,* in which he announces his third law of planetary motion; Sir Walter Raleigh, a favorite of Elizabeth I, is put to death for treason against James I.

1619

Calvinism, related in religious style to the English Puritan movement, increases its power on the European continent; A Dutch ship brings the first African slaves to British North America.

1620

The Pilgrims, after a three-month voyage on the *Mayflower*, land at Plymouth Rock; Francis Bacon publishes the *Novum Organum*, which promotes the use of inductive reasoning.

1623

The States-General of the Netherlands organizes the Dutch West India Company, a trading and colonizing company that establishes many colonies, including Fort Amsterdam located on the southern tip of Manhattan Island, now New York City; Iemitsu becomes the third shogun of Japan and intensifies insulation of Japan from external influences. Spaniards are banned from the country in 1624, Japanese are forbidden to travel abroad in 1636, and Portuguese traders are confined to Deshima Island off Nagasaki in 1641.

1624

Richelieu becomes first minister of France. His twin aims, to secure universal obedience to the Bourbon monarchy and to enhance France's international prestige, are achieved at the expense of resistant groups in French society.

1625

Charles I succeeds to the throne as king of England. He is popular at the time of his coronation but offends his Protestant subjects by his marriage to the Catholic Henrietta Maria, sister of Louis XIII of France. His reign is a bitter struggle for supremacy between the king and Parliament that finally results in the English civil war.

1627

Composed by Heinrich Schütz, *Dafne*, the first German opera, is produced in Torgau. Schütz is regarded as the founder of the baroque school of German music, introducing Italian styles such as instrumentally accompanied choral compositions.

1628

The English Parliament issues the Petition of Right against the perceived tyranny of Charles I, who dissolves Parliament, pursues his own means of raising funds, and rules autocratically from a room called "the Star Chamber"; William Harvey, an English physician, publishes his work on the circulation of blood.

1630

The Massachusetts Bay Colony is established during the great migration of Puritans and other seekers of religious freedom; Emperor Ferdinand

II dismisses Albrecht von Wallenstein, a Bohemian general who became commander of the imperial armies and won a series of victories during the early battles of the Thirty Years' War. He is later reinstated to defend the empire but is defeated in 1632 at Lützen by the Swedish king Gustavus Adolph. His intrigues lead to an imperial proclamation of treason, resulting in his assassination by Irish mercenaries.

1632
The Swedish king Gustavus Adolph is killed in battle, but the Swedish army is victorious in the Battle of Lützen during the Thirty Years' War.

1633
The Inquisition forces Galileo to recant his belief in the Copernican theory.

1636
René Descartes publishes *Discourse on the Method of Rightly Conducting the Reason and Seeking for Truth in the Sciences.*

1639
Shogun Iemitsu implements Sakoku Rei, a policy of total exclusion of all foreign influence in Japan.

1642
After Charles I attempts to arrest five members of Parliament, the Cavaliers, also known as Royalists, supporters of Charles I go to war against the Roundheads, or parliamentary forces, beginning the English civil war; Rembrandt paints *Night Watch.*

1643
Emperor Shāh Jahān erects the Taj Mahal, a mausoleum to honor his beloved wife Mumtāz Mahal after her death.

1644
A bandit general captures Peking, China; summoned to aid Ming troops, the Manchu enter Peking and take over the government, ending the Ming dynasty and founding the Ch'ing dynasty, which lasts from 1644 to 1911.

1645
Oliver Cromwell establishes the New Model Army during the English civil war; under General Fairfax, the army defeats the Royalists at Naseby.

1646
Under the leadership of Cromwell, the Parliamentarians defeat the Royalists.

1648

The Peace of Westphalia ends the Thirty Years' War in Europe; The English civil war ends, and the interregnum period begins; A series of insurrections known as the Frondes break out between 1648 and 1653 when Louis XIV is just a boy. The Frondes are initiated by the French parliament, discontented nobles, and the financially burdened French people; Muhammad IV becomes the sultan of Turkey.

1649

Parliament, now reduced in number and controlled by the powerful enemies of Charles I, establishes a special high court of justice, which tries and convicts Charles of treason for levying war against Parliament. He is beheaded on January 30, 1649. To the Royalists, he becomes the martyred king, but his opponents consider him a double-dealing tyrant; Cromwell establishes the Commonwealth of England.

1651

Thomas Hobbes publishes *Leviathan*, in which he argues that man is by nature a selfishly individualistic animal at constant war with all other men and that fear of violent death causes men to create a state by contracting to surrender their natural rights and to submit to the absolute authority of a sovereign.

1653

Cromwell dissolves the Rump Parliament, the remnants of Charles I's Parliament, and becomes lord protector of England.

1654

Kang Xi, also known as Hsüan-yeh, becomes the second emperor of the Ch'ing (Manchu) dynasty at eight years old and is considered one of the most important monarchs in China's history because of his triple role as military commander, statesman, and scholar. He organizes the compilation of a Ming history and a large encyclopedia and adds parts of Russia and Outer Mongolia to the empire; Diego Rodríguez de Silva Velázquez paints *Las Malinas*.

1655

Christiaan Huygens, a Dutch mathematician, develops a method to make telescope lenses more powerful, whereupon he discovers a moon and the rings of Saturn. Huygens also designs a pendulum and adapts it to the first reliable mechanical clock.

1657

Parliament offers the kingship to Cromwell, who declines.

1658

Molière, the pseudonym of actor and playwright Jean-Baptiste Poquelin, acts before King Louis XIV; after the publication of his comedy *Les Précieuses ridicules* (*The Affected Young Ladies*), no year passes without at least one major dramatic achievement, such as *L'École des femmes* (*The School for Wives*), *Tartuffe, Le Misanthrope,* and *Le Bourgeois gentilhomme;* Cromwell dies, his son Richard resigns, and the Puritan government collapses.

1659

Anglo-Irish physicist and chemist Robert Boyle develops an air pump for creating vacuums, confirming Galileo's view that bodies in a vacuum fall at the same rate, regardless of weight; The Peace of the Pyrenees ends the war between France and Spain.

1660

General George Monck engineers the restoration of Charles II to the throne. Charles promises a general amnesty in his conciliatory Declaration of Breda. During his reign, the power of Parliament increases and the Whig and Tory Parties emerge. Charles also sets the tone of the brilliant Restoration period in art and literature.

1661

Louis XIV begins rule as absolute monarch in France. He centralizes bureaucracy and forces the nobility into financial dependence on the Crown, creating a court preoccupied with ceremonial etiquette and petty intrigues. Louis patronized the foremost writers and artists of his time. Because of the brilliance of his court, Louis is called *"Le Roi Soleil"* ("the Sun King").

1662

The Church of England (Anglican Church) is restored.

1665

Charles II becomes the king of Spain, Naples, and Sicily. The last of the Spanish Habsburgs, he was physically crippled and mentally retarded. His mother, Mariana de Austria, acts as regent and continues to rule after his majority; The Great Plague in London kills seventy-five thousand; Englishman Robert Hooke publishes *Micrographia*, in which he reveals drawings of insects viewed through a microscope and his speculations on the origin of the lunar craters and fossils.

1666

On September 2, the Great Fire of London destroys St. Paul's Church and causes £10 million in damages; Isaac Newton develops calculus.

1667

John Milton publishes *Paradise Lost*, considered the greatest epic poem in English; Jean Racine, widely regarded as the master of tragic pathos, produces *Andromaque,* the first of seven verse tragedies.

1674

Antoni van Leeuwenhoek discovers one-celled bacteria in marsh water using his microscope.

1675

Gottfried Leibniz develops differential calculus.

1676

Kara Mustafa Pasa becomes the grand vizier under Sultan Muhammad IV of the Ottoman Empire (Turkey). Ambitious and belligerent, he allies himself with the Hungarian rebels under Imre Thököly against Holy Roman Emperor Leopold I and leads the unsuccessful siege of Vienna in 1683.

1677

Friends of Baruch Spinoza publish his *Ethics* and *On the Improvement of the Understanding* after Spinoza's death.

1681

In payment for loans made to the Crown, King Charles II makes William Penn, a devout and active Quaker, the sole proprietor of Pennsylvania. In 1682 Penn writes a "Frame of Government," which grants religious freedom to all colonists. He also cultivates and maintains warm, friendly relations with the Indians.

1683

The Ottoman Empire makes its last advance in Europe when the Turks invade Austria, but the three-month siege of Vienna ends with the defeat of the Turks by European powers; Henry Purcell becomes the keeper of the king's instruments in England. In his official capacity, he produces a number of pieces in celebration of royal birthdays, St. Cecilia's Day, and other occasions. Purcell is best known for his vocal and choral works and wrote a great deal of incidental stage music.

1685

Despite opposition by the Whig Party, James II, a converted Catholic, succeeds his brother Charles II to the throne of England. James issues two declarations of indulgence, suspending the laws against Catholics and dissenters. The birth of a son, who would have succeeded instead of Protestant William and Mary, brings about further opposition to James; King Louis XIV of France revokes the Edict of Nantes, which granted freedom of worship to the Huguenots (French Protestants), driving many from France, including merchants and skilled artisans, which intensifies the kingdom's economic decline and further alienates the Protestant powers.

1687

Isaac Newton publishes *Philosophiae Naturalis Principia Mathematica*, setting out his three laws of motion.

1688

William of Orange is invited to England by Whig and Tory leaders to replace James II. The unpopular, autocratic, and Catholic king had few loyal followers and was unable to defend himself. He flees, is captured, and is allowed to escape to France, and William and Mary take the throne in the Glorious Revolution; The Moguls complete their conquest of India; The Genorku age, centered in Kyoto and Osaka, begins the first major cultural expansion in Japan.

1689

Parliament confirms the English Bill of Rights; Peter the Great becomes czar of Russia and shortly thereafter begins his travels through Europe, hoping to westernize Russia and develop Russia's military power.

1690

William III of England defeats former king James II and Irish rebels at the Battle of the Boyne in Ireland; John Locke publishes his *Essay Concerning Human Understanding* and *Second Treatise on Government.*

1692

During the Salem witch trials, eighteen people and one dog are executed.

1693

Prince Eugene establishes the Austro-Hungarian Empire after winning the campaign against the Turks.

1699

Before his death, the childless Charles II of Spain names Philip of Anjou as his heir. A grandson of Louis XIV of France, Philip, is the first Bourbon on the Spanish throne, provoking the War of the Spanish Succession in 1700, which severely reduces Spanish power.

General Studies

Thomas Garden Barnes, *Renaissance, Reformation, and Absolutism, 1400–1660.* Boston: Little, Brown, 1972.

Charles Blitzer, *Age of Kings.* New York: Time, 1969.

Maurice Braure, *The Age of Absolutism.* New York: Hawthorn Books, 1963.

Nicholas Henshall, "The Myth of Absolutism," *History Today,* June 1992.

John Miller, *Absolutism in Seventeenth-Century Europe.* Basingstoke, England: Macmillan Education, 1990.

Leo Weinstein, ed., *The Age of Reason: The Culture of the Seventeenth Century.* New York: G. Braziller, 1965.

Art, Literature, and Music

Giulio Carlo Argan, *The Europe of the Capitals, 1600–1700.* Trans. Anthony Rhodes. Cleveland: World, 1965.

Harald Busch, *Baroque Europe.* New York: Macmillan, 1962.

David Carroll, *The Taj Mahal.* New York: Newsweek, 1973.

Roland E. Fleischer and Susan Scott Munshower, eds., *The Age of Rembrandt: Studies in Seventeenth-Century Dutch Painting,* University Park: Pennsylvania State University, 1988.

Abraham Marie Hammacher, *Flemish and Dutch Art.* New York: Franklin Watts, 1965.

Frederick Hartt, *Art: A History of Painting, Sculpture, and Architecture,* New York: H.N. Abrams, 1976.

Eberhard Hempel, *Baroque Art and Architecture in Central Europe.* Baltimore: Penguin Books, 1965.

Michael Kitson, *The Age of Baroque.* London: Hamlyn, 1966.

John Howard Bertram Masterman, *The Age of Milton*. London: G. Bell, 1927.

Jonathan Philips, "Titian and van Dyck: The Prince of Painters and the Painter of Princes," *American Artist*, March 1991.

Jakob Rosenberg, *Dutch Art and Architecture: 1600 to 1800*. Baltimore: Penguin, 1966.

Howard E. Smither, *A History of the Oratorio*. Chapel Hill: University of North Carolina Press, 1977.

Peter C. Swann, *The Art of Japan from the Jomon to the Tokugawa Period*. New York: Greystone, 1966.

Christopher White, *Rembrandt*. London: Thames and Hudson, 1984.

Rudolf Wittkower, *Gian Lorenzo Bernini: The Sculptor of the Roman Baroque*. London: Phaidon, 1966.

George Edward Woodberry, *Great Writers: Cervantes, Scott, Milton, Virgil, Montaigne, Shakespeare*. Freeport, NY: Books for Libraries, 1967.

Colonization

Carl Bridenbaugh, *Jamestown, 1544–1699*. New York: Oxford University Press, 1980.

Wesley Frank Craven, *The Southern Colonies in the Seventeenth Century, 1607–1689*. Baton Rouge: Louisiana State University Press, 1970.

John Fiske, *The Dutch and Quaker Colonies in America*. New York: Houghton, Mifflin, 1900.

Maud Wilder Goodwin, *Dutch and English on the Hudson: A Chronicle of Colonial New York*. New Haven, CT: Yale University Press, 1919.

W. Keith Kavenagh, ed., *Foundations of Colonial America*. New York: Chelsea House, 1973.

Douglas Edward Leach, *Roots of Conflict: British Armed Forces and Colonial Americans, 1677–1763*. Chapel Hill: University of North Carolina Press, 1986.

Wallace Notestein, *The English People on the Eve of Colonization, 1603–1630*. New York: Harper, 1954.

Alison Gilbert Olson, *Anglo-American Politics, 1660–1775: The Relationship Between Parties in England and Colonial America.* New York: Oxford University Press, 1973.

Francis Parkman, *France and England in North America.* New York: Viking, 1983.

Pamela Smit, *The Dutch in America, 1609–1970.* Dobbs Ferry, NY: Oceana, 1972.

George McCall Theal, *History of South Africa Under the Administration of the Dutch East India Company, 1652 to 1795.* New York: Negro Universities Press, 1969.

Alten T. Vaughan, *The American Colonies in the Seventeenth Century.* New York: Appleton-Century-Crofts, 1971.

William Harrison Woodward, *A Short History of the Expansion of the British Empire, 1500–1930.* Cambridge, England: University Press, 1931.

England

Maurice Ashley, *James II.* Minneapolis: University of Minnesota Press, 1977.

Philip Caraman. *The Years of Siege: Catholic Life from James I to Cromwell.* London: Longmans, 1966.

Antonia Fraser, *Faith and Treason: The Story of the Gunpowder Plot.* New York: Anchor Books, 1997.

———, *Royal Charles: Charles II and the Restoration.* New York: Knopf, 1979.

Pieter Geyl, *Orange and Stuart, 1641–1672.* New York: Scribner, 1970.

Ronald Hutton, *Charles the Second, King of England, Scotland, and Ireland.* New York: Oxford University Press, 1989.

J.R. Jones, ed., *The Restored Monarchy, 1660–1688.* Totowa, NJ: Rowman and Littlefield, 1979.

Clayton Roberts, *A History of England.* Englewood Cliffs, NJ: Prentice-Hall, 1980.

Conrad Russell, *The Crisis of Parliaments: English History, 1509–1660.* New York: Oxford University Press, 1971.

Lawrence Stone, *Social Change and Revolution in England, 1540–1640*. New York: Barnes and Noble, 1968.

George Macaulay Trevelyan, *England Under the Stuarts*. London: Methuen, 1965.

————, *The English Revolution, 1688–1689*. New York: Oxford University Press, 1965.

Stephen Saunders Webb, *The Governors-General: The English Army and the Definition of the Empire, 1569–1681*. Chapel Hill: University of North Carolina Press, 1979.

Cicely Veronica Wedgwood, *Oliver Cromwell*. New York: Macmillan, 1956.

Europe

Norman Davies, *Europe: A History*. New York: Oxford University Press, 1996.

Otto Friedrich, "German History, More or Less as Germans See It," *Smithsonian*, March 1991.

Stephen Jay Gould, "The Diet of Worms and the Defenestration of Prague," *Natural History*, September 1996.

David Kirby, "Imperial Sweden: Image and Self-Image," *History Today*, November 1990.

Peter Limm, *The Thirty Years' War*. New York: Longmans, 1984.

James Nathan, "Force, Order, and Diplomacy in the Age of Louis XIV," *Virginia Quarterly Review*, Autumn 1993. Available from VQR, PO Box 400223, Charlottesville, VA 22904-4223.

J.V. Polisensky, *The Thirty Years' War*. Berkeley and Los Angeles: University of California Press, 1971.

Orest A. Ranum, *Paris in the Age of Absolutism: An Essay*. New York: Wiley, 1968.

Susan Roa, "Catholicism in Seventeenth-Century Scandinavia," *Catholic Historical Review*, January 1993. Available from Catholic Historical Review, Catholic University of America Press, 620 Michigan Ave. NE, 240 Leahy Hall, Washington, DC 20064.

Cicely Veronica Wedgwood, *The Thirty Years' War*. London: J. Cape, 1944.

Russia and Asia

E.M. Almedingen, *The Romanovs: Three Centuries of an Ill-Fated Dynasty*. London: Bodley Head, 1966.

M.S. Anderson, *Peter the Great*. London: Thames and Hudson, 1978.

John D. Bergamini, *The Tragic Dynasty: A History of the Romanovs*. New York: Putnam, 1969.

Charles O. Hucker, *China's Imperial Past: An Introduction to Chinese History and Culture*. Palo Alto, CA: Stanford University Press, 1975.

Milton Walter Meyer, *Japan: A Concise History*. Boston: Allyn and Bacon, 1966.

Om Prkash, *The Dutch East India Company and the Economy of Bengal, 1630–1720*. Princeton, NJ: Princeton University Press, 1985.

Merle Ricklefs, "Balance and Military Innovation in Seventeenth-Century Java," *History Today*, November 1990.

Sir George Bailey Sansom, *Japan: A Short Cultural History*. London: Cresset, 1936.

Benedict Humphrey Sumner, *Peter the Great and the Emergence of Russia*. New York: Collier Books, 1962.

John E. Wills, *Pepper, Guns, and Parleys: The Dutch East India Company and China, 1622–1681*. Cambridge, MA: Harvard University Press, 1974.

Science and Philosophy

Michael Guillen, *Five Equations That Changed the World: The Power and Poetry of Mathematics*. New York: Hyperion, 1995.

A. Rupert Hall, *The Scientific Revolution, 1500–1800: The Formation of the Modern Scientific Attitude*. New York: Longmans, Green, 1954.

James Jacob, *The Scientific Revolution: Aspirations and Achievements: 1500–1700*. Atlantic Highlands, NJ: Humanities, 1998.

Eugene M. Klaaren, *Religious Origins of Modern Science: Belief in Creation in Seventeenth-Century Thought*. Grand Rapids, MI: Eerdmans, 1977.

Patrick Moore, *Watchers of the Stars: The Scientific Revolution*. London: Joseph, 1974.

Lance Morrow, "Isaac Newton (1642–1727)," *Time*, December 31, 1999.

Steven Shapin, *The Scientific Revolution*. Chicago: University of Chicago Press, 1996.

Richard Westfall, *The Construction of Modern Science: Mechanisms and Mechanics*. New York: John Wiley and Sons, 1971.

Michael White, *Isaac Newton: The Last Sorcerer*. Reading, MA: Addison-Wesley, 1997.

Philip K. Wilson, "Origins of Science," *National Forum*, Winter 1996. Available from National Forum, Honor Society of Phi Kappa Phi, Box 16000, Louisiana State University, Baton Rouge, LA 70893.

R.S. Woolhouse, *Descartes, Spinoza, Leibniz: The Concept of Substance in Seventeenth-Century Metaphysics*. New York: Routledge, 1993.

Society and Culture

Robin Blackburn, *The Making of New World Slavery: From the Baroque to the Modern, 1492–1800*. New York: Verso, 1997.

Madeleine Burnside, *Spirits of the Passage: The Transatlantic Slave Trade in the Seventeenth Century*. New York: Simon & Schuster, 1997.

Bernard Capp, "Serial Killers in Seventeenth-Century England," *History Today*, March 1996.

Victor De Kock, *Those in Bondage: An Account of the Life of the Slave at the Cape in the Days of the Dutch East India Company*. Port Washington, NY: Kennikat, 1971.

Philippe Erlanger, *The Age of Courts and Kings: Manners and Morals, 1558–1715*. London: Weidenfeld & Nicolson, 1967.

Charles Harding Firth, *Cromwell's Army: A History of the English Soldier During the Civil Wars, the Commonwealth, and the Protectorate*. London: Methuen, 1962.

Margaret George, *Women in the First Capitalist Society: Experience in Seventeenth-Century England*. Urbana: University of Illinois Press, 1988.

Frances Hill, *A Delusion of Satan: The Full Story of the Salem Witch Trials*. New York: Doubleday, 1995.

David Maland, *Culture and Society in Seventeenth-Century France*. New York: Scribner, 1970.

Sheila Rowbotham, *Hidden from History: Rediscovering Women in History from the Seventeenth Century to the Present*. New York: Pantheon Books, 1975.

Craig Spence, "Accidentally Killed by a Cart: Workplace, Hazard, and Risk in Late Seventeenth-Century London," *European Review of History*, Spring 1996. Available from Taylor & Francis, Dawson Ltd., Back Issues Division, Cannon House, Folkestone, Kent, England CT195EE.

Gladys Scott Thomson, *Life in a Noble Household, 1641–1700*. London: J. Cape, 1940.

David Underdown, *Revel, Riot, and Rebellion: Popular Politics and Culture in England 1603–1660*. Oxford: Oxford University Press, 1987.

Original Documents

Francis Bacon, *"Advancement of Learning"* and *"Novum Organum."* New York: Willey Book, 1900.

Gerhard Benecke, ed. and trans., *Germany in the Thirty Years War*. London: Arnold, 1978.

Albert Bushnell, ed., *American History Told by Contemporaries*. Vol. I. *Era of Colonization, 1492–1689*. New York: Macmillan, 1897.

Thomas Carlyle, ed., *Oliver Cromwell's Letters and Speeches: With Elucidations*. London: Chapman and Hall, 1885.

Charles I, *The Letters, Speeches, and Proclamations*. Ed. Sir Charles Petrie. New York: Funk & Wagnall, 1968.

René Descartes, *"Discourse on the Method"* and *"Meditations on First Philosophy."* Ed. David Weissman. New Haven, CT: Yale University Press, 1996.

Charles W. Eliot, ed., *American Historical Documents, 1000-1904: With Introductions and Notes*. New York: Collier, 1938.

Marie Boas Hall, *Nature and Nature's Laws: Documents of the Scientific Revolution*. New York: Walker, 1970.

Stuart Hampshire, ed., *The Age of Reason: The Seventeenth-Century Philosophers, Selected, with Introduction and Interpretive Commentary.* New York: G. Braziller, 1956.

William Harvey, *The Circulation of the Blood, and Other Writings.* Trans. Kenneth J. Franklin. New York: Dutton, 1963.

Robert Hooke, *Micrographia.* Ed. R.T. Gunther. London: Dawsons of Pall Mall, 1968.

Samuel Jeake, *An Astrological Diary of the Seventeenth Century.* Ed. Michael Hunter and Annabel Gregory. New York: Oxford University Press, 1988.

Sir Isaac Newton, *The Mathematical Principles of Natural Philosophy.* Trans. Andrew Motte. London: Dawson, 1968.

Samuel Pepys, *The Diary of Samuel Pepys.* Trans. Mynors Bright. New York: Random House, 1946.

Herbert Harvey Rowen, ed., *From Absolutism to Revolution, 1648–1848.* New York: Macmillan, 1963.

Abel Janzoon Tasman, *The Journal of Abel Jansz Tasman, with Documents Relating to His Exploration of Australia in 1644.* Ed. G.H. Kenihan. Adelaide, Australia: Australian Heritage, 1960.